EXCELLENCE IN BRAND ADVERTISING

EXCELLENCE IN BRAND ADVERTISING

JIM OSTERMAN

Visual Reference Publications, Inc., New York, NY

Copyright © 2007 by Visual Reference Publications, Inc.

All rights reserved. No part of this book may be reproduced in
any form or by any electronic or mechanical means, including
information storage and retrieval systems, without permission
in writing from the publisher.

Visual Reference Publications, Inc.
302 Fifth Avenue
New York, NY 10001
www.vrpubs.com

Distributors to the trade in the United States and Canada
Watson-Guptill
770 Broadway
New York, NY 10003

Distributors outside the United States and Canada
HarperCollins International
10 E. 53rd Street
New York, NY 10022

Library of Congress Cataloging in Publication Data:
Excellence in Brand Advertising

Printed in China
ISBN 978-1-58471-081-3

Cover Design: Eric Mower and Associates
Cover Photography: Scott Le Voyer
Book Design: Judy Shepard

CONTENTS

The Value of a Brand

Some believe the birth of the modern-day branding movement occurred right after World War II with the proliferation of hundreds of thousands of new consumers, but we now know one of the first known branding efforts can be traced back to 1877.

In that era folks who bought oats never knew where they originated, but one smart entrepreneur put the name "Quaker" on his, and shortly thereafter he realized an illustration of a Quaker on his bags and boxes of oats became a symbol of quality to buyers. Here was one of the first marketers who wasn't afraid to say he was proud of his crop— and by trademarking his, no other farmer could use that symbol of quality.

From such a simple but insightful beginning, generations of advertising professionals have evolved, investing billions of dollars every year to attract consumers and build loyalty.

Today, over 11,000 ad agencies are busy building brands for their clients, literally 24 hours a day 7 days a week. They dig into the history of the brand, past and present consumer attitudes, and competitors' positioning and advertising. The smartest agencies totally immerse themselves in every nuance of their client's organization and products. Experience has taught them there is no more powerful influence for creating a positive brand awareness and image than brilliant advertising that is *true to the brand.*

And conversely, the old axiom that the fastest way to kill a bad product or brand is to advertise it heavily, remains true. Misleading advertising and overblown expectations outstripping the reality of the product or service never prevail.

It's virtually impossible to build a positive brand image with advertising alone. Every consumer experience touching a brand reinforces it positively or negatively. And the brightest agencies help clients understand the importance of a strong favorable experience at every level.

The book you are about to enjoy celebrates excellence in brand advertising— thought by some to be focused *only* on brilliant creative executions. But as you read the case histories highlighting these award-winning campaigns, you will quickly come to learn the importance of understanding the consumer mind long before any ads are concepted. These in-sights give the agency direction and the advertiser strategies for product development and service delivery—all the elements that ultimately craft and shape that elusive positive brand experience. Here you will learn how these great ads and commercials come into being...and who does them. You may see some new agency names here...and quickly learn that great advertising can come from shops of all sizes.

But how do advertisers find the right agencies they need? If you read *Advertising Age* and *AdWeek* you know how many lead stories deal with account changes, highly competitive new business chases, and near-perpetual games of client musical chairs. Client loyalties to their agencies can be fickle at best. Stakes are high, with the cost of entry to play a round in a pitch running tens of thousands and up into the hundreds of thousands of dollars in out-of-pocket costs alone.

Some experienced professionals in the advertising business can read a list of the top 100 agencies and recall their best campaigns. Others would simply put the "agency's own brand" into one of three categories: "I know their work and admire most of it; I know their work and I'm not impressed," or "I don't know anything they've done."

Helping advertisers evaluate and select agencies to build their brands is the work of my firm, Wanamaker Associates, a pioneer in a genre of highly specialized firms known as "advertising agency search consultants." Savvy advertisers are reluctant to change agencies. It's a grueling, time-consuming exercise that diverts energy from brand-building programs. Yet, with the average client/agency marriage lasting under 6 years, it's now all-too-routine a task.

When the brand begins to falter and sales decline, pressure builds and the drumbeats for change become too loud to ignore. As the search for a new agency... new thinking... begins, clients seek out shops who have a history of building brands for others. They want to see a proven track record. During the four to six months of a well-organized search, client/agency chemistry becomes a major issue. Our firm has a very simple credo: "likes attract." Every agency, like every client, has its own DNA...its own culture. Agencies that become chameleon-like to adapt to every prospect fall to the bottom of our rankings. An agency that can't be true to its own brand simply can't be trusted.

I have sat through hundreds of new business pitches, as they are lovingly called. Branding case histories are heavily emphasized in these presentations, because virtually every advertiser must focus on building a brand, regardless of their need for quick sales increases or immediate direct response results.

Agencies build reputations for brand-building skills almost exclusively by doing so for their clients. Their work for advertisers is just about the only way they can build a brand for themselves. Amazingly, advertising agencies rarely commit to long-term advertising campaigns for themselves.

All of this adds up to the fact that advertisers, search consultants, and students studying the craft will use this book to research the best in the business. This is what is heralded in this first volume of *Excellence in Brand Advertising*. Here is recognition of brilliant advertising built on a solid foundation of consumer insights. All with proven results in line with objectives. And the good news is, in dozens of cases, this great work has built long-lasting relationships between advertiser and agency. Which, as any advertiser knows, is the backbone of brand loyalty!

Ken Bowes is president of Atlanta, Georgia based Wanamaker Associates (www.wanamaker.net) an advertising management consulting company which he founded with partner Rod Hanlon in 1986.

INTRODUCTION

The New Landscape of Brand Excellence

There are a lot of acronyms in this book. Enough to rewrite an eye doctor's chart or word search your way through the entire advertising alphabet. But they're here with good reason and great intentions. GSD&M, SS+K, BVK, C+M: they're all people. People make ad firms, and those firms make ads for people. It's the creative universe in perfect balance.

At least that's what the folks in this book will tell you—and who wouldn't believe them? In the world of brand building, in the pages of the new brand communications bible, they're testament to not only taking the path less followed, but also generating a giant gigawatt light so that others can follow. If they can keep up.

Don't expect to see the poster boys and dust jacket stars of the mainstream advertising world here, though. Donnie Deutsch is too busy hanging out with Matt Lauer; Pat Fallon's got his own books to think about. Nor will you read about firms who chase every award down the street, or whose growth strategy revolves around hefty media and production markups. Instead meet the real game changers, going around, rather than through, the motions of mainstream brand marketing to alter, or shatter, the rules and win big for their clients' brands.

GSD&M

These are the agencies that are rapidly becoming the distinct new voices of brand excellence today, voices that, from boutique to giant, are echoing through a vibrant new communications landscape never before seen in the United States.

The New Landscape

Time was when an adman wore grey flannel and would be in one of three places: the executive washroom, in front of a Martini, or pitching some cockamamie jingle in a smoky boardroom. Now you need a GPS to find him—or her. In a world where we're increasingly unplugged, we're even more ready to play. In any market, anywhere and anytime.

Taxi

Just as media has fractured and splintered and regrouped into new channels and avenues, the agencies that service clients are further flung than ever before. They live and breathe and thrive in a new landscape where size and location truly no longer matter and where clients see that, too. The firms in this book attract, retain and help build the reputations and images of some of the biggest, hottest, and most impressive consumer brands in our culture today. Pick just a few examples: MINI. Converse. Nike. Back in the day, the size and caliber and cultural cache of these brands would absolutely require an old guard agency; today these and other savvy clients seek out the new brand builders wherever and whoever they are. This book is about the intersections of great brands and unprecedented brand strategists. About the rare kind of work that happens when the two come together.

In the new landscape of brand excellence there's a lot of ground to cover and a new, developing language to translate: collaboration, relevancy, engagement, emotion, purpose-driven branding. All of them help explain what make the firms in this book successful and their work so good.

Each firm is very different to the next, but from juggernaut to jump-started new shop, there's one theme that truly stands out among them all: creativity is the driving force. Whatever the brand category or challenge each firm here delivers creatively in both form and function. Countless

Venables Bell & Partners

shops can produce a slick, colorful and eye-catching print insert or a bold billboard, but what sets the truly great brand builder aside from the collective is creativity spelled out in the unusual and hammered home in the unexpected. Giant inflatable game pieces that overtake a city's side streets, curbside "art installations" of cars crushed by Powerball and many more twists and turns that keep us smiling and guessing.

But creativity alone is pointless. It's a light shining without a subject. So, to understand how these agencies successfully build their clients' brands, you'll find an "A-Z" guide of bright, cuttingly insightful agency processes in many forms. All are designed to sideline the expected or the ordinary, to clear the brand planning table for new ideas and ultimately to focus all that creative energy, all those ideas and team members on one thing: building the client's brand. In the whirl of world-class work, industry accolades and successful business growth, no agency in these pages forgets that. If creativity is king, the brand is the throne on which it always sits.

It has to be. At the job site, in the plants, on the shop floor of modern brand building, it is all about the work. And it's a simple mantra to follow: the

mcgarrybowen

work builds the brand, the brand builds the client, both build the agency.

So what does all of this tell us as we accelerate on our journey through the new landscape of brand excellence? What's the one thing to take along on the trip? That, if anything, great brands today are built without rules and engineered by the very best rule breakers.

Enjoy the ride.

Class of Whatever

Like size, age doesn't matter. At least not in the new brand-building landscape. Agencies no longer need to punch the clock for twenty years to earn the respect of clients from the ground up. They can pay their way into the fast moving, success-hungry new establishment with the hardest working of currencies: ideas. And when that works, it really works. Just ask the folks behind the wheel at mcgarrybowen. Based in New York and founded as recently as 2002 by partners John McGarry, CEO, and Gordon Bowen, Chief Creative Officer, the agency is now the largest independent shop in New York. Called by many the most successful startup agency in history, mcgarrybowen has annual billings of $1 billion and clients including Crayola, Pfizer, Reebok, and Disney.

The secret to at least some of that success, according to John McGarry, is rejecting the "masses

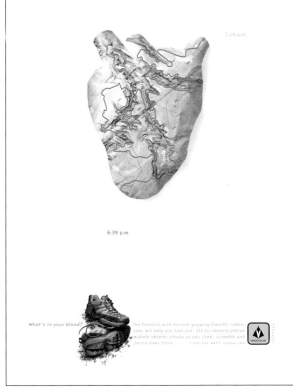
Colle+McVoy

Sullivan Higdon & Sink

BOATS FOR THOSE WHO FISH RELIGIOUSLY.

BVK

THE NEW OCEAN'S EDGE EXHIBIT
IT'S LIFE UNDERWATER, SURPRISINGLY CLOSE.

MONTEREY BAY AQUARIUM

BuderEngel and Friends

lobby. Their message? Unfailing drive to steer their clients' brands away from the flock. Austin, TX-based GSD&M started as four friends right out of college and now boasts a staff of 800, clients such as AT&T and the PGA Tour, and an agency mantra: "Winning on Purpose." Cute expression, but the agency practices what they call "Purpose-Based Branding", essentially determining a brand's purpose for its consumers and building everything else off, and around, that. Other firms take note: clients are in business for a reason.

Something In a Name?

Clichéd, but true. Your name can say a lot about you. Take Buder Engel and Friends, for instance. Not associates or partners, and that's deliberate, so says Wayne Buder of the San Francisco firm he founded in 2003. In their work for clients such as MTV2, Save San Francisco Bay.org, and others, the agency taps an extended and intricate network of "friends" that includes world travelers who help to bring a street-level, global perspective to account teams by briefing them on cultural trends and observations from their travels.

Then there's TAXI, the 210 person, Toronto-based agency whose name has become an operational philosophy. According to Paul Lavoie and Jane Hope who founded the firm in 1992, a core brand team should really be no more people than can comfortably fit in a cab: a strategic planner, an account lead, a creative director, and so on depending on the client and their needs. Simplistic idea? We don't think so, not when the firm grew rapidly to

of asses" approach (as he puts it) to agency staffing. Truly exceptional brands and the clients that steer them require seasoned, senior hands on their business, not junior teams. At mcgarrybowen that's exactly what they get. The young firm has excelled in building a model that not only flies in, but also slaps, the face of the old hierarchical way of thinking. The other part to success could be the firm's incredible, single-minded focus on what every program for every client needs: a Big Idea and an Organizing Idea. Ideas that work as well in a million-dollar TV spot as they do on a napkin.

At the other end of the age spectrum, witness Colle + McVoy, a thousand or so miles away in Minneapolis. Born back in 1935, the shop's mantra is now more than ever "Inventing the Future." And the work for clients such as Nestlé Purina, Red Wing Shoes, and the Minnesota State Lottery is anything but your granddad's advertising. Ask Group Creative Director Dave Keepper how fast, and how smart, an agency has to move to build a brand these days, and, oh, he'll tell you. His team turned around a program to promote a new client's (The Minnesota State Lottery) scratch cards as gift ideas just three weeks ahead of the holidays.

Carol H. Williams Advertising

The Sell

If you can't sell yourself, you'll never sell. Since the days of door-to-door aluminum, that's a god-given truth handed down to each brand-building generation. Everyone needs an angle. But to succeed in brand communications today, the best agencies take that angle, internalize it, give it life and it becomes a core of who they are, how they think, and how they treat their clients' brands. Sullivan Higdon & Sink in Wichita, KS, say "We Hate Sheep" and even have a (fake) sheep's head with an arrow through it in their

SS+K

Guest Relations Marketing

now include a thriving New York office and count names such as Nike and MINI on their long roster of big brand clients.

Process

Nobody's going to admit it. And don't ever ask, but the dirty secret of success behind all jaw dropping brand creative is outstanding process. And there are agencies in this book that excel at both. It's easier to see and measure creative that captivates and moves, but how can process ever excite? Not subscribing to symmetrical thinking can help according to management at SS+K in New York, where they've come up with an approach to brand building termed Asymmetric Communications™ or the "art and science of building brands and opinion in a fractured world." The agency hires people from wildly varied backgrounds including speechwriters, a former drag queen, and journalists, as well as creating multi-disciplined teams to bring completely different strategic perspectives to the issue of building a client's brand. Multiple viewpoints, from every angle, bring a brand into sharp focus.

The approach pays off with off-the-charts ideas such as ConQwest for Qwest Communications, a five-city street game for teenagers where teens download clues by cell phone to enable them to move giant 20-foot inflatable game pieces around city

streets to reach the finish line. It also helps teams maximize opportunities for brands. When Song airlines launched their JFK to LAX route, it was the team at SS+K who thought of targeting the Long Beach Jet Blue terminal with a chauffeur holding a sign: "if you'd flown Song, you would be in LA by now."

For BVK, the Milwaukee-based firm founded in 1983 by Mike Voss and Dan Birdsall, the process of creating brand excellence translates physically into what the agency calls "Respond 360." Picture a cross-disciplined "engagement process" where a brand team gathers in a rotating meeting area and brainstorms a brand's issues for an hour as the room rotates through 360 degrees. When they're back where they started, the meeting is over.

For other firms such as Eric Mower and Associates, with six thriving offices, successful brand communications is about keeping it simple—or human. The agency's own credo is "To drive action, talk human." And it's a refreshing approach to process that has amassed 200 employees and $170 million in annual billings. Each brand is put through

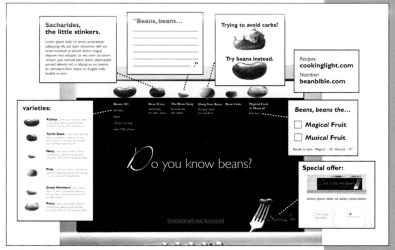

Gabriel deGrood Bendt

Eric Mower and Associates

Martin | Williams

for their clients' brands. It's about understanding how customers view and interact with each brand that provides the basis for what Merkley calls the GBI, the "Governing Brand Idea." The process works. Single-handedly the agency has reinvigorated the stale Arby's restaurant brand and matched Mercedes with aging Gen Xers usually too cynical for luxury brands.

The Specialists

Walking in your clients' shoes, on their turf, and living their life can be at the heart of brand-building excellence. Look up specialist in the ad agency dictionary and you'd find firms like St. Louis-based Osborn & Barr Communications sitting there. Founded back in 1988 by Joe Osborn and Steve Barr, the firm hung its shingle with just one client.

Today their roster includes the

Butler, Shine, Stern & Partners

Brand Studio, a process where teams focus on finding a brand's voice and then communicating that in very human ways.

Minneapolis-based Gabriel deGrood Bendt sums up the essence of process about as well as any agency could or should: "always-thinking." It's a phrase that's in the agency DNA, etched into the boardroom table, and representative of a process that embodies constant, and often unsolicited, idea-generation for clients. It's helped GdB grow from a small Minneapolis start-up eight years ago to a busy creative boutique.

Merkley + Partners believes most brands follow a predictable pattern they call the "BIG FAT S"—a variation of the classic business school model—and so challenge themselves to invent the next S-curve

Environmental Protection Agency, John Deere, Michelin, and the National Pork Board to name a few clients that have helped build an unrivalled reputation, track record, and a 140-person agency staff dedicated to the brands of rural business. Joe Osborn will tell you the seed of their success lies in planting deep agency roots in a few core markets, where their people can breathe the same air and daily challenges as their clients and offer far more than simple communications skills.

Then there's Guest Relations Marketing, a spin-off of Cole Henderson Drake, and a firm that travels hand-in-hand with a client's brand. Based in Atlanta, GA, and headed up by Michael Tyre, formerly of ValuJet, Guest believes in building a brand from the inside out by connecting in very personal ways with a client's customers. New in 2006, the firm and its approach has already attracted Mauna Lani, a four-diamond resort in Hawaii, and the West Places Hotel Group.

Osborn & Barr Communications

Sedgwick Rd.

Lopez Negrete Communications

True partnerships can also lead to brand-building success. Glenn Pere, President and Chief Creative Officer, believes that so much he put it in the name of his firm, The Pere Partnership. Founded in 1988, the firm is one of the nation's leading entertainment specialists for clients such as A+E, AMC, TNT, and many of the country's most beloved cable networks. Pere learned the value of real relationships working for his family's business in consumer packaged goods with designers, packaging specialists and printers. His focus on partnership has paid off with clients such as HBO, a now-giant brand that joined the firm as a project client and which, 20 years later, is one of Pere's marquee names.

Ethnic Branding

With the Hispanic population growing faster than any other demographic in the United States, and the cross-cultural nature of media today, marketers are no longer sidestepping the need for multicultural branding. They can't ignore the nuances, beliefs and preferences of an increasingly fragmented population or their brand building efforts will ultimately miss. In fact, they're clamoring for help to quickly adapt and translate their brands into the new, complex and booming marketplaces. And if they're asking anyone for that help, it's the ethnic branding specialists in this book.

Lopez Negrete Communications, Houston, TX, started life as Third Coast Marketing in 1985 and has been helping bridge the gap between corporate America and the Hispanic community ever since. "Colors are big, emotions are big. And best of all our sense of family is big," says Cathy Lopez Negrete of understanding even some of the simplest contextual differences in translating a brand's image for the

La Agencia de Orcí & Asociados

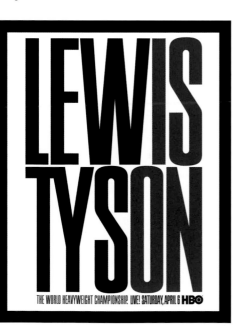

The Pere Partnership

Hispanic market. And the management at La Agencia de Orci & Asociados in LA agrees. With Latino customers, brand marketers must really understand emotion. Which is why the agency, founded in 1986 by Hector and Norma Orci, talks to clients about "Delivering Latino Share of Heart"™ tapping into the social, familial, and consumer customs of varying segments of the Hispanic community to create Hispanic cultural relevance for a more mainstream brand.

Based in Oakland, CA, and founded in 1986, Carol H. Williams Advertising asks clients "whose eyes are you looking through when you view the world?" This disarmingly simple precept should be one of the first questions all agencies ask all clients. It's certainly working for CHWA. The firm has built a stellar reputation as the leading African American agency in the country and landed Clorox, Coors, General Motors, Proctor & Gamble, and Disney on the client roster plus $365 million in annual billings. It's also driven some of the most successful African American brand advertising ever conceived.

The Idea Junkies

Creative capital, the currency of excellent brands comes from process, from dedication and knowledge, and pinpoint expertise. But, it also sparks from the idea. The one notion, boiled down, that just clicks and powers everything else.

Ideas can solve every single problem, so says Venables Bell & Partners in Los Angeles. But, they caution, those ideas had better work hard and be nothing less than great. Their dedication to the daily light bulb popping overhead for all of their clients has brought in five EFFIEs in just three years of eligibility. Sedgwick Rd., formerly McCann Seattle agrees, but insist on ideas being rooted in, and anchored to, pop culture. Their ongoing ability to tap into popular culture for clients has proven enormously successful, helping take financial clients such as Washington Mutual from $30 billion to $300 billion in sales.

Martin/Williams in Minneapolis, specialists in retail, like their ideas big. Devotees of what they term the 20-ton idea, they strive to wrestle intensive brainstorming and ideation sessions to the floor where they can get their arms around that one behemoth of an idea that can form the heart of everything they do. Payless Shoes, the once-tired, worn-at-the-heel, cost-conscious retail shoe brand is just one client to benefit from the firm's stellar work to kill the buy-one-get-one-free (BOGO) philosophy and help them try on a certain new hipness.

And, in the world of ideas, budget doesn't matter. Witness Richter7 in Salt Lake City whose beautiful, smaller-budget work for Jackson Hole Mountain Resort focused brand image on the area's historic, western-sensibilities and stampeded traffic by a staggering 104 percent. Their work for Zions First National Bank also reinvented that bank's image with faltering consumers so well that it gave it the largest market share of any bank in Utah today.

Some agencies are founded on one simple idea that becomes the life-force, motivation and reason for being for the firm. Take Butler, Shine, Stern & Partners in Sausalito, CA, founded in 1993 after

Mullen

Merkley + Partners

four ad friends returned from a fishing trip with a clear idea of what they wanted. The result? An agency founded on, and dedicated to, ideas that flow as freely as the ocean breeze. It may sound a little rose-tinted, but less than fifteen years later, clients include Priceline, LucasFilms Entertainment, and Converse, for whom the agency created a customer movie contest in 2004. Today 2000 films are viewable online at the brand site, which still receives 40,000 hits a day. Online sales are up a very rosy 35 percent.

But let's give the last word before the work to Joe Grimaldi, CEO of creative juggernaut Mullen, one of the most successful agencies in the United States today. What's it he says, what's his big, over-arching, simple, direct idea? Something every brand builder of excellence should take to heart. That a brand shouldn't sell, it should say who it is and what it believes. And that a brand is every single encounter a product has with its customer.

So turn the page. In the new landscape of brand excellence built by rule breakers, encounters are waiting, and they sell themselves. —Jim Osterman

Richter7

BuderEngel and Friends

Question the Expected.
Create the Exceptional.

Founded in 2003

128 King St.
San Francisco, CA
415-658-2800
www.buderengel.com

KEY NEW BUSINESS CONTACT:
Wayne Buder, Co-Founder/Managing Director

SENIOR MANAGEMENT:
Vince Engel, Co-Founder/Executive Creative Director
Andy Narraway, CFO/General Manager

BuderEngel and Friends

That's BuderEngel and Friends. Not BuderEngel and Partners. Not BuderEngel, a division of Omniglobcorp. Just BuderEngel and Friends.

Wayne Buder, agency Co-Founder and Managing Director, expands on the agency philosophy. "A lot of us have worked at big agencies, but we got sick of the red tape, politics and complacency. They lacked any kind of inspiration. We believe we are in the inspiration business. And we draw that inspiration from our independence and our disaffection with where we believe the industry has underserved its clients."

Buder continues, "As the agency world becomes more corporate and conventional, we invite every person who works with us to take a personal interest in the agency's success. Which explains why we hire those with an entrepreneurial sensibility and who take their work more seriously than they take themselves."

BuderEngel offers their employees an open and collaborative environment that allows this inspirational thinking to flourish. But beyond that, their offices are right across the street from San Francisco's new AT&T ballpark. How much more inspiration would they need than that?

"Inspiration is Creativity," says Co-Founder and Executive Creative Director, Vince Engel. "It is the difference between good and great. It is thought, insights, vibrations and mental images. It's the

A

B

C

18

printed word and moving pictures. You have to follow them. Chase them down and bring them to life."

Engel adds, "Inspiration is an ongoing journey. It has the power to motivate consumers, which in turn leads to action. It is always moving forward. Striving for a greater good, elegance, grace and exhilaration. Sometimes it appears like magic. More often than not it appears out of hard work. It's years of experience that tells us what to look for and what to discard. How to use it. Each time we learn something new. Each time it leads us, and our clients, to somewhere we've never been before. And that's powerful."

And so, under this call for a new way to inspire brands and the clients who manage those brands, Buder and Engel have assembled a group of trademarked superheroes (their characterization of their fellow employees) to form BuderEngel and Friends.

Now, as long as there are couches to be sat upon and potato chips to be eaten, there will always be a place for the 30-second TV commercial. But explains Engel, "today's advertising landscape involves more than just TV, print and radio—what we commonly accept as 'advertising.' There's brand design. Branded content. Outdoor. Online. Viral. Guerilla. Consumer-created content. You can buy advertising space in places that I can't mention in mixed company, and in places that don't even exist yet. And

A. Campbell Brothers — Promoting in-store the Bonzer line of surfboards.

B-C. Clown Alley — Studies show people fear clowns more than public speaking. Here, they become a powerful tool for selling hamburgers.

D. MTV 2 — Connecting with the masses by celebrating the marginalized weirdo.

E. Virgin Mobile — Taking a stand against misleading fine print in phone contracts.

F. Mavi Jeans — The most important thing about a pair of jeans is the way they fit.

D

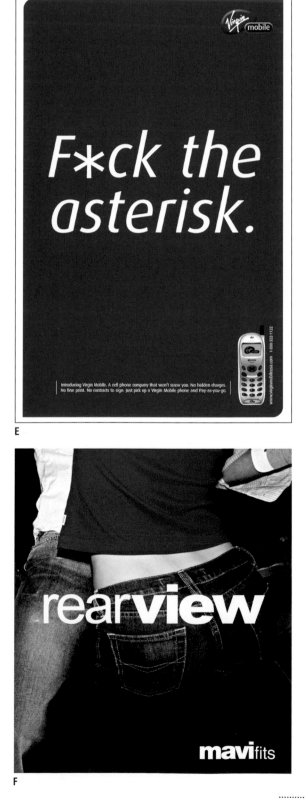

E

F

BuderEngel and Friends

that's why our approach to advertising is not about making ads, but about creating fresh, thought-provoking communications ideas."

So, where do they start the process? Engel is quick to point out that "the world is littered with marketers who have chosen the road to 'more-of-the-same' as the safe alternative to 'never-been-done.' But there's nothing safe about allowing brands to become irrelevant. And that's why we use 'never-been-done' as the launching pad for any project we undertake."

Of course, there's more to it then "never been done." And so, the agency's approach is not to be formulaic, but to treat each project for each client and for the unique opportunity that it presents. They talk to the target audience. They listen to their stories. They dig for brand truths. They examine cultural trends. They study relevant media. "We've never found the time to sit down and write some fancy book like 'The BuderEngel Way to Better Advertising' or to trademark some hokey methodology," says Buder. "This business changes too fast to justify a formula. What we believe in are big ideas that will connect with consumers in surprising and compelling ways."

And finally, even the biggest idea needs to be executed flawlessly. And that means the BuderEngel team is completely obsessive about every part of the

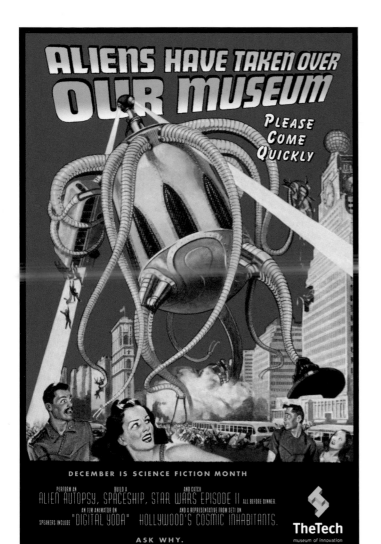

A

B

A. Tech Museum — A premise ordinary people can instantly relate to: invasion from space.

B. bewaresamfisher.com — A real world invitation to participate in an online conspiracy for Ubisoft's Splinter Cell video game.

C. SaveSFBay.org — Recognizing the potential of the storm sewer as a media vehicle.

production process: choosing the right directors, photographers, programmers, editors, artists, retouchers, and musicians. They count many of these professionals among their network of friends, and, according to Engel, "we're unafraid to beg them like dogs for favors to get the job done right."

What kind of clients does BuderEngel work with? Andy Narraway, the agency's third equity partner and General Manager puts it simply: "Ones we like.

And ones we respect and who respect us." He continues, "After that, we seek out clients whose products we admire even if they never choose to join our roster. And who, in turn, admire our own work. Then we build those relationships from a point of mutual respect."

Mike Lee, Senior Art Director, adds, "too many client/agency relationships in this business are antagonistic. Agencies resent clients for dictating creative. Clients accuse agencies of pushing their

own agendas rather than solving problems. But agencies and clients who are emotionally committed to, trust, and respect each other behave in ways that defy logic and produce results that go beyond expectations. They pursue impossible dreams, work ridiculous hours, and solve unsolvable problems."

And so BuderEngel and Friends challenge the definition of their client relationships every single day. They strive to constantly improve and safeguard the integrity and values that surround a brand. They believe in their clients' brands, support them and use them. They watch them, wear them, play with them and enjoy them. And should they no longer believe in a brand, they resign the account.

This kind of commitment is reinforced every day when employees arrive at work. "We have a credo posted on the entrance of the agency," says Engel. "It reads: 'Be accountable. Share ideas. Accept ideas. Build on each other's ideas. Help each other. Particularly when you are not asked to. Embrace change. Demand more of yourself first; then of others. Listen. Try something different. Expect something different. Converse more. Email less. Listen some more. Go to the movies. Challenge everything. Enjoy each other. Respect each other. Listen some more. Take time off. Respect those for whom we create our work. Enjoy your craft. Be open. Listen some more. Commit. Inspire. Make something better than it was. Make yourself better than you were. Have fun.'"

"Wow, it's pretty high up on this soapbox," he adds. "Maybe I'd better get down now."

c

CASE STUDY: Monterey Bay Aquarium

The Monterey Bay Aquarium is one of the world's leading marine habitats. It's a center for research with an important message about conservation, as well as a fascinating destination for families or anyone interested in taking a closer look at life beneath the waves. For BuderEngel & Friends, the challenge in creating communications for the aquarium lies in adequately conveying the sense of wonder that this world-class attraction inspires in visitors each year.

BuderEngel & Friends' Sharks campaign illustrates how an agency can use traditional media to create a non-traditional environment for a high profile client. The Monterey Bay Aquarium, despite its notoriety, had experienced sluggish growth since 2001. BE&F met this challenge with a strategy to dramatically convey the unique experiences that were on offer at the Aquarium and to do so in unexpected ways.

The agency focused on a new exhibit, Sharks: Myth and Mystery, featuring 24 different species of sharks and rays from around the world. The exhibit provided a completely immersive experience, allowing visitors to touch and interact with sharks. It was an opportunity to experience first-hand the wonder of these misunderstood animals.

BE&F devised an expansive media strategy that would deliver a big impact on a relatively small budget in order to leverage the completely unique appeal of this exhibit. To reach the largest concentration of consumers within the client's market, the agency focused on parents who live and work in San Francisco's Greater Bay area. The density of this area allowed for multiple types of outdoor placements that would showcase the creative in different ways and achieve high impact. Complementing the outdoor campaign, a base radio buy achieved further coverage over a larger geographic area. The integrated outdoor campaign, headlined "A World of Sharks. Up Close and Personal," immersed unsuspecting onlookers in downtown San Francisco into a world of sharks that perfectly reflected the exhibit experience. The high-impact messages allowed the campaign to make a huge impression despite a relatively low media frequency.

The supporting radio campaign, called "Sharks come from Canada" used live recordings of children candidly discussing their fascination with sharks. The kids generated a lot of comedy while at the same conveying the sense of wonder an aquarium visit can inspire.

A final whimsical stunt was staged to generate even more interest in the exhibit. On a weekday, during the lunch hour, ten "Shark" taxis "swam" through the streets of San Francisco, handing out tickets to see the new exhibit. Several local television stations covered the swimming taxi event, creating even more publicity for the client.

A

A. Sharks; Bus window wrap – Bringing the premise of sharks up close and personal to life on bus ads.

B. Sharks; Taxi wrap – Bringing the premise of sharks up close and personal to life with a fleet of cabs.

C. Sharks; Billboard – Bringing the premise of sharks up close and personal to life in wall paintings.

B

C

Subsequent campaigns have also relied on creative insight to dramatically convey just what makes a visit to the Aquarium such a unique experience. For 2005, the Aquarium needed to announce the opening of yet another high profile exhibit. Ocean's Edge gave aquarium visitors a look beneath the waves at the diverse community of sea life coexisting in a kelp forest. The exhibit had been consciously designed to give visitors an unprecedented impression of being underwater face-to-face with the teeming aquatic life. The resulting advertising campaign illustrated the premise of the exhibit by creating oversized portraits of ordinary people in startling proximity to sea life. The tagline for the campaign, "It's life underwater surprisingly close," completed the thought presented by the whimsical portraiture perfectly and also served as a concise summation of the experience that awaited the exhibit's visitors.

In 2006, unlike the previous two years, the Aquarium was not debuting a new exhibit. For the agency, this seeming lack of news was actually seen as an opportunity to reinforce the core attributes of the Aquarium brand. The resulting campaign celebrated 2006 as "A Year of Exploring" with a strategy emphasizing the power of an aquarium visit to ignite the imagination and turn anyone into an explorer. This premise was paid off in print ads that depicted packaging for an instant marine biologist and an instant oceanographer, touting the Aquarium's unique ability to turn "ordinary kids into intrepid adventurers." In addition to the print executions, the campaign also included a viral component built around a website where visitors could view short films ostensibly created by "The Monterey Bay Explorers," a band of plucky if somewhat amateurish young adventurers inspired to share their own observations about the ocean.

In the end, in addition to creating a distinct and memorable brand voice for the Aquarium, BE&F's measure of success was significant. The client's total attendance climbed to 1.9 million in 2004, a jump of 15% over the previous year. As a result of the success, the Aquarium increased and subsequently exceeded attendance goals over the course of both of the following years. Not bad for a bunch of underwater animals.

D. 2006 Oceans Exhibit – Discovering the ocean explorer in each of us.

E. Oceans Edge Exhibit; Outdoor & Print – Promoting an exhibit that brings people closer to the ocean.

D

E

CASE STUDY: Disney Mobile

Get all the control you want completely free of any unpleasant control freak connotations.

Disney Mobile: the new wireless service with Call Control to let parents decide when phones can and cannot be used. Disney mobile.

Visit disneymobile.com or call 1-866-DIGNEY2 to learn more.

A

Respecting your kid's independence is a lot easier when you can track their every move.

Disney Mobile offers families peace of mind with a Family Locator that uses GPS to let parents view a map of kids' locations. Disney mobile.

Visit disneymobile.com or call 1-866-DIGNEY2 to learn more.

A. Print – Launching a brand designed to help mom's controlling nature.

B. Collateral – The details of a brand that gives kids what they want and parents what they need.

C. Website – Launching a website designed to help families stay connected.

With the debut of Disney Mobile in 2006, one of the world's best-known brands made an entry onto the crowded and fiercely competitive wireless marketplace. Disney Mobile was a new kind of wireless service designed specifically to meet the needs of busy, multitasking families, offering innovative features that would grant parents greater control and flexibility. BuderEngel was selected as agency of record to create the advertising that would support the launch of this new brand.

The agency's challenge was to articulate these very real and unique product benefits in a way that would make them compelling to parents while still appealing to their kids. Additionally, the advertising needed to be consistent with the larger Disney brand. The solution the agency arrived at was summed up in the line, "Where your worlds connect," which referred to both the wireless service that helps families stay connected and the unique way Disney has consistently brought families closer together.

This line became a common element in an integrated campaign of print, television, online and direct mail communications. The advertising took a lighthearted view of family interactions that emphasized the phone's utility by placing its unique features in the context of everyday family situations. The products are ads that wryly acknowledge the many obstacles to family togetherness that exist today while still remaining grounded in the traditional appeal of Disney storytelling.

In a print ad focusing on the phone's GPS function, the

B

headline reads, "Respecting your kid's space is a lot easier when you can track their every move." A television ad highlighting the same feature presents an unusually business-like boy presenting a very efficient and detailed itinerary of his activities for the day to his visibly astonished parents. The resolution of the ad explained that in real life kids were never like this, which is exactly why Disney had created a phone that could supply parents with the same information. Across all media, care has been taken to present characters and situations that families will readily relate to. This emphasis on presenting family situations with a humorous twist was intended to lead consumers to the conclusion that Disney Mobile offers a real solution to the dilemma of family communication.

C

The early response to the work has been overwhelmingly positive leading into the brand's first holiday season. And the first spot in the television campaign was cited by *Advertising Age* as one of the top ten most-liked spots in a survey of viewers during the month of the launch.

Butler, Shine, Stern & Partners

Advertising, Design, Interactive and Strategic Consulting

Founded in 1993

20 Liberty Ship Way
Sausalito, CA 94965
415-331-6049
fax: 415-331-3524
www.bssp.com

NEW BUSINESS CONTACT:
Patrick Kiss, 415-339-1215

SENIOR MANAGEMENT:
John Butler
Mike Shine
Greg Stern
Greg Richey
Patrick Kiss
Lynda Richardson
David Blum
Ed Cotton
Neal Zimmerman

CLIENTS: MINI, Priceline, Converse, Sun Microsystems, Diageo Chateau & Estates, Nike, Verisign, LucasArts Entertainment

FULLTIME EMPLOYEES: 122

Butler, Shine, Stern & Partners

Most advertising agencies create campaigns, but at Butler, Shine, Stern & Partners, they don't stop there, they strive to create movements, says John Butler, Creative Director of BSSP, "Campaigns come and go, but movements incite people to shift thinking, change behavior, and if we do our job right, get people involved in the marketing."

It's no wonder clients like MINI, Converse, Priceline, Sun and LucasArts Entertainment have sought out BSSP for their unique approach to branding.

Nothing about this agency is typical. Not even the way it began. The idea to create BSSP was conceived on a fishing trip out in the Pacific ocean. Creatives John Butler, Mike Shine, and account person Greg Stern, breathing the fresh ocean breeze, were inspired to create an ad agency of a different kind, a place that encourages ideas to flow as freely as the ocean breeze. After returning to dry ground, they followed through on their plans and left Goodby,

Silverstein and Partners in 1993 to form Butler, Shine and Stern in the picturesque setting of Sausalito, California.

The team's early realization that targeted, one-way media was joining the endangered species list was key in influencing the interactive approach of the agency. The passive audiences marketers enjoyed since the 1950s were evolving. "We felt that brands that engaged consumers with two way communication would surpass those that didn't," says Butler.

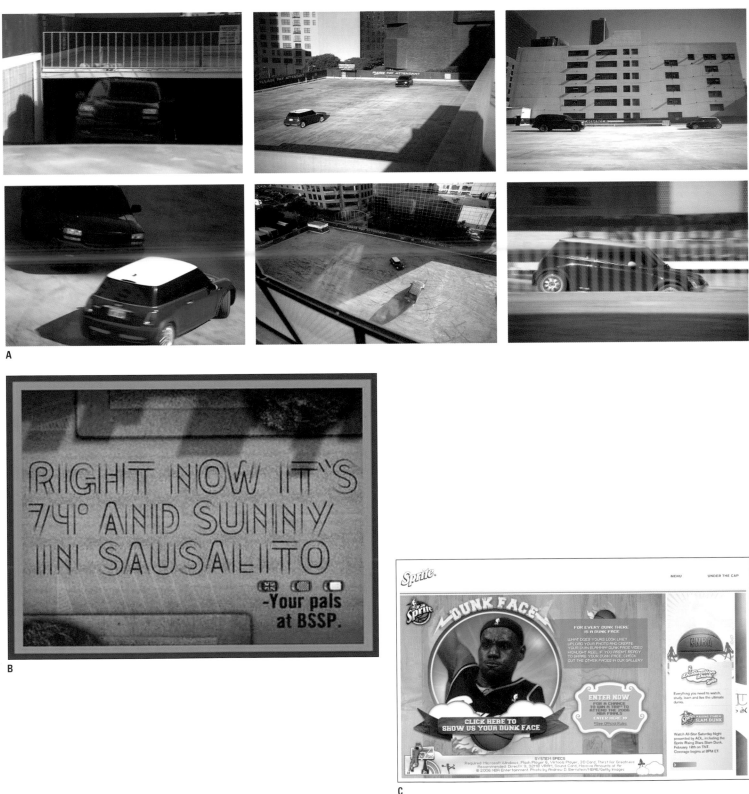

A

B

C

In today's marketplace it takes a powerful idea to create the driving force behind a successful branded movement. Finding the key to incite consumers into action takes fresh, strategic thinking. BSSP looks at it as an all out offensive to capture the minds and hearts of consumers. Creativity isn't merely limited to the creative department, in fact, it's expected from every department. Thus, you won't find your stereotypical account team, media people, or creatives at Butler, Shine, Stern & Partners.

"We tend to hire that unique breed of person who works hard, yet has an interesting personal life," says Shine, an avid surfer himself, "artists, musicians, writers, filmmakers and athletes, to name a few. We find that those who are passionate on the outside are most likely to be passionate in the workplace. Plus, they're a hell of a lot of fun to be around."

Throughout the agency they've created "war rooms" where media, interactive, design and creative teams can work togeth-

er to plan, execute and ignite the spark to move the targeted consumers into action. But by no means does "war room" connote the attitude that the creative takes. "We approach branding the way great architects approach building," says Shine. "Architects like Frank Lloyd Wright designed not only the structure itself, but often the furniture, lighting, rugs, even the flatware. To enter a Wright building is to immerse yourself in a cohesive 'branded' experience. We believe brands should be experienced the same

D

E

A. MINI, USA — "The Sun also Rises." In an homage to the Hemingway days of old where swift and agile Matadors faced off against giant lumbering beasts, MINI pits a Cooper S against a lumbering SUV. In an urban area the maneuverable MINI proves that bulk is no match for handling. Olé.

B. MINI, USA — Online

C. Sprite — Dunk Face website in conjunction with NBA Slam Dunk contest

D-E. LucasArts Entertainment — Poster, Star Wars Episode III, video game

Butler, Shine, Stern & Partners

way. We set out to build a marketing 'Bauhaus,' that combines identity, design, strategy, creative—and more recently, online—all beneath one roof."

Sun Microsystems was a visionary technology company that led the dot-com charge during the late Nineties. During the bust, however, it was written off as a has-been with no clear vision or consistent communications. People thought it was too expensive and just a "box" company. All of this led to waning employee morale. The

challenge was intense competition from deep-pocketed competitors such as IBM, Dell, HP and Microsoft. Products were becoming commoditized.

BSSP decided that Sun needed a movement, not just a campaign. They needed to give customers, analysts and partners a reason to reevaluate Sun. The solution was to deliver a brand platform to unify all communications—a platform that was inherent to Sun and its company philosophy.

On June 1, 2005 BSSP relaunched the

Sun Microsystems brand with the mantra: "Share." Print, outdoor and interactive media supported the campaign, which was well received by analysts, press and internally at Sun.

The agency prides itself on finding unique ways to engage customers and create a movement, many times without any broadcast or print advertising at all.

Such was BSSP's approach to creating a branded movement for Cricket, a wireless carrier that offered unlimited local calls for

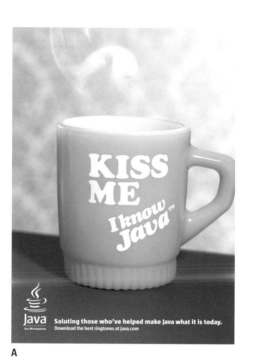

A

B

C

A. **Sun Microsystems** — Wild posting

B. **Sun Microsystems** — Magazine ad

C. **Sun Microsystems** — Magazine ad

D. **EA Lifestyle** — Logo

E. **Nike** — Store interior

F. **Nike** — BattleGrounds truck

G. **Cannondale** — "The Prophet," POP in environment

a fraction of the budget of the big carriers. "We created a contest/event that "advertised" the company's unlimited calling benefit, but without advertising at all," noted Shine. "We created the "Motormouth Madness Marathon," where 12 finalists kept phone conversations going for days on end. Last ones to end their conversations won. The winners lasted past 3 days. Needless to say, the press had a field day, and our client enjoyed extensive free media coverage. And anyone who witnessed the news coverage quickly understood the 'unlimited minutes' brand benefit."

How does BSSP gauge success? "While winning awards is good for creative morale, it is not our end goal. Helping brands grow into movements that translate into buzz, relevance, and ultimately, sales, makes us very happy people. So we measure much of our success by eavesdropping. We monitor blogs, press, and dialogs. Because that's where a brand's truest 'relativity barometer' will exist. How are people relating to the brand? The advertising? A new product launch? The truth is out there in the ether, in a way that can't exist in a focus group, survey, and even at the cash register," says Shine.

Look at BSSP as the MINI of advertising. There have always been cars, just as there have always been advertising agencies. But one look at the MINI and you know it's one of a kind. One look at this agency's work and you'll know BSSP is a one-of-a-kind agency.

E

D

F

G

CASE STUDY: Converse

Converse shoes have been around for over a century, and have been worn by inspiring originals through the years. Individuals like Jackson Pollack, Curt Cobain, John Belushi, Dr. J, and Joey Ramone have embraced Converse as a mark of self expression, but one that exists outside the mainstream. Which posed an interesting dilemma; how do you advertise such an iconic brand without creating a backlash among its fiercely independent fans?

As the agency team began thinking, an interesting truth emerged. Technology was liberating the core target. Creative expression was exploding. Skateboarders were making films, girls were designing clothing, art was being created on computer, music composed in bedrooms. A democratization of creativity made self-expression more accessible than ever before.

Butler, Shine, Stern & Partners convinced Converse to take a leap of faith with them, and invited consumers to participate in the first ever "open source" advertising campaign. They were asked to create 30-second films inspired by Converse, and the winners would be aired on TV and on a special website. The commercials would be consumer inspired and generated, instead of corporate brand statements.

The idea was promoted on Converse.com and the call for entries was seeded in chat rooms. Then BSSP crossed their collective fingers, chewed pencils, developed ulcers, and waited.

The initial response was incredible. Over 450 films were received. Eleven of them were put on MTV in August 2004, and an additional 9 films on Conversegallery.com.

In the years since, the campaign has proven to be a rather radical success. More than 2,000 films have been received from fans. Conversegallery.com gets an average of 40,000 unique visitors daily. And online sales have shot up over 35%.

The campaign has been featured in dozens of business, trade, and consumer magazines, from the *Wall Street Journal* to *Entertainment Weekly,* to *Thrasher* (skateboard mag). And it has led to a rash of similar campaigns by other brands. "Consumer Generated Marketing" has become a new buzzword.

The Converse campaign continues on, and has morphed and changed to involve other art forms beyond film. And the brand is stronger today than ever before in its century long history.

A

A. Converse, magazine ad

B, G-H. Converse, posters — Around the world, Converse brand democracy

C-E. Converse, sceen shots — Among the 2000+ consumer generated films

F. Converse, TV spots — "Game face"

B

C

D

E

F

G

H

CASE STUDY: **MINI**

How does one create a movement to drive people to some of the most unique cars to hit the road today?

Develop something so compelling, so motivating, everyone wants to be a part of it. And then make it so exclusive by only letting a select group in on it.

That's exactly what Butler, Shine, Stern and Partners did when they won the MINI business in a pitch against some of the country's top advertising agencies.

What impressed MINI USA Chief Jim McDowell was that the BSSP team understood the branding, as well as the dealer aspects of the MINI. BSSP even assembled a special dealer creative team to address the retailer issues.

The "big" idea for branding MINI didn't just fly in the window of a MINI Coupe. "We did our homework. We had extensive conversations with MINI USA HQ staff, MINI USA regional staff, along with interviews of the dealers," said CEO Greg Stern.

"Early on, in all of the research, it became incredibly clear to us that MINI has built a passionate community of over 150,000 owners," said Creative Director Mike Shine. "They spend a great deal of time online, talking to each other on message boards. They are members of car clubs that rally every weekend. They talk to anyone who will listen, and they're not afraid to profess their love for their MINIs. We realized that MINI had a

A

powerful cult-like following and they had the potential to cultivate that into a vital, ongoing culture. A culture that would be very appealing to prospects as well." With the entire team assembled in one of the agency's War Rooms they quickly

agreed on a strategic course of action to give this community of MINI owners special information and previews, and to use them to help attract new users to the brand.

Then came the "big" idea.

The agency created a "secret campaign"—a series of creative programs directed first at owners, and secondarily at specific prospects—to let them see that cool things happen when you're part of the club.

150,000 owners' kits were mailed exclusively to existing MINI owners with special tools to let them see messages hidden in the ads. Outdoor advertising, direct mail, online and search engines helped to surround the target with a 360 degree media experience.

The initial result of BSSP's campaign for MINI has been extremely positive. While it's too early to see movement in key brand metrics, word of mouth among customers has been extremely favorable. The dealers are also very happy with the campaign, and report that it is successfully driving traffic into the showrooms.

A. MINI USA, magazine ad — Covert campaign

B. MINI USA, magazine ad — Covert campaign

B

Founded in 1983

250 W. Coventry Court
Milwaukee, Wisconsin, 53217
414-228-1990
www.bvk.com

KEY NEW BUSINESS CONTACT:
Michael Voss (Milwaukee)
414-228-1990

SENIOR MANAGEMENT:
Mike Voss, Founder, President
Larry Swanlund, EVP/COO
Joel English, EVP/Account Services
Gary Mueller, EVP/Creative Director
Ron Gudinskas, VP/Account Planning
David Kelly, VP/Media Director
Bob Gessert, President/BVK/G
Bret Stasiak, President/Respond/360
Herman Echevarria, Managing Officer, BVK/Meka
Gonzalo Gonzalez, Managing Officer, BVK/Meka
Tricia Lewis, Director, BVK/Chicago
Mary DeLong, Sr. VP/BVK/Tampa

Napoleon Dynamite, Charlie Brown and Ralph Kramden: Underdogs, all. And if BVK had them as clients, who knows what companies or countries they'd be running by now.

If anyone believes in the power and potential of the underdog, BVK does. In fact, the agency proudly lives by these words: "Size is no match for insight, passion and creativity." The agency also believes in the power of surprise and unconventional thinking, both easy to see on a first visit to its offices.

Creative Director Gary Mueller's desk is the front end of an old truck with a stuffed deer head lying underneath the front end. Other offices feature everything from rustic beach cottage settings to mannequins coming out of the walls. The showpiece of the agency is a genuine Wisconsin log cabin, built inside the agency and that serves as one of the many eclectic conference rooms. Then there's the conference room located in the agency's CRM division, called Respond 360. This is the room where brainstorming sessions are held on the consumer engagement process. Its name reflects a self-imposed time limit on brainstorming: The floor actually rotates 360 degrees in an hour; when you end up back where you began, the meeting is over.

Icons of BVK's clients are also scattered around the agency. Riding lawn mowers, hospital gurneys and airline seats line the halls. The agency's philosophies are painted on the walls; hidden messages catch

FIGURE EIGHT BAREFOOT WATER SKI CHAMPIONSHIPS.

AUGUST 20-22 • CLEAR LAKE • CRANDON, WI • 414.444.3958

A

INTRODUCING V28 BATTERY TECHNOLOGY.

Milwaukee

B

A. Figure Eight Barefoot Water Ski Championships — The largest event of its kind in the world. Good news for outdoor fanatics, bad news for fish.

B. Milwaukee — We'd like to state for the record that no outlets here were harmed in the making of this poster. Neglected, maybe, but not harmed.

C. National Ace — Maybe it's just us, but we don't believe your hardware store should have its own zip code.

D. LifeBridge Health & Fitness — Sometimes the best spokesman for your brand is an everyday loser. His loss was our gain.

E. Princecraft — And to take the religion metaphor one step further, worship service begins as soon as you enter the showroom.

F. Southwest Florida International Airport — Ambition will take you places. New York, Los Angeles, heck, even Denver.

people by surprise in the bathrooms and the lobby.

Mike Voss, founder and president of BVK, prides himself in creating an environment that supports and celebrates untraditional thinking. And as the agency grows, Voss is also constantly trying to tear down walls between disciplines. In fact, he's created a process he calls the engagement process, a weekly, one-hour brainstorming session between six to eight members of the staff from different agency disciplines.

The sessions try to find new and surprising ways of engaging consumers.

Voss's quest to engage consumers began in 1983. A former AT&T marketing exec, he teamed up with Don Birdsall, a more seasoned local agency veteran, and founded the agency Birdsall-Voss. Their first client was a small vacation brand called Funjet Vacations, an account valued at less than $1 million in billings. (It's since grown to become a $1 billion-plus company and the country's largest vacation

packager. And yes: It's still with BVK.)

Seven years later, Birdsall and Voss met Gary Mueller, an up-and-coming young copywriter, who they soon pegged to run the still tiny creative shop. Mueller brought along art director partner Scott Krahn and almost overnight, they raised the creative department's reputation to a new level.

In 1992, the agency bought another local agency, Kloppenburg & Associates, to become Birsdall, Voss & Kloppenburg.

"We realized that as we grew, acquired

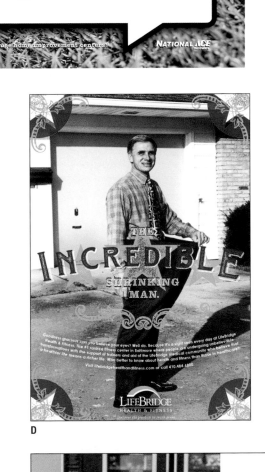

C

D

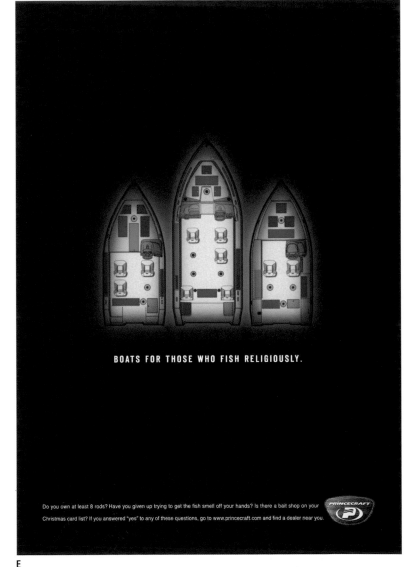

E

F

agencies and added names, we'd have to shorten our name or our receptionist would quit. So we shortened it to BVK," says Voss.

BVK merged with another large Milwaukee agency, McDonald Davis, in 1995. It was the largest agency merger in Wisconsin history, and overnight created the city's second largest shop, with $80 million in billings. Suddenly, BVK was in the big leagues.

Now that the shop was more powerful, it had the kind of critical mass it needed to expand. The agency built a network of offices across the country, bought Hispanic agency Meka, in Miami, and added dozens of new resources.

At the same time, the agency also landed a series of plum branding assignments. There was Gehl's Main Street Café, a small, national iced cappucino brand that competed with Starbucks. Milwaukee Tool, a dusty, 100-year-old national power tool brand was trying to compete with deep-pocketed De Walt. And Sun Country, a tiny, upstart airline in Minneapolis that was being launched in the hub of Northwest, the country's third largest airline.

The similarities were obvious. They were all underdogs: Challenger brands that had to compete with less money against behemoths; small brands that needed to reinvent themselves to survive. And nobody was more up to the challenge of reinventing an underdog than BVK, a once tiny agency that had itself survived long odds to succeed.

As such, the agency describes itself as one of the new breed of ad agencies, idea-driven and nimble, constantly changing and adapting to the new technology that is changing the way consumers get their information.

For BVK, the old, conventional agency model, which is based on media commissions driving profits, is no longer an effective way to go about building brands. "We believe in surrounding consumers with the brand, building relationships with them and making the brand personal. That means embracing emerging technology, customer relationship marketing and guerilla marketing tactics. You need to create new and surprising brand touchpoints and to go where you can cultivate deeper relationships between the consumer and the brand," explains Mueller.

"We're good at breaking the rules of a category and essentially re-framing the discussion about a brand or brand category," Mueller continues. "The brands we work with don't have the luxury of pounding home a single message through repetition of endless media. The brands we work

with are Davids taking on Goliaths. They have to be smarter. More creative. More personal. That means forging deeper, more emotional connections between consumers and the brand, and owning a bigger idea that goes beyond simple product features or benefits. We shift the focus from what a brand offers to what a brand stands for."

In the case of Sun Country Airlines, a Minneapolis-based air carrier, BVK's creative team tapped into the anger and frustration which, research showed, travelers

had with Northwest. They decided to make Sun Country the polar opposite. Northwest was a big, faceless airline that didn't care. So the agency made Sun Country a small, caring friend that was always there for them. And they did it in a way nobody expected: by turning to the airline's potentially biggest liability, its 31-year-old president, Bill LaMacchia, who'd never worked a day of his life in the airline industry. "Bill became the icon of care and compassion in an industry dominated by apathy and disre-

A

B

spect. Bill was the wildcard."

The strategy paid off. In the first year alone, Sun Country went from tenth to second in top-of-mind awareness in Minneapolis, ahead of airline giants United, American and Delta. Passenger volume doubled.

But, as Voss puts it, the only way to truly beat a giant is to keep changing the rules and become a moving target. Sun Country held town hall meetings, thank-you picnics and smile-off contests that continued creating publicity—and keeping Northwest off balance.

Even their approach to web business was unconventional. They launched the quirky website, HeyBill.com, using bill-boards showing only Bill's body parts (feet, head and tie). They also ran :10 TV outtakes of Bill flubbing lines in commercials. Online bookings increased from $15 to $40 million in just six months.

In 2006, Sun Country was still doing well and flying out of Minneapolis. And Northwest had just filed for bankruptcy.

"Big, bold, industry-changing ideas are the currency of our agency," says Voss. "I think working with clients that have less money to compete has trained us to be more creative than our competitors at finding untraditional ways of engaging consumers and uncovering universal human truths that no one has discovered. We believe in the power of big ideas, because they work, no matter what size you are."

Underdogs, meet your champion.

C

D

A. MATC — A technical college asks the question, Wouldn't it be cool to actually be what you said you'd be in the fourth grade?

B. Wisconsin Tobacco Control Board — Secondhand smoke: much more dangerous then running with the bulls, yet only slightly more dangerous than being a Big Tobacco executive these days.

C. Houdini Historical Center — Few people realize that Harry Houdini once lived in Appleton, Wisconsin. Predictably, he escaped.

D. Sun Country Airlines — Uncovering a universal truth about visiting relatives. Uncle Lou, you're not reading this, are you?

E. Cruisers Yachts — A strong craftsmanship message. Okay, so maybe Detroit was an easy target.

E

CASE STUDY: The Beaches of Fort Myers/Sanibel

To say the Beaches of Fort Myers/Sanibel is one of the country's most unlikely tourism success stories would be an understatement.

When BVK won the account in 1997, it found that its client was nowhere near paradise. This tourist destination on the West Coast of Florida was facing a double-digit decline in national consumer tourist spending, slumping inquiry numbers and research indicating that consumers thought of Florida as all being the same. And, they were being outspent 10 to 1 by larger, in-state rivals like Orlando and Miami.

One of the first things BVK did was to help their client realize that they needed to make the brand more personal, more emotional. They needed to shift from simply being another me-too Florida destination to a place 180 degrees from every other vacation out there. BVK started by convincing the client that they were selling the wrong things. They were selling features of the place when what they really needed to be selling was exploration. They were pushing amenities when they needed to be pushing connections, such as families and couples.

BVK's strategic planning guru, Ron Gudinskas, observes, "Research told us that, to our customers, the Beaches of Fort Myers/Sanibel are more than just a destination, more than seashells, beaches and palm trees, Jimmy Buffet music and colorful local art. The Beaches of Fort Myers/Sanibel are the opposite of just about every man-made vacation available."

For BVK, its client had the answer to what had been missing in people's lives and the hectic world they live in: Calm. Peace.

Quality time spent together. So the agency positioned them as being "What's right with the world."

The result? Since 1997, a 45% increase in visitor expenditures. Web inquiries increased 511%. More than 2 million visitors a year come to the area now, a whopping 14% increase since 1996. Unique user sessions on the website exceeded 1.5 million in 2003, compared with 26,770 in 1997.

Even after the famous hurricane season of 2004, which ravaged the area, visitation for the year was up over 3% while virtually every other tourism destination to Florida was down by double digits. To help the local tourism industry get back on its feet, BVK launched a special "U Can Help" recovery campaign. The campaign encouraged residents to visit local restaurants, continue buying local art, and to shop at souvenir shops so the economy could stay alive. A special website was set up that attracted 165,000 unique visitors during the first six weeks of the campaign. Local businessmen reported a dramatic increase in traffic and inquiries.

D

C

So how did this Florida client come to choose a Milwaukee agency? BVK's response: Who better to speak to visitors than a bunch of visitors? Creative Director Jeff Ericksen explains, "We can speak to the unique personal experiences and feelings that a vacation conjures up, because much of our staff were and still are regular vacationers there. It was easy to tap into the deep-seated feelings people have about Sanibel. It's so much more than a vacation. If you've ever been there, you know it gets in your blood."

Words to get amazing results by.

A

B

REMEMBER YOUR OTHER TITLE

Call **888.231.7073** or visit **fortmyers-sanibel.com** for more info and your free visitor guide.

the beaches of FORT MYERS SANIBEL
What's right with the world.

E

F

GO ENJOY YOURSELF. HOW'S THAT FOR A TIP?

When the place you live thrives on tourism, the perception that you haven't fully recovered from a natural disaster can severely harm the local economy. So what can you do? For starters, let friends and family know that the majority of our attractions, hotels and resorts are open and ready for business. While you're at it, remind them our restaurants are serving just as delicious meals as ever. For other things you can do, visit fortmyers-sanibel.com. Kelly Perry. Longtime waitress, Mucky Duck, Captiva.

HURRICANE HELP

G

....

A-B. These spots remind us all that family reunions should happen a lot more than every ten years.

C. Website

D. An opportunistic idea with a simple message: Hey, coffee lovers— wake up and smell the cocktails.

E. Sometimes simple humun insight trumps mounds of statistical research.

F. T-Shirt sales: one small step toward reviving a bettered economy.

G. A timely ad communicating that it's business—er, pleasure—as usual in Fort Myers/Sanibel.

CASE STUDY: Giving Back: Serve

BVK had long been known for its philanthropic work in the community, donating time to as many as seven or eight non-profits a year. But for agency Creative Director Gary Mueller, it wasn't enough.

One day, while listening to a sermon at church explaining that each person has a higher calling in life, Mueller conceived the idea of Serve, a non-profit organization dedicated to creating marketing and advertising programs that would give a voice to causes low in awareness, popularity and funding. It was something BVK had been doing for years.

The key was staffing. Mueller believed that to have a bigger impact, the fledgling non-profit needed a dedicated staff. So Mueller approached Mike Voss, whom he had often turned to in the past to

back the agency's philanthropic efforts, and asked him to provide funding for two full-time staffers.

"He never batted an eyelash," says Mueller. "Mike believes that giving back is an obligation of successful companies. Not only did he offer to give us two people, he offered Serve the agency's full resources: research, web development, digital printing and pre-press work, editing, P.R, analytics, everything. There are not many agency owners that give back as much as Mike." In 2004 and 2005 alone, the agency donated over $2 million of time to Serve projects, and another $1.2 million in services.

There was, however, a catch to all this. According to Mueller, all Serve work had to go through the same rigorous strategic planning process that paid client work was subjected to.

"Branding is just as important to an unknown non-profit organization as it is to a major corporate brand. That means that the advertising has to be smart as well as creative."

For the Partnership for a Drug Free America's Drug Treatment campaign, Serve conducted focus groups with addicts, support groups and families that had been affected by drug addiction. That research led to Serve dramatically repositioning drug addiction as a disease no different than heart disease or cancer. Addicts are not bad people who deserve to be cast out, but sick people who need treatment. The message was that if you treated them as sick, people would seek help sooner, which gives them a better chance at recovery.

The Partnership campaign, like most of Serve's campaigns, comes with a three- to five-year commitment. "Branding a cause isn't something that happens overnight," says Mueller. "It takes time and a close relationship with your agency. We teach our clients about the importance of looking long-term."

According to Mueller, BVK's ability to create awareness for underdog companies with little money to compete fits right in with the kind of challenges they face with many of their Serve clients. Like small companies, pro bono clients don't have big budgets for traditional advertising, so they must look for innovative, non-traditional ways to create awareness.

One day, a small start-up organization, the Shaken Baby Association, came to Mueller's office and asked if he could help get the message out that people should never shake a baby. The organization didn't have a penny in marketing money available. So Mueller created a radio spot featuring a baby crying non-stop for 50 seconds. At the end of the spot a voiceover tells people that no matter how frustrated they get, they should never, ever shake a baby.

Mueller then talked every radio station in Milwaukee into airing the commercial at the same time. It was impossible for any radio listener to miss. The result was weeks of radio, television and newspaper coverage about shaken baby syndrome, including national attention. And the most important result? No reported shakings in Milwaukee for six months following the campaign.

"Big non-profits have ad agencies lined up to do their work. But who's offering to tackle the more difficult, less popular issues? Crisis nursery care. Epilepsy. Gang violence. Without the same kind of professional marketing support, these causes don't have much hope of ever registering even a blip on the public's radar screens," says Mueller.

That makes Serve the perfect fit for underdog causes. And, as Mueller adds, "It's a heckuva lot more rewarding when you succeed."

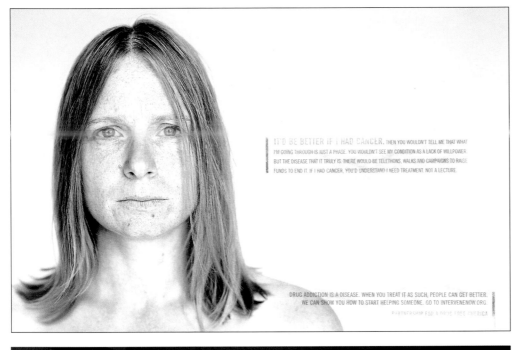

IT'D BE BETTER IF I HAD CANCER. THEN YOU WOULDN'T TELL ME THAT WHAT I'M GOING THROUGH IS JUST A PHASE. YOU WOULDN'T SEE MY CONDITION AS A LACK OF WILLPOWER. BUT THE DISEASE THAT IT TRULY IS: THERE WOULD BE TELETHONS, WALKS AND CAMPAIGNS TO RAISE FUNDS TO END IT. IF I HAD CANCER, YOU'D UNDERSTAND I NEED TREATMENT, NOT A LECTURE.

DRUG ADDICTION IS A DISEASE. WHEN YOU TREAT IT AS SUCH, PEOPLE CAN GET BETTER. WE CAN SHOW YOU HOW TO START HELPING SOMEONE. GO TO INTERVENENOW.ORG.

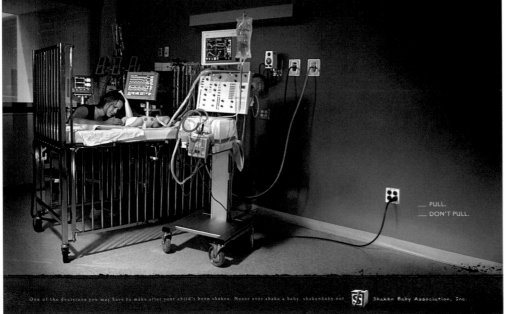

PULL.
DON'T PULL.

Carol H. Williams Advertising

Whose eyes are you looking through
when you view the world?™

Founded in 1986

LOCATIONS:
OAKLAND
555 12th Street, Suite 1700
Oakland, CA 94607
510-763-5200
fax: 510-763-9266

CHICAGO
875 N. Michigan Ave., Suite 2750
Chicago, IL 60611
312-836-7900
fax: 312-836-7919

www.carolhwilliams.com

KEY NEW BUSINESS CONTACT:
Robert Birks, 510-622-8054
robert.birks@carolhwilliams.com

SENIOR MANAGEMENT:
Carol H. Williams, President, CEO & Chief Creative Officer
Ray Clemons, Senior VP, Executive Creative Director
Tsegereda Habtu, VP, Chief Financial Officer
Larry Hancock, Senior VP, Account Director
Kay Lucas, Senior VP, Director of Media Services
Carlton Taylor, Senior VP, Creative Director
Dan Katsin, VP, General Manager
Robert Brown, Director of New Business

CLIENTS: The Clorox Company, Coors Brewing Company, General Motors National &
Regional (Cadillac, Chevy, GMC, Hummer), GMAC Finance, McNeil Consumer &
Specialty Pharmaceuticals/Nutritionals, National Basketball Players Association, Pfizer,
Procter & Gamble, Sunny Delight Beverage Co., U.S. Army, The Walt Disney Company,
Washington Mutual

FULLTIME EMPLOYEES: 155

Carol H. Williams Advertising

"Whose eyes are you looking through when you view the world?"™

At Carol H. Williams Advertising this question isn't simply a motto, it is the path to the firm's extraordinary success. There's no question for founder Carol H. Williams that looking at advertising challenges from multiple perspectives is critical to brand building.

Williams' advertising career began as a copywriter at Leo Burnett in Chicago in the early 70s. Soon after joining the agency she penned several lines that have stood the test of time and are etched into American pop culture, including "Strong enough for a man, but made for a woman," a line that took Secret anti-perspirant from #9 in its market to #1 within just seven months. In writing the campaign "Say hello to poppin' fresh dough," Williams re-introduced Pillsbury's Doughboy and gave him something to giggle about.

Williams' advertising expertise with blue chip clients, combined with her insightful understanding of African American consumers, led her to open her own agency in 1986. Today, CHWA is the largest privately held African American and urban advertising agency in the country, with earnings of more than $365 million in annual revenues. CHWA has two full service offices in Oakland and Chicago, and satellite offices in Atlanta, Dallas, Detroit, and New York.

Williams points out that the agency's

A   B   C

D

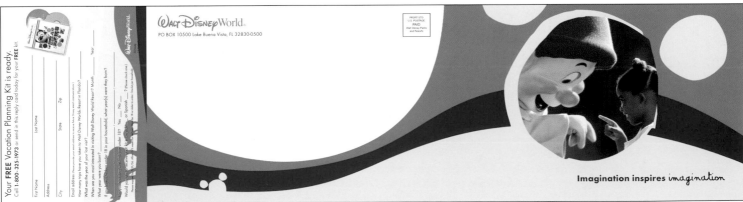

E

continued growth is the result of quality work. The agency prides itself in helping clients revitalize and build strong brands by effectively communicating with African American consumers in a meaningful and relevant way that is also synergistic with a client's general market campaign.

"We focus on African American and urban markets, but we're also highly diverse," says Williams. "We seek out and embrace people from all walks of life. As a result, we're able to see advertising challenges from different perspectives."

Although several of CHWA's employees are African American, the firm believes the best solutions for clients come from diverse teams that produce diversity in thought and creativity.

For the agency, perspective is a critical tent pole of its branding philosophy. "We always look at our clients' brands from both a strategic and creative point of view," Williams observes. "In fact, one of our greatest strengths is our ability to develop creative excellence powered by insightful, strategic thinking. Creativity and strategy must work hand-in-hand to build strong, lasting brands."

The opportunity to help clients sell products still excites Williams today.

"Passion, communication, clarity and courage are the intellectual components of the creative process," Williams says. "It's probably impossible to be an effective creative without deep strategic insights and a passion for finding the answers."

F

A-C. Disney — TV, "Imagination"

D-E. Disney — Direct Mail

F. GM — Print Ad

G-H. GM — Print Ad

G

H

Carol H. Williams Advertising

This philosophy comes to life in how the agency executes work daily. The agency begins by immersing themselves in the brand to understand it better. Employees study the product's history, category and competition, core brand equities, goals and objectives. After digging deep into the brand, the agency focuses on better understanding the consumer.

"We often supplement whatever our client knows about the consumer with consumer research," Williams says. "We also look for learning available through our historical experience and through our personal network of connections—family, friends, and neighbors. Through this exhaustive process, we identify current consumer perceptions of a brand and the company, both positive and negative, to identify its unique relationships with African American consumers and thereby connect the dots."

Lactaid Milk is one brand that has benefited greatly from CHWA's branding philosophies, strategic processes and creative juices. In 2004 McNeil Nutritionals' Lactaid brand team hired CHWA to help increase sales of Lactaid Milk among African American women. While approximately 75% of African Americans are lactose intolerant, they're highly likely to put up with the symptoms given their strong love of dairy products.

The immediate challenge for CHWA was to uncover key African American consumer insights related to the category, product and brand to determine important behavior motivators and barriers. Research revealed that while milk has an important health benefit, for some consumers its sensory pleasure—delicious milk with tasty foods and treats—is even more compelling.

Using insights gathered from the research, CHWA developed the African American targeted "Pass Those Cookies" campaign. The campaign, which was synergistic with the general market's strategic messages, took an honest approach to effectively address consumer-perceived taste issues, while countering those perceptions with beautiful product shots and a gratifying taste demonstration.

The spot tested extremely well, significantly exceeding key purchase behavior scores and ASI norms for key attitudinal measures among both African Americans and the total general market sample. And the commercial's effectiveness? It topped the charts by being the second highest score ever achieved in ASI's database of 1,500 spots tested via their on-line methodology. The client was so pleased with the results they decided to use the "Pass Those Cookies" campaign

as a general market execution.

"I believe that all CHWA creative work must have an intelligent, emotional hook that gets inside consumers' minds and motivates, educates and inspires them," Williams says.

An outstanding example of the agency's skill at finding the hook a brand needs is its success with Allstate. An established brand recognized as a leader in the insurance industry, Allstate faced the onslaught of price-driven competition.

Market activity in the industry led to a lack of differentiation between brands, and a commoditizing of insurance in the minds of African Americans. In 2004 the company decided to reestablish its brand equity and reinforce the value of being in "Good Hands" with consumers in all segments.

To understand African American consumer attitudes about the insurance industry and the history of those attitudes, CHWA conducted qualitative research.

A

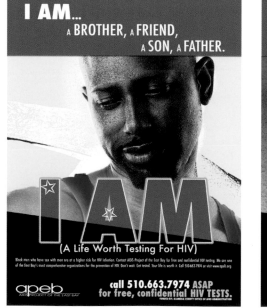

B

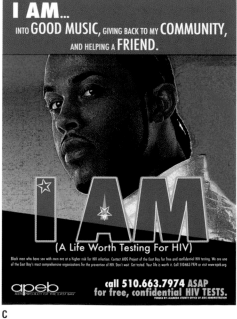

C

Through the strategic and creative development process, they strove to use cultural insights to communicate directly and specifically with African Americans.

CHWA developed three targeted executions that were launched as part of Allstate's first fully integrated, African American media plan. Each execution was designed to drive brand consideration among consumers in a straightforward, compelling way. Each was synergistic with the general market creative in that it featured Dennis Haysbert, an authoritative figure who spoke to consumers in a credible, respectful way, with a consistent brand voice.

All three TV spots achieved commercial test scores that significantly exceeded norms across numerous measurements; TV ad awareness of Allstate among young African Americans increased by 72%. African American consideration of Allstate grew by 12 share points in four weeks. In early 2006 the three TV spots won a "Best in Show" award from the Insurance Marketing and Communications Association. The same year, CHWA's Allstate effort won an EFFIE Award.

Where will the agency turn its eyes next? As CHWA continues to produce innovative and insightful work for Fortune 500 clients, the answer is clearly toward a bright, successful future.

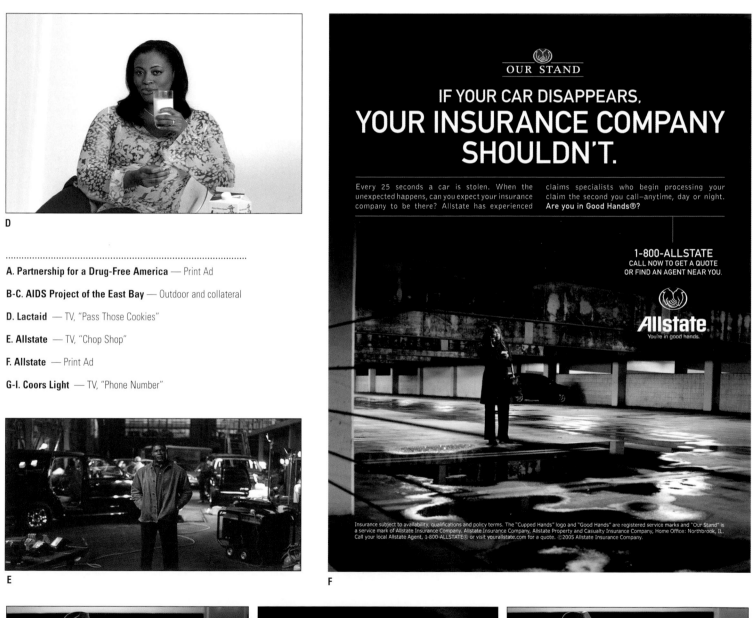

D

A. **Partnership for a Drug-Free America** — Print Ad

B-C. **AIDS Project of the East Bay** — Outdoor and collateral

D. **Lactaid** — TV, "Pass Those Cookies"

E. **Allstate** — TV, "Chop Shop"

F. **Allstate** — Print Ad

G-I. **Coors Light** — TV, "Phone Number"

E

F

G

H

I

CASE STUDY: GMC

What is the African American market looking for in an SUV? To find the answer, General Motors chose Carol H. Williams Advertising.

GMC gave CHWA marching orders to get more African American (AA) consumers excited about GMC's SUV models by bolstering their brand awareness and generating interest. CHWA's solution also had to remain synergistic with the general market "Professional Grade Engineering" campaign.

For the general market, "Professional Grade" meant the vehicles had uncompromised strengths (towing capacity, horsepower, comforts and refinements) as evidenced by GMC vehicles being used by professionals such as construction contractors. To help understand AA perceptions about GMC's "Professional Grade," as well as its sub-brands, CHWA conducted extensive consumer research.

"We learned that style and self-expression in this category is very important to African American consumers," The agency explains. "Their decision to purchase an SUV or truck is not driven by function, but by its ability to reflect a positive self-image and sense of style, as well as for its comfort and amenities. African Americans aspire to drive a quality vehicle that conveys to their friends and family 'they've arrived' in an unpretentious way."

The agency found GMC needed to realign the meaning of "Professional Grade" for AA consumers. CHWA translated "Professional Grade" to speak to a higher level of quality and achievement for those who excel in their professional and personal lives. GMC represents not only a brand that's aspirational, or "top shelf," but also a brand that's authentic. GMC is for the individual who knows he has made it, but doesn't need to broadcast his success at maximum volume. The GMC consumer appreciates the head nod, but is not seeking the head turn.

Once the agency translated Professional Grade, they applied their strategic thinking to help launch the new GMC Envoy Denali. Prior to this, the agency supported the Envoy and Yukon Denali models. However, the Envoy Denali represented a combination of the two, and CHWA wanted to leverage the benefits of each. The Envoy Denali presented the design and amenities of the Yukon Denali at a more affordable price now available as the next level in the midsize SUV segment.

CHWA knew the AA consumer for this brand kept up with latest trends and enjoyed discovering new products and features. With the Envoy Denali's innovation, amenities and style, the agency recommended the Envoy Denali be positioned as a superior choice for those in the know, creating the desire to be one of the first to purchase the new model.

To launch the product to AA consumers, CHWA created the campaign "Poetry in Motion." The advertising features Mos Def, who is relevant and influential with the AA target audience and embodies the essence of the brand. As a celebrity, Mos Def is aspirational, but unlike many celebrities, he is also considered to be real and genuine. He is also widely recognized as an innovator within his field, often at the core of the latest movements, and therefore regarded as someone "in the know."

Images in the TV spot were based on a simple black background that revealed Mos Def, as distinct parts of the car floated into place and created the Envoy Denali. Soulful hip-hop music played in the background as Mos Def recited his poem for GMC Envoy Denali.

In addition to TV, the agency developed an integrated campaign to achieve the greatest comprehensive brand impact.

Overall, the Poetry in Motion campaign delivered on the brand team's objectives to create a higher-end Denali sub-brand, reinforcing GMC as "professional grade." In addition, the client felt the creative was a perfect fit with new urban culture. Apparently, others did as well, since "Poetry in Motion" received the best AA campaign award in 2006 from Urban Wheels.

The agency was not content to rest on their laurels. In 2006, the agency recommended evolving the campaign to extend the idea of being an innovator or "in the know." Rather than focusing on a spokesperson, like Mos Def, as the one in the know, the agency wanted to give credit to and acknowledge those consumers who are in the

A

know. Instead of taking an obvious approach, CHWA created the campaign, "Do You Know," which flipped the script by having the GMC vehicles seeking out savvy and well-informed drivers and thereby recognizing that the vehicle has chosen the consumer because of the fit with the brand.

The TV spot showcased three GMC vehicles, through stylized black and white footage, canvassing an urban city. The interactive creative took this idea a little further with a stronger graphic treatment though animation that provided a more engaging, and urban approach to draw in the consumer. The effort is also supported by print which launched in first half 2006.

A. TV — "Do You Know?"

B. Interactive — "Do You Know?"

C. Magazine — "Poetry in Motion"

D-E. TV — "Poetry in Motion"

B

CONFIDENCE. STYLE, WITH VISION FOR MILES.
INNOVATIVE. SHARP, FRESH, CLASSIC AND NOW.
V-8 STRONG, PROFESSIONAL CHARM. I'M RIDING WITH YOU.

PRESENTING THE NEW 2005 ENVOY DENALI BY GMC. WORDS BY MOS DEF.
300-HORSEPOWER VORTEC V-8 ENGINE. BOSE AUDIO SYSTEM. LEATHER SEATING SURFACES.®
AVAILABLE SPRING 2005.

* First and second rows only. OnStar is available on select 2005 GMC vehicles. Call 1-888-4ONSTAR or visit onstar.com for details.
OnStar and its emblem are registered trademarks of OnStar Corp. © 2005 General Motors Corp. All rights reserved.

WE ARE PROFESSIONAL GRADE. | **ENVOY** DENALI
VISIT GMC.COM

C

D

E

CASE STUDY: St. Joseph Aspirin

Oh, baby. How does an agency sell a trusted brand of infant medicine to a sophisticated, adult, African American audience? After winning the St. Joseph Aspirin business, the agency's marching orders were to increase the client's business with African American men and women.

CHWA applied its creative philosophy and research methods to the challenge to uncover target consumers' brand perceptions of St. Joseph Aspirin: its equities and strengths, its weaknesses, and the role the product could play in benefiting heart health. The agency conducted internal brainstorming sessions to identify various advertising strategy statements. Afterward, consumer research helped determine which statements had the strongest potential to generate trial among African Americans, and, further, to achieve the brand's business objectives.

Results of this process revealed consumers' true perceptions of St. Joseph. Most knew St. Joseph as the aspirin for children and babies, and recognized it as a flavored, orange-colored pill. They saw the brand as accessible, down-to-earth and honest, and a name that meant trust, quality, heritage, and efficacy.

Having a healthy heart was also perceived as a challenge, given the stresses of life, but respondents also recognized aspirin therapy as a benefit to heart health. After the agency identified a strategy, they began exploring and testing several creative executions.

"We wanted to determine which executions, and what elements in each, resonated strongest with consumers," the agency explains. "Our creative development strategy was to remain synergistic with the general market creative effort, but tailor it to the African American consumer with the incorporation of relevant cultural insights."

The brand's tagline, "America's Original for the Heart," remained the same for the African American

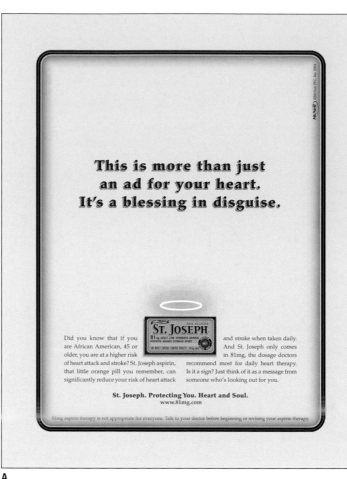

This is more than just an ad for your heart. It's a blessing in disguise.

Did you know that if you are African American, 45 or older, you are at a higher risk of heart attack and stroke? St. Joseph aspirin, that little orange pill you remember, can significantly reduce your risk of heart attack and stroke when taken daily. And St. Joseph only comes in 81mg, the dosage doctors recommend most for daily heart therapy. Is it a sign? Just think of it as a message from someone who's looking out for you.

St. Joseph. Protecting You. Heart and Soul.
www.81mg.com

81mg aspirin therapy is not appropriate for everyone. Talk to your doctor before beginning or revising your aspirin therapy.

A

target. The brand positioning statement, however, was made more relevant.

"The little orange pill you remember is the dose doctors recommend most for daily aspirin therapy," used in general market advertising, became, "The little orange pill you remember is the dose (81 mg) doctors and the Association of Black Cardiologists (ABC) recommend most to reduce the risk of a heart attack or stroke."

Thus, the African American message was designed to supplement the general market plan with a unique strategy that heavily relied on local market media and extended national media buys in highly targeted consumer magazines such as *Ebony* and *Essence*.

Guerilla marketing played a key role in the campaign, as well. The brand team developed an integrated surround sound strategy that included community event sponsorships, consumer outreach (via sampling and outreach at churches), PR initiatives, and retailer support. For instance, to help establish synergy between St. Joseph and local African American communities, the brand chose to sponsor family-oriented events with a spiritual component, such as large gospel concerts.

In addition, activity components included exhibit booths, radio remote van hits at local market retail locations with high African American traffic, sampling programs at churches and PR initiatives.

Yardsticks used to measure success included ASI as a commercial testing tool and IRI for actual in-market sales data. Results showed the brand's African American targeted effort was extremely successful: the TV ad "Movin' Smooth" scored within the top 1% of all ads ever tested by ASI.

St. Joseph realized an incremental sales lift among African Americans within its targeted local markets, as measured by IRI. This lift ranked in the top quartile of all IRI ethnic market tests ever conducted. In addition, St. Joseph generated a share lift in local markets and nationally among African Americans.

....

A. Print Ad

B-E. TV, "Movin' Smooth"

B

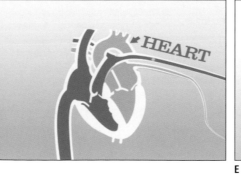

D

E

Colle+McVoy

Inventing the Future

Founded in 1935

400 First Avenue North
Suite 700
Minneapolis, MN 55401
612-305-6000 (phone)
612-305-6500 (fax)
www.collemcvoy.com

HOLDING COMPANY
MDC Partners Inc., Toronto

NEW BUSINESS CONTACT:
Christine Fruechte, President, 612-305-6200
christine.fruechte@collemcvoy.com

SENIOR MANAGEMENT:
Christine Fruechte, President
Phil Johnson, Chief Operating Officer
Lisa Miller, Chief Financial Officer
Mike Fetrow, Executive Creative Director
Tom Lindell, Director of Client Services
Riff Yeager, Managing Director, Exponent Public Relations

CLIENTS: Aveda, Case IH, Cenex, CHS Inc., Courage Center, DuPont, Erbert & Gerbert's, Farm Credit Services, Johnson & Johnson Vision Care, Minnesota State Lottery, Nestlé Purina, New Holland, North American Olive Oil Association, Northern Tool + Equipment, Novartis, Red Wing Shoe Company, Schell's Brewery, Taubman Centers, Time Warner, Vasque

Colle+McVoy

Every Friday morning at 8:30, the 160+ employees of Colle+McVoy in Minneapolis file into the agency lunchroom. Some walk right in and grab a seat. Others, bleary-eyed, line up at the coffee machine or soda fountain looking for their first jolt of caffeine.

They're gathered for Future 411, a weekly look at the world of information, technology, media and the social forces that are helping shape the future. For thirty to sixty minutes they're treated to an entertaining presentation by someone from the agency or a guest from outside the company. It may be a look at the latest consumer-generated content that's revolutionizing the way brands and consumers interact. It may be a review of the latest buzz marketing techniques, technology trends, web innovations or street-level guerilla tactics.

At the end of each presentation, energized employees of Colle+McVoy spread out, armed with new ways to help their clients address the future.

"That's what we do best," says Christine Fruechte, president of Colle+McVoy. "We help our clients invent their future. We look for ways to help them imagine and shape what's next, what's going to help their brand succeed, what's going to keep their brand steps ahead of the competition. No one really knows what the future holds, so we're always reminding them the best way to predict the future of a brand is to invent it."

A

A. New Holland — Magazine ad

B. New Holland — Magazine ad

C. Schell's Beer — In-bar sign

D. Schell's Beer — Six pack

E-G. Schell's Beer — T-Shirts

B

Fruechte says the time is right for clients to be thinking this way. "Everything is changing so fast. Today's hot trend will be overexposed and in the dustbin next month. Companies have less control than ever before over how their brands are being defined in the marketplace." Most clients are looking for help in coping with the rapid pace of change, and most agencies are woefully ill equipped to accommodate them.

"Every agency has a few people or a department they can point to and say 'look at how forward-thinking we are.' We decided we needed an entire organization thinking that way."

Over the years, Colle+McVoy became known for great client service, creative thinking and its wide range of talented and experienced employees. "We stand apart from a lot of Minneapolis agencies," says Phil Johnson, chief operating officer and long-time employee. "We're smart, driven and passionate about our business and our clients, but humble and genuine too.

Companies see the benefits of working with a group of smart people who don't let personal egos and creative agendas get in the way of driving a client's business forward."

"We've brought in top talent from across the country, our creative work is getting the attention of everyone from award-show judges and prospective clients to journalists and bloggers, and we've built a culture of future-thinking people who collaborate across disciplines without

C

D

E-G

thinking it's anything but ordinary," says Fruechte.

The agency recently moved to the warehouse district of downtown Minneapolis, taking over the top two floors of an old office/showroom. The light-filled, open-office environment is anchored by a 32-foot-long paste-up table in the center of the agency where new work is created, debated and celebrated. Around the two floors, small, informal meeting places abound, perfect for a quick discussion when inspiration strikes.

"We have creativity flowing in all directions at all times from every corner of the agency. We didn't want a lot of walls impeding that flow," says Fruechte.

Those ideas are coming from everywhere. For example, Colle+McVoy boasts one of the most highly awarded PR firms in the country in Exponent, a 25+person group that works hand-in-hand with the advertising, direct, graphic design and interactive groups. "There's no reason all these disciplines shouldn't be under one roof," says Riff Yeager, managing director of Exponent PR. "There's enormous power when strategy links together these initiatives in branding, tone and content. No matter what discipline takes the lead, we're always in agreement that we'll leverage whichever ones make sense to invent a future our clients' brands can thrive in."

But inventing the future takes more than knowledge of trends or technology or people who know how to collaborate. It requires a willingness to get under the skin of a brand and its consumers and discover the insights that connect the two in a meaningful way. "Connecting the soul of a brand with the heart of its consumer is key to everything we do," comments Mike Fetrow, executive creative director of Colle+McVoy. "Everyone talks about planning and insights, but so often those things get lost in the execution. There's no heart to it. It's just creative for creative's sake. The best work leaves an impression, you feel the time spent with it was worth your while—even if it was only a few seconds, or even a glance."

For example, the soul of the state of Minnesota is its 10,000 lakes—a place to relax and reconnect with family and friends. At the heart of the traveler is a need to escape the 24/7, can't-get-away-from-voicemail-and-email world we've created for ourselves. As a result, Minnesota was the first state to move away from the all-too-familiar strategy of "Come here because of us" and say "Come here because of you" instead.

The soul of a Vasque hiking boot is an experienced climber or day-tripper who doesn't want to worry about what's on his or her feet. In the heart of the Vasque consumer is the desire to go further, faster or higher the next time out.

The soul of Nestlé Purina is research, research and research. Nothing is put on the shelf that isn't the result of years of testing and know-how. In the heart of the veterinarian is a desire to do the best for every animal that comes into the office.

"Perhaps it would be more accurate to talk about reconnecting that product's soul," says Fruechte, "because many times over the years Colle+McVoy has found itself working with products and services that, once established, had started to lose some of their luster." New Holland farm equipment was seeking to reestablish itself in the wake of a corporate merger. The agency discovered that the company's new-found passion for innovation fit perfectly with the smaller, more entrepreneurial grower, the kind of person driven by harnessing technology and brainpower to

A

B

A. **Winnebago** — Poster

B. **Winnebago** — Poster

C. **Nestlé Purina** — ProPlan ad

D. **Explore Minnesota Tourism** — Print ad

E. **Red Wing Shoes** — Men's motorcycle boot ad

F. **Vasque Outdoor Shoes** — Print ad

get the job done and less concerned about the brand.

Winnebago, practically a generic name for motor homes, had lost its position atop the RV world. The agency found, in traveling around the country and talking with owners, that people had a bias toward products built in the heartland of America. Less than two years after launching a "Midwest values" branding campaign, Winnebago was once again the leading seller of recreational vehicles.

Another hallmark of the agency is its corporate motto: "Fortune Follows the Brave." Imprinted on t-shirts, notebooks and signage throughout the company, that phrase is a constant reminder to employees and clients alike to expand their thinking and look for brave, inventive solutions. It's even spawned a "Brave it Out" club that meets several times a year outside the office. No one is told what the evening's event will be, just when and where to meet. As a result, you may find yourself at a lutefisk dinner, a drawing or ballroom dancing class, or a hot air balloon event.

"It definitely keeps people on their toes," says Fetrow. "And shouldn't that be the goal of each of us every day? This business is changing too fast to get complacent. If you're smart and passionate about what you do, you want to embrace the unknown challenge of every new day."

Then again, when you invent the future, you usually know what that new day will look like.

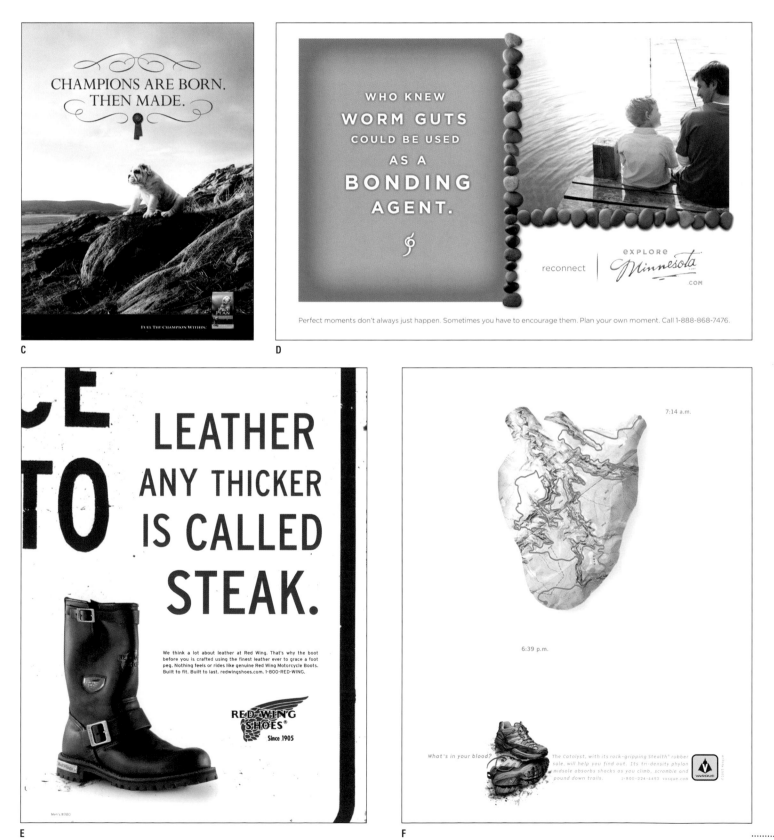

C

D

E

F

CASE STUDY: Minnesota State Lottery

It was November 4th, only three weeks before the start of the holiday season, and the Minnesota State Lottery was asking its brand new agency, Colle+McVoy, for a campaign to sell Scratch Game tickets as a gift item.

So much for a honeymoon period.

The Lottery team at the agency dug in and did what it does best—think bravely, improve on the past, and invent a new future for its client. The strategy quickly came together: position Scratch Game tickets as an extra touch that would make any gift a great gift.

Within three weeks the campaign was on the air, in the newspaper, shouting out from bus stops throughout the state. After its first week, the campaign achieved its goal of a 25 percent sales bump. The next week it saw a 50 percent bump and set an all-time record in sales. And it continued to beat projections for the rest of the campaign.

A

"That pretty much set the bar," Dave Keepper, group creative director on the Minnesota State Lottery at Colle+McVoy, said. "And we haven't looked back since."

Breaking a tradition of promoting each new Scratch Game, and running the occasional television spot, the team at Colle+McVoy set out to have a constant presence in the marketplace and make sure that every piece of communication promoted fun and surprise.

So when it came time to reinvigorate Powerball, the Lottery's most prominent game, the agency team came up with the phrase, "Don't belittle Powerball. It's always big." That came out of research that revealed that people don't take the Powerball game seriously until the jackpot hits $100 million or more. Traditional media—including outdoor boards crushed by huge red balls—was employed, but it was the non-

traditional variety that really caught the attention of people all over the state.

A number of cars and trucks were "crushed" by larger-than-life Powerballs and driven around Minnesota to attract media attention. When parked outside festivals, concerts, sporting events or the Minnesota State Fair, people did a double take. Or two. Past winners were invited to pose by the cars. Prizes and discounts were offered when the cars showed up at retail locations. And the message was delivered: Powerball is always big. Online, the agency contracted with several popular local sites to have their home pages crushed by a huge red ball when visitors arrived. As a result, Powerball sales increased 35 percent very shortly after the campaign broke.

A campaign for Scratch Games used the tagline "Surprise is good," and included buses painted to look like a Lottery game cards with the windows "scratched" off and surprises revealed. A campaign for the "Second Chance" game (a game where players could send in losing scratch cards for a second chance at winning) included garbage cans located through downtown Minneapolis and St. Paul with protruding arms holding thrown-away Lottery cards. In that case, over 270,000 entries were received and the Lottery sold 32 percent more scratch games than during the same period a year earlier, beating its targeted goal by 12 percent.

"Having gotten a taste of non-traditional media, the Lottery continues to challenge us to bring something new to the table every time," says Steve Thomas, director of contact planning at Colle+McVoy. "We've wrapped trains, crushed cars, put garbage cans in skyways, created messages out of

flowers along the highway, taken over department store windows, covered elevator doors and much more. It's certainly kept us on our toes trying to invent new media."

What's next? Already in the formative stages are a reality television show and a full-length documentary film about a small group of players around the country who collect mint-condition lottery game cards.

Most gratifying of all is the fact that in its first year of handling the account, Colle+McVoy helped the Minnesota State Lottery reach a new record in sales, over $408 million, and saw $106 million given back to the environment.

"As our television spots say," explains Keepper, "when you play the Lottery, nature thanks you." And he shows his favorite spot of the year. It opens on a hiker out for a quiet walk through the woods when he suddenly stumbles upon a huge black bear lumbering toward him. And what does that fearsome creature do? He wraps the hiker in a giant bear hug, of course..

B

C

D

A. **Powerball** — Crushed billboard

B. **Scratch Games** — Bus wrap

C. **Second Chance** —Garbage can placed in skyways

D. **Powerball** — One of several crushed cars postitioned around town

E. **Lottery Beneficiary** — "Nature Thanks You," TV spot, a part of all lottery proceeds go to help the environment

E

CASE STUDY: Nestlé Purina

"Sure he's a little big, but he's my baby. I love to spoil him."

"Oh, just look at her! She's so cute and chubby!"

"Does he look fat to you? Not to me. He's just a cute little ball of fur!"

Obesity in children is a national issue, debated in academic and social circles from coast to coast. Unfortunately, obesity in pets doesn't have quite the same profile. Yet, it's every bit a concern—or should be. As with humans, proper nutrition and weight management can add years to a pet's life, studies by Nestlé Purina have shown.

And much like with children, addressing a problem like obesity often starts with getting the attention of the key decision makers. (Perception studies showed that owners see their overweight pets as significantly thinner than they really are.) So when Nestlé Purina took on the challenge of raising the issue of obesity in dogs and cats, Colle+McVoy went right after moms—and veterinarians.

"Both are highly receptive to in-person communications, and both respond favorably to programs that provide solutions," says Jennifer Gove, account director at Colle+McVoy.

The key was walking that delicate line between informing and embarrassing the pet owner. And then finding a way of communicating that message one-to-one.

Engaging the local sales force with detailed materials about Purina OM, a prescription weight-management pet food, Nestlé Purina took the effort right to the streets. The Purina "Pet Pounds Patrol" mobile marketing unit visited with pet owners at shopping malls, playgrounds and dog parks, talking about the importance of learning a pet's body condition score.

A media tour was organized using a third-party spokesperson. Trade efforts provided clinic staff with education and materials about pet obesity. And traditional media like television and print were used in each market to raise broad awareness of the issue.

"It was exciting—and gratifying—to see," says Gove. "In market after market we saw significant interest from both the TV and newspaper media. We reached hundreds of thousands of pet owners through street marketing, we saw double-digit awareness of Purina OM among veterinarians and product sales increased more than 50 percent in some areas."

The future is looking a lot brighter for Purina Veterinary Diets—and Colle+McVoy —as a result.

....

A. **Purina OM** — Magazine ad

B. **Purina OM** — Mobile marketing vehicle

C. **Purina OM** — "W-A-L-K" television spot

A landmark Purina study showed that lean-fed dogs live longer, happier lives. That's why it's important to ask your veterinarian if a weight-loss diet like Purina OM Overweight Management® brand Formula is right for your dog or cat. OM and other Purina Veterinary Diets® brand formulas are available only at participating veterinary clinics. To learn more, visit purina.com/OM. And for a certificate good for $10 off your next purchase of OM, call 1-866-264-3319.

Knows he's going on a W-A-L-K.

Clueless he's on a D-I-E-T.

PURINA VETERINARY DIETS®

A

B

C

Eric Mower
and Associates

··

To drive action, Talk Human[SM]

Founded in 1968

www.mower.com
800-724-0289

LOCATIONS:
ALBANY
7 Southwoods Boulevard, Suite 300
Albany, NY 12211

ATLANTA
7000 Central Parkway, Suite 1020
Atlanta, GA 30328

BUFFALO
50 Fountain Plaza, Suite 1000
Buffalo, NY 14202

CHARLOTTE
1001 Morehead Square Drive, Suite 500
Charlotte, NC 28203

ROCHESTER
28 East Main Street, Suite 1960
Rochester, NY 14614

SYRACUSE
500 Plum Street
Syracuse, NY 13204

NEW BUSINESS CONTACT:
Eric Mower, 315-413-4200
emower@mower.com

CLIENTS INCLUDE: Bojangles', Charlotte Pipe and Foundry, Eastman Kodak Consumer Photography, Eastman Kodak's Graphic Communications Group, FedEx, First Niagara Bank, Fisher-Price, Ford, George Little Management, Georgia-Pacific, Hand Held Products, Honeywell, I Love New York, LENOX, Motorola, Nucor, Pass & Seymour/Legrand, Shurtape, Sorrento, Welch Foods

FULL-TIME EMPLOYEES: 200

Eric Mower and Associates

"How often does an ad make you want to pick up your phone and make a call, much less get in your car and drive somewhere to buy that product?" asks Eric Mower, chairman and CEO of Eric Mower and Associates (EMA). "Not often. That's because most marketing messages talk to 'target markets' and 'demographics,' and not to people."

EMA, on the other hand, believes in a "Talk Human" approach to marketing communications. "To Talk Human requires listening first, to understand not only what and how audiences think, but why they think the way they do and how they feel," explains Michael Cunningham, EMA senior partner and executive creative director, "then crafting communications that speak to both their heads and their hearts."

Why heads *and* hearts? "Because it takes both rational and emotional communications to motivate people to take action," Cunningham continues. "The rational provides essential information about features and benefits, while the emotional involves the customer, shapes beliefs and drives behavior. And driving behavior is what gets results and builds brands."

Finding the brand voice.
One of the first things EMA tells its clients is the importance of finding a loud, clear and consistent voice for the brand. The process begins with Brand

Kodak

Now it's easy to pick the right partner to help grow your business.

To succeed today, print providers not only need to provide excellent service, but also communicate that excellence to customers and potential customers. Kodak **MarketMover** business development services can help with proven marketing and promotional resources to drive growth and increase profitability. Discover **Kodak** and take your business to the next level. **To learn how, visit graphics.kodak.com.**

See us at Booth # 1901.

A

Portfolio

A. Kodak — trade ad

B. Levine & Dickson Hospice House — outdoor

C. Shurtape — trade magazine

D. Kodak — any caption

E. Hand Held Products — direct mail

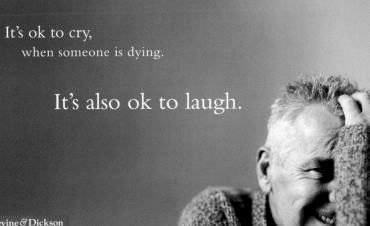

It's ok to cry, when someone is dying.

It's also ok to laugh.

Levine & Dickson
HOSPICE HOUSE
DonateHospice.org

B

Studio, a proprietary tool that digs deep into the different brand experiences that exist inside and outside of a client's company.

Through a suite of strategic planning exercises, Brand Studio reveals:

- What people within the client's organization are saying about the brand.
- What the client's competitors are saying about the brand.
- What people outside of the client's company believe about the brand.

- What the client wants its brand to stand for.
- The most differentiating, most motivating brand positioning opportunity within the client's competitive environment.

Armed with these insights, EMA's brand strategists move on to crafting the branding message and developing an integrated approach that effectively and consistently connects the message with customers. They seek the intersection of the customer's rational mind and emotional self—

the sweet spot where a message gets noticed, digested and put into play.

Connecting with today's moms.
One example of EMA's Talk Human approach is its work with Sorrento Lactalis, a leading U.S. maker of cheese products.

In 2005, Sorrento Lactalis was ready to introduce a reduced-fat version of its Stringsters string cheese. Although it had traditionally targeted moms with young

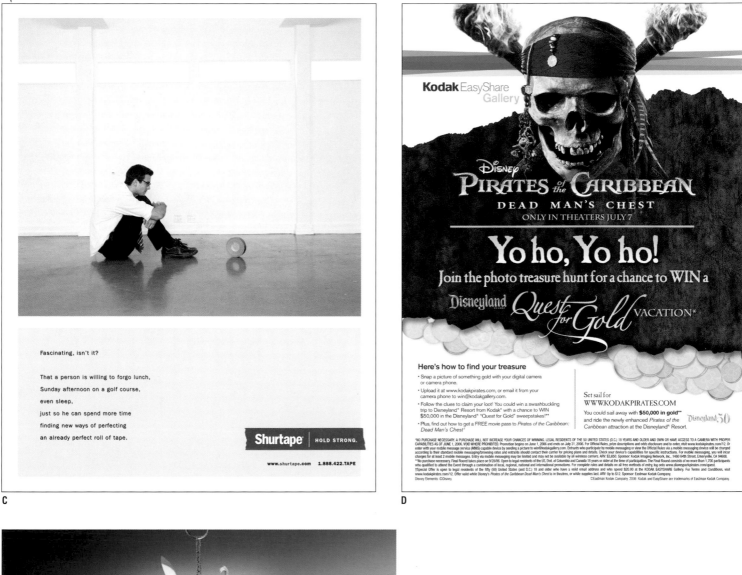

Fascinating, isn't it?

That a person is willing to forgo lunch,

Sunday afternoon on a golf course,

even sleep,

just so he can spend more time

finding new ways of perfecting

an already perfect roll of tape.

Shurtape® | HOLD STRONG.

www.shurtape.com   1.888.422.TAPE

C

D

SMALL.
MULTIFUNCTIONAL.
EASY TO USE.

HandHeld
PRODUCTS

E

Eric Mower and Associates

children for its line of snack cheese, market trends—including the prevalence of low-carb diets—presented a perfect opportunity for the manufacturer to expand its customer base.

Driving EMA's strategic launch plan was a key consumer insight: Today's moms want to orchestrate smart lifestyle choices for their entire families. That insight, combined with the popularity of mountain biking and the buzz created by Lance Armstrong's seventh Tour de France victory, led EMA to create an integrated marketing program that connected snack cheese—a healthy, on-the-go snack—with bicycling—a healthy, on-the-go family activity.

The result was the "Smart Snack on Wheels" program. Designed to position the company's snack cheese as the smart snack for the whole family and to generate trial of new reduced-fat Stringsters, the program was extensive. Special events, sweepstakes, premiums, FSIs, a dedicated website and more worked together to send a consistent message.

Like Lance Armstrong, the Smart Snack on Wheels program was a winner. Sales of Sorrento and Precious brands snack cheese grew 6.61% over the previous year—outpacing growth for the entire snack cheese category by more than two-and-a-half times.

A universal approach.
While it's easy to see how Talk Human applies to consumer marketing, the approach is the foundation for all four of the agency's practices—the Consumer Advertising Group, the Brand Promotion Group, the Public Relations and Public Affairs Group, and EMA Group B2B.

"Even when you're talking to businesses, you're talking to people," says John Favalo, managing partner of EMA Group B2B. "So the principles behind Talk Human are just as important—maybe more so—in the B-to-B space."

That was certainly the case when the agency worked with LENOX, a division of Newell Rubbermaid that manufactures blades and hand tools, to launch its new LENOX Gold utility blade.

Although testing had shown that the blade outlasts any competitive product, the contractors who were the prime audience for LENOX Gold saw utility blades simply as commodities. For the launch to be successful, that perception would have to be overcome.

EMA Group B2B began by building on its deep knowledge of the construction market. Then, in-the-field ethnographies showed that while trade pros are loyal to time-tested brands, they're willing to try a product proven to be better.

The goal was to get the product in their hands. So the agency created an integrated program that combined advertising and PR in key trade publications with media tactics typically reserved for consumers, such as point-of-sale materials at retail, mobile billboards circling active construction sites, and radio spots.

To help generate trial—as well as attention, interest and excitement in a product category that's often ignored—EMA Group B2B also targeted top U.S. construction markets with a sampling and spotting promotion called "Get Caught with the Gold."

LENOX spotters visited jobsites, giving away 6,000-plus LENOX Gold blades. A month later, they returned. Because even LENOX Gold wasn't likely to last a month under heavy use, spotters could assume that workers seen using the blades had purchased them. Those workers then

---

Campsite

Two campers are sitting at a picnic table eating Bojangles' chicken.

Two bears come running towards them and the campers get up and run.

The bears take off their heads revealing it's just a bear costume. They sit down and start eating the Bojangles'.

Two hunters with shotguns come running, firing shots. Scare off the bears in costume.

The hunters remove their costume heads revealing they're really bears.

A

B

C

received an "everyone's a winner" game piece entitling them to an American Express gift cheque on the spot.

Supporting the promotion was a range of local advertising and PR, from radio and outdoor to media alerts, announcements on major winners and trade press releases.

EMA's combination of traditional and non-traditional marcom methods proved to be a blockbuster. Nationwide, sales of LENOX Gold increased 59%. In the first market targeted, sales increased 231%. And at Home Depot stores across the U.S., sales increased between 102% and 167%.

Talking success.

With its work achieving such outstanding results for its clients, it's no wonder that EMA has grown to 200 employees in six offices—Atlanta, Ga.; Charlotte, N.C.; and Albany, Buffalo, Rochester and Syracuse, N.Y.—and $170 million in capitalized billings. In fact, the agency is ranked among the nation's top 100 agencies by *Adweek, Ad Age, BtoB, PR Week,* and *PROMO* magazines.

"Everything a client shares with the outside world says something about its brand," adds Mower, summing up the importance of Talk Human. "That's why every message the client sends needs to be so strategic and so compelling, that it makes prospective customers stand up and say, 'Yes, I want that and I want it now.'"

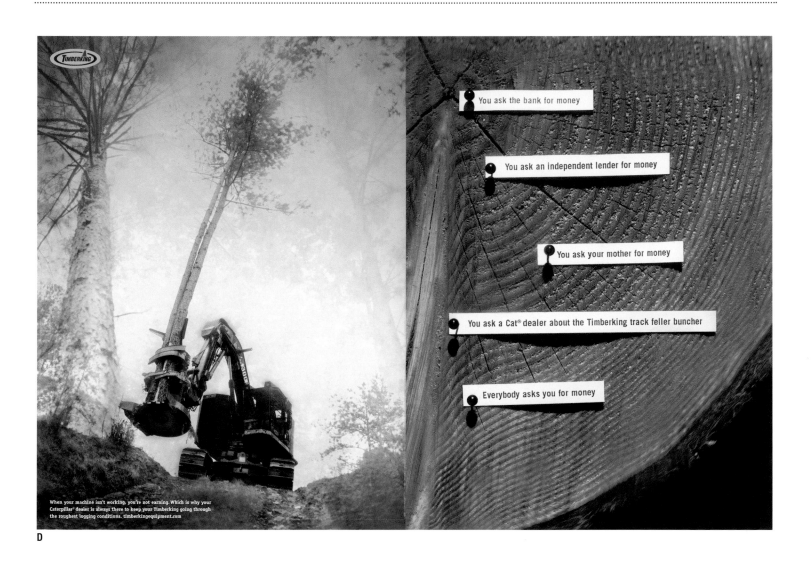

D

Portfolio

A. **Bojangles'** — TV

B. **Motorola** — trade magazine

C. **FedEx Kinko's** — in-store display

D. **Timberking** — trade magazine

CASE STUDY: Nucor

We started recycling steel with an electric arc furnace,
when everyone else was using a century-old method to make steel.
We pioneered the technology to pour steel into thin slabs, while others were pouring
thicker slabs and flattening them. Again, the way it had always been done.
Along the way, we made steel mills smaller and more efficient. We streamlined management
and gave the decision-making power to the plants, the people closest to our customers.
And managed to make something the steel industry hadn't made in a while. A profit.
www.nucor.com

It's Our Nature.

When the agency was awarded the account, Nucor was a true underdog in the world of Big Steel, a fraction of the size of behemoths like Bethlehem Steel and US Steel.

"Even though Nucor wasn't the biggest company out there, we believed it was one of the best," says EMA Senior Partner Tom Eppes. "Its management practices, culture, innovation and get-it-done attitude were unparalleled. We felt if we could get the message right, the outside world would believe it, too."

For the first dozen years or so of the relationship, advertising and marketing communications targeted individuals who specify and purchase steel, including purchasing agents, architects, auto and appliance designers and the like. The B-to-B advertising was among the industry's best, frequently winning top readership scores and awards for creative excellence. And Nucor grew faster than any other steel company.

As the company grew, it became more important to influence broader audiences, including senior executives at steel-consuming companies, potential investors, opinion leaders, and the broader public. With the expansion of the campaign audience in mind, the EMA team set out to revitalize the Nucor brand positioning and ele-

vate Nucor above the morass of the struggling steel industry. Through research of Nucor employees and customers, a theme emerged.

"We found that people who know Nucor see it as more than just a steel company," says Matt Ferguson, EMA partner and account director. "It's actually a catalyst to making things better. It's built into Nucor's DNA as a company. It's just the way they are. So 'It's Our Nature' emerged as a fitting theme line."

The agency team saw it as an idea that could resonate with every audience—from B-to-B to corporate and ultimately to consumers who could influence political decisions about fair trade. Steel buyers could be assured their projects would run smoother and better because of Nucor's top customer-satisfaction and on-time delivery ratings. Investors could feel confident their portfolios would perform better, since Nucor has been the only steelmaker to turn a profit every year and issue a dividend every quarter for more than 30 years. Opinion leaders could be assured that Nucor, the world's number-one recycler, was making the world a better place. And employees' lives would be better because of Nucor's pay-for-performance structure and industry-leading benefits.

"Sure, we're talking to people in different walks of life who each need something different from Nucor, but they're still people," says EMA Partner and Executive Creative Director Seth Werner. "We still needed to, as we like to say, Talk Human."

To dramatize the fact that Nucor is a catalyst to making things better, the EMA team decided to simply tell real stories about how Nucor does just that, each unified by the "It's Our Nature" theme.

With such a highly targeted audience for both the corporate and trade campaigns, select print and online media proved to be the most cost-effective tools to use. Corporate ads were placed in publications such as *The Wall Street Journal, Business Week, Fortune* and *USA Today,* as well as online venues, including wsj.com, businessweek.com and usatoday.com.

Nucor's website was re-branded with consistent graphics and messages. The brand message was infused into public relations outreach, and PR was utilized as a tool to tell more Nucor "stories." Everything reinforced the brand, from employee orientation DVDs to newsletters, and from tradeshow displays to sales presentations. The agency also recognized big potential in using Nucor's employees as a medium for the message.

"One of our biggest 'guerilla marketing' opportunities was to help Nucor employees articulate and live out the Nucor brand essence every day," says EMA Partner Laura Mercer. "Their employees are their biggest ambassadors. So we helped introduce the new brand positioning with a mailing from the CEO that went to every employee household, including a personalized letter, a postcard-sized version of one of the print ads, and a decal of the logo and slogan for car windows or hardhats."

Results were beyond expectations. Unaided brand awareness for Nucor rose 85% after the first year of the broader campaign. Nucor's overall corporate reputation jumped 35%. Ad recall scores were among the highest of all advertisers in the publications in which Nucor advertised.

"When our ads for this steel company started beating sexy brands like Armani and Hummer, we figured we must be doing something right," says Werner.

And, by the way, Nucor has gone from underdog to big dog in the corporate world. It's now America's largest steel manufacturer and one of Fortune's 100 Most Admired Companies. It hit number one on the 2005 BusinessWeek 50 list of best performing companies, its stock has performed exceptionally well.

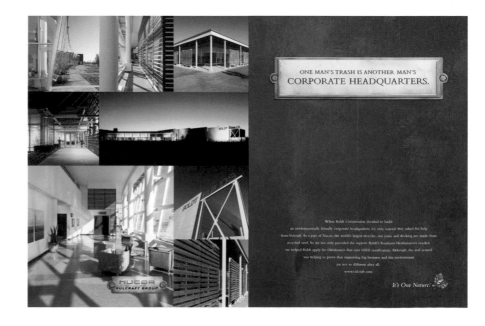

CASE STUDY: Fisher-Price

The best thing to happen to 1ˢᵗ birthdays since chocolate cake.

Ask any parent, and you'll hear how quickly time flies as a child grows from newborn to toddler to kindergartener. No company knows this better than Fisher-Price, the world leader in children's products and toys.

Unlike most consumer products, a young child is only "in the market" for a particular toy for a short time. Extending that time for even six months can make a huge impact on business. And that's just what Fisher-Price did, redesigning Little People playsets to be appropriate for children as young as 12 months, as opposed to the previous age grade of 18 months.

EMA saw the assignment from Fisher-Price as an opportunity to show its stuff and win the account away from the former agency of record.

"Fisher-Price challenged us with this assignment," said Doug Bean, managing partner. "They wanted to see what we could do with this. We saw a chance to show Fisher-Price that we would get to know them, their business and their customers. And develop strategies that would accomplish their goals."

As such, EMA was being asked to take a big brand and make it even bigger. Sales volume for Fisher-Price Little People toys topped one million units each year. The 40-year old brand had a solid lead in the playsets category, with seven of the top 10 best sellers.

"Our mission was clear and simple," said Bean. "We needed to reach out to that very narrow target of moms with babies seven to 10 months of age. We needed to raise her awareness of the new 12-month age grade for Little People toys, and affect her decision to enter the Little People 'family' at an earlier stage in her child's development."

EMA attacked the problem with its "Talk Human" branding approach: listening to consumers, understanding what they say and how it

drives them, and then reaching out to them on a human-to-human level.

"We started with the fact that the toys were now appropriate for children as early as 12 months. That led us to think about first birthdays," said creative director Rob Neiler. "From there we unearthed a deep-seated human truth—new parents approach the first birthday party as a way to celebrate with family and friends that they, and their baby, survived the first year."

In other words, while one-year-olds don't think much about their first birthday party, their parents do. It's a rite of parental passage.

Thus, the goal became for Little People to "own" the first birthday celebration. Based on what the

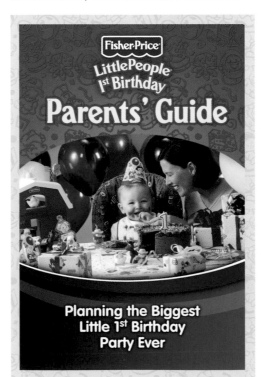

Parents' Guide

Planning the Biggest Little 1ˢᵗ Birthday Party Ever

EMA team learned from listening sessions with consumers, the team's game plan was three-pronged:

- Play to mom's pride—she loves showing baby pictures.
- Ignite a viral reaction—tell mom about Little People, and she'll share the news with other moms.
- Drive multiple purchases—let friends and family know that Little People toys make a great birthday gift.

The primary offer was a free kit for parents— "The Parents' Guide to Throwing a Great Little First Birthday Party." This touched on two human traits—the pride surrounding the first birthday, and the fact that brand-new moms are voracious readers of how-to literature.

The campaign theme promised it would be "The best thing to happen to 1st birthdays since chocolate cake." The kit included nine Little People themed party invitations, ready to be customized with the birthday child's photo. Kodak was brought in as a partner, enclosing a coupon giving mom the chance to make the nine pictures needed to complete the invitations at a Kodak Picture Maker kiosk.

And, since the invites featured Little People characters, it provided a tacit "suggestion" to guests that Little People toys might be a great idea for a birthday gift.

Fisher-Price supported the program with party tips on its website, and a paper goods company licensed Little People characters for plates, napkins, party favors, etc., so mom could carry the theme throughout the party.

The birthday kit was the first in a series of mailings that included premiums and dollar-off coupons for Little People playsets.

The prime medium EMA used was direct mail, owing to the narrow and specific target for the effort. Even ads in parenting magazines would have hit too broad an audience for effective use of media dollars.

The media expenditure was approximately $105,000 for direct mail; $20,000 for online.

The program drove record-breaking sales in its first year. Both Fisher-Price and Kodak saw coupon redemption rates near 10%, compared to the typical 0.25% to 0.50%. Moms even called Fisher-Price to ask if they could buy additional packages of the promotion's customizable party invitations.

The promotion delivered $6 million in sales for Fisher-Price, enough to convince the toy company that EMA deserved to be named promotions AOR. EMA is now part of the Fisher-Price team when it comes to strategic business development, brand marketing, key account planning, licensed products and visual merchandising.

Gabriel deGrood Bendt

Always Thinking®

Founded in 1997

608 2nd Avenue South,
Suite 129,
Minneapolis, MN 55402
612-547-5000
www.always-thinking.com

KEY NEW BUSINESS CONTACT:
Jim Bendt, 612-547-5050

SENIOR MANAGEMENT:
Tom Gabriel, CEO, Creative Director
Doug deGrood, Partner, Creative Director
Jim Bendt, Partner, President

CLIENTS: Andersen Windows, Activision games, Antron carpet, Best Buy, Danze faucets, Del Monte/Gedney Pickles, Gold'n Plump chicken, MacPhail Center for Music, Mortenson Construction, Science Museum of Minnesota, Sempra Energy, Valleyfair amusement park and Zebco fishing gear

Gabriel deGrood Bendt

A lot of agencies talk about "out of the box" thinking, but Gabriel deGrood Bendt (GdB) is one agency that literally wrote the instruction manual for it. Just click onto GdB's website and you'll get an interactive version of their user's guide. It tells you everything you need to know about working with the agency, complete with definitions and simple line drawings. There's also a printed version for clients who'd like to keep one on hand. According to CEO Tom Gabriel, "Toasters and DVD players come with an owner's manual, why not an agency?"

From the beginning, the agency had a simple plan—to build client's brands by providing extraordinary thinking and creativity across a broad range of disciplines. While others were exploring the idea of "integrated marketing," GdB was practicing it. To this day, the agency has no separate departments and has minimized layers—all for the sake of cultivating great ideas.

Founded in 1997, the agency early on proved that a nimble, resourceful company could compete with anyone by winning the DuPont Corian® account, previously with BBDO/New York. Based on that win and others during the dot-com boom, the agency grew to more than 30 people in

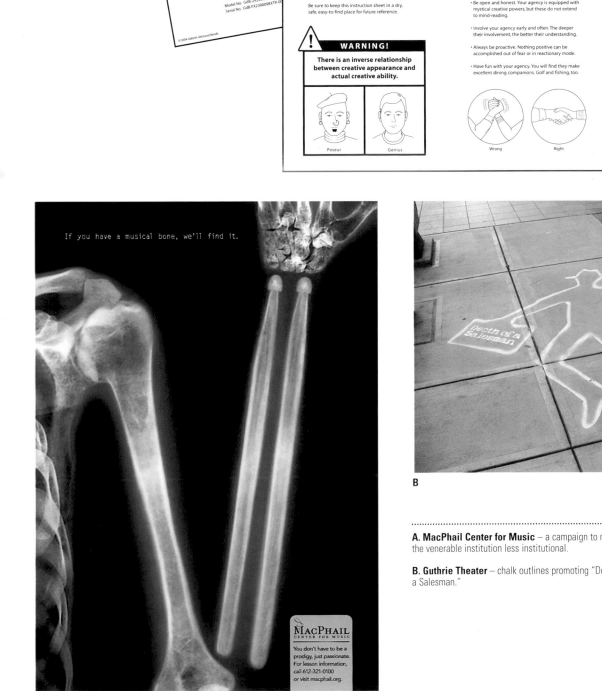

A

B

A. **MacPhail Center for Music** – a campaign to make the venerable institution less institutional.

B. **Guthrie Theater** – chalk outlines promoting "Death of a Salesman."

little more than three years.

In 2001, the original agency merged with Kaleidoscope, another Minneapolis agency whose founder and President was Jim Bendt, a former colleague of Tom Gabriel's. Together, they formed Gabriel deGrood Bendt, the name also reflecting the important and growing role of Creative Director/Writer Doug deGrood, a former Adweek All-Star at Fallon Worldwide.

Though quite a bit larger these days,

GdB is still all about great creative and non-traditional solutions. What makes this agency unique is that those solutions are coupled with the hands-on involvement of senior management in an environment where everyone literally works side-by-side. The offices of creatives, account people, media planners, PR folks, etc. are all interspersed to encourage the open exchange of ideas.

"Our culture and environment inspires and rewards fresh ideas and inventive

thinking," says Gabriel. In fact, as you enter the GdB offices, you can feel the energy in the building. Set in a ground-floor, formerly retail space, the vibe is bright, open, and contemporary.

The agency's mission statement, Always Thinking®, can be seen and felt throughout the agency. Everything from conference room tables to business cards and lobby signage to the website (www.always-thinking.com) showcases the importance of these two powerful words.

C

C. **Science Museum** – TV for "Body Worlds" exhibit.

D. **Gedney** – outdoor.

E. **Danze** – print for America's fastest growing faucet brand.

FIVE GAY MEN AND A CAMERA CREW BARGE INTO YOUR BATHROOM. THEY'RE SPEECHLESS.

Life is too short to settle for boring faucets. And you don't have to with Danze. To see our full line of more than 1,000 faucets, showerheads and accessories, visit Danze.com.

E

NOBODY CRAVES A CARROT.

EXTRAORDINARY PICKLES

GEDNEY
KOSHER DILL
BABIES

D

Gabriel deGrood Bendt

"I've always believed that building brands is fundamentally a simple business," says Gabriel. "It starts with both the client and the agency listening. Listening not only to each other, but more importantly, to the voice of the customer, whether that customer is an end user or an employee on the factory floor. While this isn't exactly radical thinking, it's amazing how often that little voice is, in the end, slighted or just plain ignored. Whenever we, or our clients, have temporarily veered off course, it's been a direct result of overcomplicating things and losing sight of this simple truth."

It's this kind of thinking that helped GdB win the Andersen Windows account from the agency that held it for 72 years. After being invited to pitch the business, GdB presented a simple, compelling solution that involved taking a fresh look at one of the company's once-famous themelines, Come home to Andersen.

Unlike most of the category advertising flaunting Architectual Digest style room shots, the GdB campaign focuses on the simple, intimate relationship people have with their windows.

"So many clients and agencies look to great branding successes like Nike and Apple, and want to emulate those strategies," says Gabriel. "What they don't realize is that what worked for those companies isn't necessarily what's best for them. It's our job to help them discover

A

B

A-B. Andersen Windows

what's unique about their brand. To find their own true story. We don't necessarily create it, we just help it evolve."

Does the agency have aspirations to grow? "We've always held to the belief that it's not the size of the agency, but the size of the idea," says Jim Bendt, GdB's President. "That's not an argument for small. Nor is it an argument for big. Size is irrelevant. Our goal is not to get bigger. It's to get better." Those motivations have helped the agency create a history of

working with big brands that were previously with much larger agencies.

For example, Gold'n Plump, the Midwest's largest poultry producer, came to GdB seeking fresh thinking and greater attention. The agency looked at the business from a neutral perspective and developed a campaign that placed as much emphasis on the meat case dividers as it did on the 30-second TV spots. The work also included a wide range of interactive and new media vehicles.

"We're not afraid of the changes in our business and the world. In fact, we embrace them," says Creative Director Doug deGrood. "It's still all about using creativity to make a strong connection." Speaking of creativity, GdB does have an impressive award show record. Yet the bottom line is always the client's bottom line.

"I'd never sacrifice what's best for a client's business just to win a creative award," says deGrood. "As much as we live for great ideas, we would never be content if those ideas didn't lead to significant differences in our clients' businesses. The Effie Awards are important to us because they're all about results. The O'Toole Awards, which honor creative consistency across a range of clients are also meaningful. And all the awards we do win help us attract the best talent."

If you haven't been tallying the winners at the award shows, GdB has consistently been the recipient of Effies and O'Tooles for their work. In fact, for five of the last seven years GdB has won or been runner-up in the O'Tooles.

Want an agency that's always thinking on your behalf? Start by visiting www.always-thinking.com.

C

D

E

C-D. Gold'n Plump – outdoor for the Midwest's largest chicken producer.

E. Freschetta – TV promoting their brick oven frozen pizza.

F. Black Forest Inn – outdoor.

G. Valleyfair – outdoor.

F

G

CASE STUDY: Northarvest Bean Growers Association

"Beans, beans, the magical fruit, the more you eat, the more you…" Yup, we've all heard that one before—not to mention the many other amusing little ditties at the expense of the poor, oft-maligned bean. But how many people are aware of the amazing health and nutritional benefits inherent in beans (Low in fat/cholesterol. High in foliate/fiber?) Or that, in actuality, the more you eat, the less you…well, you know.

The Bean Growers Association partnered with Gabriel deGrood Bendt (GdB) to change the negative perceptions that have been deeply seeded in most people since childhood.

Using the latest trend data, MRI, PRIZM and secondary resources, the agency defined the target as the "Epicurious." These are people who, regardless of age, like to try new things, are on top of the latest food trends and enjoy sharing their experiences with friends and family. They crave information. And, in order to appeal to this group, the communications needed to tap into their curious and inquisitive nature.

After much debate, it was decided the best way to get around the "giggle factor" associated with beans was to tackle it head-on; to let the amusement quotient provide the power behind the majority of messaging. At the same time, it was very important to have the giggle factor lead into the many surprising health benefits inherent in beans. Not overpower it. As a result, the target saw messages that promoted the low cholesterol nature of beans (Who Cut the Cholesterol?) and the heart healthy benefits of beans (Shaped like a kidney but good for your heart).

To reach the Epicurious, the agency developed a "flypaper" strategy, and saturated popular dining and entertainment districts with a variety of unconventional out-of-home media. Vehicles included upscale street furniture, bulletins, posters, bus benches, wrapped commuter trains and wrapped delivery trucks (giving the impression beans were being delivered all over town). The effect was amazing. Everywhere people turned, they'd see an ad, giving an appearance of a much more extensive effort.

To allow the advertising to generate PR buzz, markets were carefully selected based on media efficiency indexes, creative out-of-home vehicles, and geographic dispersement across the country. The result was a "Johnny Appleseed" approach which allowed the message to spread to Boston, Chicago Minneapolis, Sacramento, Fargo and Bismarck, all with a budget barely big enough for one market.

The Magical Fruit campaign achieved record breaking results against all stated objectives. GdB increased the value of the media budget by 48 percent through press hits. The campaign was featured on CNN, ABC, NBC and CBS. It was talked about on over 800 radio stations across the country. And it appeared in papers such as the *Washington Post, Boston Globe* and *LA Times.*

The Magicalfruit website achieved a number one ranking on all major search engines and received 10 percent of all online bean searches to the site (all without paid placement)

Maybe the most rewarding part was the overwhelming amount of letters of appreciation from the industry and new Bean Evangelists praising the campaign.

A

C

Shaped like a kidney but good for your heart. Go figure.

MagicalFruit.org

B

D

A. **Bus shelters** – located in dining and entertainment districts.

B. **Bar coasters** – placed in trendy bars/restaurants.

C. **TV Coverage** – Even CNN couldn't resist helping us spread the word, at no cost, of course.

D. **Outdoor/event** – grass root efforts included school children singing a new version of the familiar beans song.

E. **Website** – Magicalfruit.org.

E

CASE STUDY: Zebco Fishing

A

B

A-B. Print

C. TV

Zebco® is the reel that taught America to fish (over 40 million people to be exact). But despite its rich heritage, the brand (and category) was experiencing a decline in sales. The root cause of the sales decline was the waning interest in fishing among kids. Apparently, iPODs and video games were pulling kids away from an American pastime. Zebco® was also celebrating their 50th Anniversary, and wanted to find a way to increase sales and get parents and kids back to the water.

Research revealed that parents felt very guilty about how electronics have taken over as the hobby of choice for kids. At the same time, parents were looking for ways to reconnect with their kids. They often recalled memories from their own childhood, which often related to fishing with their dads.

The creative strategy was built around reminding parents of the joys of fishing and how it could help them spend more quality time with their kids. As a result, ads featured headlines such as "Don't let your kid be the one that got away" and "What kids did with their thumbs before video games." The campaign included an integrated effort in consumer magazines, outdoor boards on major highways to hot fishing spots, in-store materials, bumper stickers at fishing stores and a stronger presence on their website all focusing on getting parents and kids back to the water.

The strategic and creative tactics paid off. During the course of the campaign, Zebco® was able to

increase main line sales by 30 percent. Despite the declining category, Zebco® sold out of their entire inventory and left retailers clamoring for more.

The campaign also received an overwhelming amount of requests for bumper stickers from parents who wanted to proudly display Zebco's message on the back of their minivans.

C

GSD&M

··

Winning on Purpose

Founded 1971

Idea City
828 W. 6th St.
Austin, TX 78703
512-242-4736
www.gsdm.com

KEY NEW BUSINESS CONTACT:
J.B. Raftus, SVP, New Business, 512-242-4632
Ashley Andy, Director of New Business, 512-242-4424

SENIOR MANAGEMENT:
Steve Gurasich, Founder/Chairman/CEO
Roy Spence, Founder/President
Judy Trabulsi, Founder/EVP/Executive Media Director
Tim McClure, Founder, Mythos Branding Group President

CLIENTS: Southwest Airlines, Brinker International/Chili's Grill & Bar, PGA Tour, Lennox, MasterCard Worldwide/Media, AT&T, U.S. Air Force, Kohler, AARP, American Legacy Foundation, Frito-Lay/Tostitos, BMW, Norwegian Cruise Line, Yellowpages.com, SI.com

FULLTIME EMPLOYEES: 800

GSD&M

How did four people right out of college, with no experience and no money, build one of the country's leading branding agencies in the wrong city?

Roy Spence has no doubt that a great deal of GSD&M's expertise and success with branding comes from the fact that the agency came along at the right time in the wrong place.

"Look at the evolution of branding," says Spence, founder and president of the Austin, Texas–based agency. "In the '50s and into the '60s it was about a product's attributes. In the early '70s there was a shift to what was the benefit of the product's attributes."

About the time that latter shift was taking place in corporate America, Spence and four college buddies (Steve Gurasich, Judy Trabulsi, Tim McClure and Jim Darilek) were graduating from the University of Texas in Austin. The five wanted to start an ad agency and wanted to stay in the city they'd gone to school in.

They freely admit they had little idea of what they were getting into, which was a good thing or they might never have stayed in Austin. And if they hadn't stayed in Austin, they probably never would have known the success they have achieved.

"When we first started, there really wasn't much of an advertising community in Austin, so we didn't have other agency people to hang out with," says Spence. "So we hung out with our clients. A lot of what we learned about the advertising business

A

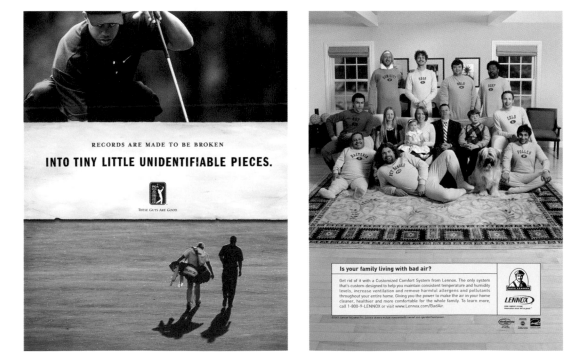

B

C

came from their perspective. And since we didn't know what the rules of advertising were, we had to use our intuition."

The benefit was that the agency formed strong partnerships with clients that were starting to grow and take off at a time brands were evolving from being driven by attributes and benefits, to being driven by something more, something beyond just profit—purpose.

"Our agency came of age in the '80s when we had a chance to work with some of the smartest people in the business world," says agency senior vice president J.B. Raftus. "People like Sam Walton (founder of Wal-Mart) and Herb Kelleher (founder of Southwest Airlines). What we learned from them helped form the essence of how we think about branding."

Raftus and Spence point to Wal-Mart and Southwest as prime examples of the sort of companies that are the prototypical GSD&M client—ones that have a purpose beyond the balance sheet.

The late Sam Walton wanted to make money, the two concede, but there was also a purpose behind Wal-Mart, which was to give the average working man access to things only upscale people could have afforded in the past.

Southwest Airline's Kelleher likewise wanted to show a profit, but he also wanted to make air travel an option to people who couldn't afford the cost of a plane ticket. In Raftus' words, he "democratized" the skies.

A. AT&T

B. PGA Tour

C. Lennox

D. Margarita Madness

E-F. Kohler

D

E

F

In each case, purpose put an additional layer onto the company's brand that gave it a position no one else could claim. If Walton simply wanted to be another big-box discounter, or Kelleher wanted to play the same game as the established major air carriers, neither would have had a defensible position.

"If you can find and communicate the purpose behind a brand, then there's no ceiling for a company," Spence says.

As a result, GSD&M's guiding light is a strategic process it refers to as Purpose-Based Branding. "If a client can work through the superficial layers of the market segment it competes in, and get to the core purpose of its organization, then it has a positioning that is virtually invincible. That company can stake a position the competition can't claim."

As a result:

• AARP isn't about offering discounts and advice on aging. Its core purpose is to create positive social change, not just for members, but society at large.

• In a world where people are looking for ways to slow down, have a little fun and get together with the people they enjoy everyday, Tostitos offers an easy way to create moments to connect. The purpose is about providing opportunities to Stop. Gather. Engage.

It's purpose-based philosophy also gives the agency an ideal filter when it considers new-business opportunities.

"If we look at a company and we can't

A

B

C

A. U.S. Air Force

B. Museum of African American History

C. UnitedHealthcare

see a purpose behind it, we know it's not going to be a good fit for us," Spence says. "Sometimes there are companies out there that have changed and don't know what their purpose is, or their purpose has changed or they have sort of lost their way. Those are clients we feel we can help."

If all the talk of purpose sounds a little too touchy-feely for some, consider that GSD&M now has billings of over $1 billion and more than 800 employees—no mean feat when one considers it is still in Austin.

"We had branch offices in [larger cities in Texas]," Spence says. "But it's tough to be a team when everyone is so spread out. We're committed to Austin."

Indeed, the agency has created its own city within the city of its birth. "For a long time we had very corporate-looking offices," Raftus says. "We did that on purpose so clients wouldn't think we were creating ads out of Roy's garage." Raftus was referring to the agency's early, lean days. According to GSD&M history, in the salad days, Spence couldn't swing rent so he slept on a mattress under an art table in the agency's one-room office and showered at a nearby health club.

When the agency wanted to grow beyond its corporate image, the partners created Idea City. Part of the inspiration for that came from a rare trip outside the agency by Spence.

"It was probably the only time I ever went to a Chamber of Commerce meeting," he says. "They had a guy making a presentation on what cities (in America) would be like in the 21st century. Austin was going to be the idea city. I liked that phrase and we decided to use it for our new home, in part as a tribute to the city that allowed us to succeed."

The agency wanted to design a space that would inspire great work by creating a marketplace of ideas. The result was a structure that includes a library, an art gallery, a rotunda and "war rooms" for creative think sessions. Another goal was to have a space that fostered spontaneous interaction among the employees across all agency disciplines, which would build a sense of community.

"The result of bringing everyone together is stronger collaboration that leads to great work for our clients," says Ashley Andy, director of new business.

Then management had the courage to place the words "Idea City" directly under its name in big letters over the front door. "If you put the words 'idea city' on your building, you'd better have some," Spence says. "It makes us rise to the occasion."

D

D. Norwegian Cruise Line

E. AARP

F. American Legacy Foundation

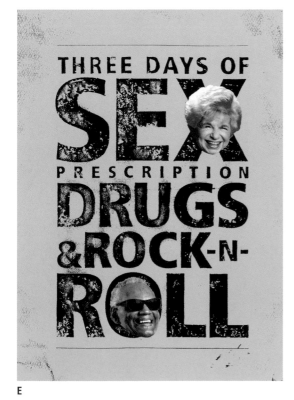

E

F

CASE STUDY: Southwest Airlines

Born on a cocktail napkin in 1967, Southwest Airlines pioneered the concept of lower airfares. The way the client was able to accomplish that was by stripping away some of the frills of traveling by plane, such as in-flight meals and assigned seats.

It worked as far as consumer interest was concerned, but it also left the impression that Southwest was the bargain alternative, which can be dangerous territory for any company. Once a brand becomes the cheaper alternative in the minds of consumers, its ability to get a broad message out is lost—the bargain brand forever represents compromise.

Thus, when Southwest chairman Herb Kelleher brought his account to GSD&M in 1981, he needed consumers to see more than just the bottom-line.

"You can do wonderful things in a cave all by yourself, but the world isn't going to know about it, won't give you credit and won't come and buy your products," Kelleher says.

"From the start our agency/client relationship has been a true partnership," says Dianna Howell, who has worked on the Southwest account for 15 of her 20 years with GSD&M. "Brand building is long term. It's not done in one campaign, so it's important that the client sees you as his partner.

"Great creative is obviously an important part of the mix and to do it right, so that the creative works to build the brand, you have to understand the client."

Applying its Purpose-Based Branding, the agency saw that what Southwest was accomplishing was giving people the ability to fly on their own terms by offering lower prices, better service and more flights.

"We realized that this company was about allowing everybody to get out there and travel," agency director of new business Ashley Andy explains. "Southwest was about freedom."

Indeed, the tagline on virtually all of Southwest's print and TV ads drives home the message: "You're now free to move about the country."

And along with consistently producing fresh creative, the agency has had a hand in creating several of Southwest's programs it would later create advertising for. To wit: a handful of agency senior officials were part of a committee that

(with the client) created the Rapid Rewards program.

"Southwest's program couldn't be like most airlines, because Southwest customers typically fly shorter trips and it would take too long to build up their miles," says Howell.

So instead of a complicated frequent-flier reward system, Southwest made it simple. Fly eight times and the ninth is free, eliminating the need to track monthly mileage statements.

In 1988, when Southwest became the official airline of Sea World of Texas, the agency came up with the idea of painting one of the client's Boeing 737s to look like Shamu, the theme park's killer whale. That concept was later carried forward with specially painted planes to commemorate other milestone events for Southwest.

Participating with a client in areas that aren't traditionally thought of as advertising is one of the goals of any agency. They go from being seen as an outside vendor to being an inside partner and the value and trust of the relationship goes up exponentially.

"Southwest has asked us to be involved in a number of things relating to their business beyond just marketing," Howell says. "Things such as their culture committee, labor relations initiatives and their annual report development and creation."

But in a relationship that was forged by the agency getting consumers to not think about numbers, it is a number that validates the agency's success in tending the Southwest brand. The client has stayed with the agency for 25 years, an almost unheard-of tenure.

And why not? The airline has posted profitable gains every year of the partnership with GSD&M. In 2005, Southwest boarded a record-breaking 88 million passengers; showed operating revenues of $7.6 billion; and has been named the highest-valued airline in the world as measured by market capitalization.

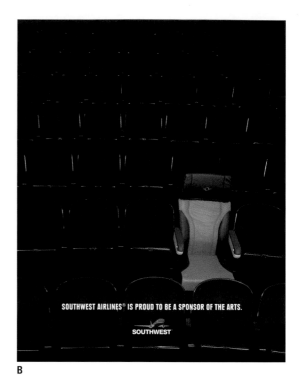

SOUTHWEST AIRLINES® IS PROUD TO BE A SPONSOR OF THE ARTS.

B

A

C

DING Search	**DING**	**DING** No more searching.	Download **DING** and our best deals come to your desktop. SOUTHWEST.COM
sound off	sound off	sound off	sound off
D	E	F	G

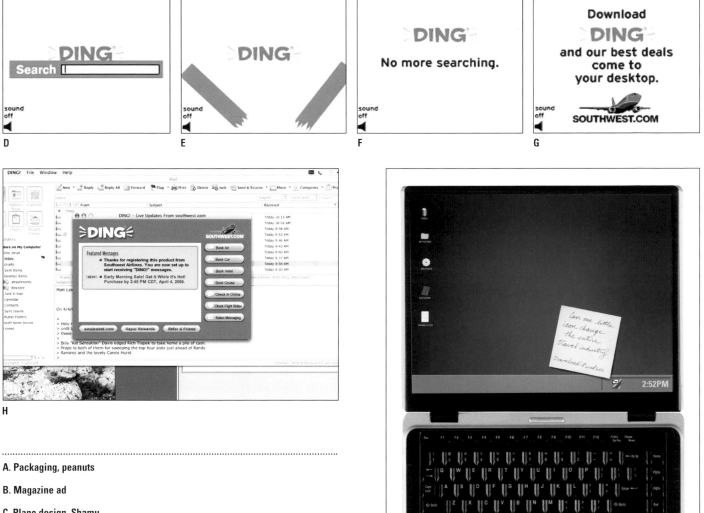

H

A. Packaging, peanuts

B. Magazine ad

C. Plane design, Shamu

D–H. Online advertising — The recent focus has been on driving purchases through the southwest.com website to capture and track important consumer information and at the same time lower overhead cost of doing business. GSD&M and Southwest developed a desktop application that allows customized messaging and product offerings on the subscriber's computer desktop. Consumers receive fare specials and engage with the brand on their terms, providing a customized and relevant interaction with Southwest. A record-breaking number downloaded the application the first month of operation. Online sales increased seven percent that same month.

I. Magazine ad

J. Rapid Rewards, outdoor

K. Web banner

I

J

K

CASE STUDY: BMW

In 2005 BMW came to GSD&M with sales up and no real glaring issues to confront. Instead of wanting a partner to help them fix something, they were looking for a team that could work with them to seize the momentum and expand the brand's relevance to a new target that had not historically considered BMW.

GSD&M needed to expand relevance; not divert it. They needed to preserve the BMW core—the BMW loyalists and considerers—while at the same time get those who were not considering BMW to consider them. The obvious answer was to go straight after those 1.5+ million people and show them more of the same old industry clichés: cars zooming along beautiful, winding, traffic-free (and probably wet) roads. But, they asked themselves, "Would this be the right approach for the brand to build momentum?" The evidence showed that while this might get short-term sales blips, this was not an approach for the long haul.

The GSD&M media and planning teams worked together to create a profile of the type of person who would be right for the brand. The team collaborated with Richard Florida, author of three recent books about the economic impact of The Creative Class. This Creative Class is a fast-growing, highly educated, well-paid segment of American society. They are progressive, tech-savvy, solutions-oriented, and paid to think. They do not believe that one size fits all and value the things BMW has been known for since the company's beginning: authenticity and independent thought.

The agency identified a subset they dubbed the Idea Class (25 million strong). These high-achieving consumers share many of BMW's principles: an independent spirit, a drive to challenge conventional wisdom, and an appreciation for a brand's ability to offer both substance and style.

Looking at the brand and the Idea Class together, ideas emerged they could bond over. The Idea Class favors an independent spirit. GSD&M would leverage the fact that BMW is one of only a few independently owned and managed automotive companies in the world. The Idea Class understands the drive to challenge conventional wisdom. GSD&M would leverage the benefit of independence—BMW can not only dream big, but also then do something about it—turning exceptional ideas into reality.

This evolved into the positioning statement that drives the creative executions: BMW is a company of ideas. At BMW ideas are everything. And because we are an independent company, we have the freedom to make sure great ideas live on to become The Ultimate Driving Machine.

The new campaigns are already generating positive responses among the target audience and have rallied BMW employees at both the corporate and dealer levels.

Give designers complete freedom
and they tend to create cars that give it right back.

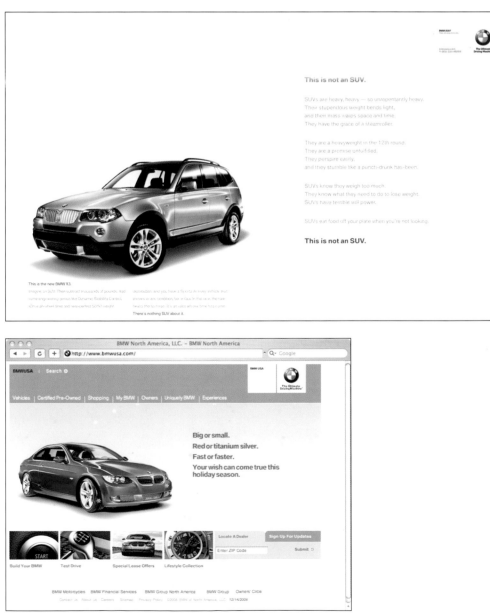

This is not an SUV.

SUVs are heavy, heavy — so unrepentantly heavy.
They stupendous weight bends light,
and their mass warps space and time.
They have the grace of a steamroller.

They are a heavyweight in the 12th round.
They are a promise unfulfilled.
They perspire easily,
and they stumble like a punch-drunk has-been.

SUVs know they weigh too much.
They know what they need to do to lose weight.
SUVs have terrible will power.

SUVs eat food off your plate when you're not looking.

This is not an SUV.

Big or small.
Red or titanium silver.
Fast or faster.
Your wish can come true this
holiday season.

Guest Relations
Marketing

···

"Transforming Prospects to Guests,
and Guests to Zealots"

Founded in 2006

1401 Peachtree St.
Suite 500
Atlanta, GA 30309
404-870-8410
fax: 404-870-8411
www.guestrelationsmarketing.com

SENIOR MANAGEMENT:
Michael Tyre, Founder/Partner, 404-663-9065 (direct)
April Voris, Founder/Partner/Director of Client Services, 678-427-8635 (direct)

CLIENTS: Mauna Lani Resort, The Lane Company, Solís Hotels & Resorts,
West Paces Hotel Group

Guest Relations Marketing

How does a well-established agency grow up to become a young, new agency rooted in original thinking and fresh, new ways of building brands?

Certainly a loaded question. But one agency is ready to fire away with the answer.

Meet Guest Relations, a brand new "seedling" firm of Cole Henderson Drake, an agency founded in 1969.

In the '80s and early '90s, CHD was likely the most awarded agency in the Southeast. Best known for its work for The Ritz-Carlton Hotel Company and Bush Beans, CHD also helped build such brands as Masland Carpets, Georgia-Pacific, Henredon Furniture, Dunlop Slazenger and Omni Hotels. It was the agency's singular focus on distinctive creative work that attracted talented people from all over the country.

Enter two people who counted themselves among that group: Michael Tyre, who came to CHD from ValuJet Airlines in 1997 to establish a separate strategic planning unit, and April Voris, arriving at the agency fresh from the University of Alabama. Following extended talks, they received the blessing of original partner John Drake to establish Guest Relations in early 2006. Guest Relations was born out of a desire to be a true marketing consultancy impacting the total relationship between a client and its customers.

"As great as CHD had always been, it became apparent that it had to change

A

B

C

with the times," says Tyre. "The agency had grown up in the '70s and '80s, when brands were largely built on advertising. Today, that's no longer the case. It seemed to make a lot more sense to start fresh than to try reshaping a well-defined, entrenched agency into a different entity. We truly valued the heritage and quality of CHD, but it was also important for us to establish a new direction."

The business started with a handful of people who had worked with Tyre and Voris at CHD, and two clients: Mauna Lani Resort, a 4-diamond resort in Hawaii, and West Paces Hotel Group, the new venture of former Ritz-Carlton CEO Horst Schulze.

From the beginning, Guest Relations has been dedicated to creating marketing programs that transform client's prospects to customers, customers into guests and ultimately, guests into zealots. "By transforming faceless customers into recognized and satisfied guests, its program creates the best marketing of all—word-of-mouth referrals," stated Voris. Thus, the name Guest Relations: "a challenge to connect our clients with their customers, or guests, in a more personal way."

So, Guest Relations was established as a marketing firm that would build brands from the inside out. "We understand zealots, because we are zealots about brands. We have a real passion for developing distinctive, lasting brand programs and then sweating the details to collabora-

D

E

F

A. Omni International — This timeless looking ad helped launch the Omni Hotel brand in 1979.

B. The Ritz-Carlton Hotel Company — Campaign to position its resort properties.

C. Halekulani — How do you say 5-diamond service? You try and put the reader literally into the setting.

D. Athens First — How to make a small budget work in taking on the industry giants.

E. Emory Medical Center — A good visual always tells a story better.

F. Slazenger — Gold EFFIE Winning Campaign.

tively build authentic brand experiences," states Tyre.

Voris continues, "We're like producers. You have a stage, you have a theater. Our job is to help you get the storyline right, find the right talent(s), ensure the program comes off as intended, on-time and on-budget. Build programs to delight the zealots and their friends will follow. Build to the extreme—the remarkable—and give people, especially zealots, something to talk about."

More than ever, people want to identify with brands that represent their values, simplify their need to make choices and connect them to a greater community.

How does Tyre describe the real value of Guest Relations? "We help our clients understand who their zealots are, craft a story for the brand that is easily understood and can be spread by zealots and employees and then reinforce the program by delivering the story to a larger prospect audience."

"Taking an inside-out approach means we also work at collaborating with our clients. Successful brands are synergistic—operations is also marketing, and marketing aids operations. For our programs to succeed, we believe it is important to understand our client's business, enlist their expertise and resources and collaborate toward shared equity in the outcome," insists Ms. Voris, who heads client services for Guest Relations.

As new as the agency is, though, it sees real value in carrying forward with branding—and advertising—lessons learned from it clients and CHD. A few examples:

Understanding and exploiting a consumer's emotional interest is critical. The CHD work for Dunlop Slazenger is a great example of understanding the competitive "kill or be killed" nature of tennis. It's timeless work. And, because the agency was so sure about the stance, they really empowered the creative team to take a strong stance and run with it.

A campaign well thought and positioned can last a long time. There were essentially three campaigns for the Ritz-Carlton in its 15-year growth period and those changes were driven more by evolving targets than by the need to update the brand.

Great photography/art is critical to a campaign. As Guest Relations puts it, the business of engaging viewers/readers with interesting, compelling visuals sells better than any amount of copy. "We've always erred on the side of photography—even for real estate projects that have not started construction. And we've had excellent results. There was an ad done

by the agency for Omni Hotel more than 25 years ago that's still visually arresting today."

Now that Guest Relations has hit the ground running, what are its next steps to successful branding and marketing for its clients?

"There are no magic short cuts to building sustaining relationships. Our primary point of difference is simple. We get more involved in our client's business," says Voris.

"We intend to be media-form neutral. That is, we'll always try and utilize the touchpoint(s) best suited to the situation. We are always looking to discover new touchpoints that previously have not been employed in our particular category. The medium can be a significant part of the message. Strategic insights and creativity can be applied to employees, POS and public relations just as easily as to a spread 4-color ad. In fact, it can be used to create new media. Our goal is to create

A

B

A. World Golf Hall of Fame — Turning a museum into a multi-generational experience.

B. River Valley Ranch — When you understand what your zealots value, campaigns like this become successful selling stories.

a 'new media form' for each client. For instance, for a hospital client, we did the research, sold in the idea and executed a brochure display to go in every participating physician's office in their system. Not only was this the best way to reach future patients (guests), but also it was a higher 'reach' media that we secured at a one-time cost. Further, the second stage of this project will allow for partner participation, thus making it a revenue opportunity as well."

Guest Relations' founding partners echo a pragmatic approach to its own growth. "Our own business growth/acquisition program attempts to mirror our approach to our clients. Create superior programs and results for our current clients. Create client relationships that are lasting and lead to referrals. We have been blessed by multiple client referrals over the years."

"Our passion to deliver great results (and in marketing that means sales) is

unrelenting. We intend to accomplish this by addressing and connecting programs to operations at the outset. Less can be more," according to Tyre.

"And perhaps, most importantly, we love what we're doing and intend to convey that to the people we contact each day. We want to refocus the journey from the future, the constant chase to get bigger or greater, to the present—making the best of what's in front of us."

C

C. **Broadlands** — Dramatic positioning led to premium price point for client.

D. **Disney Business Productions** — When you are the best, don't be afraid to show it.

E. **Delta Apparel** —Campaign that put this small niche manufacturer on the map against industry heavyweights.

D

E

CASE STUDY: World Golf Village

World Golf Village is a mega-development (retail, commercial, residential, resort) created by PGA Tour as a new home for the World Golf Hall of Fame and located in a less developed area south of Jacksonville, Florida. Simply put, the original plan was grandiose and made overly positive assumptions relating to attendance and purchase. "If you build it they will come" clearly was the attitude.

Further, the real estate development had stalled due to several factors. Realtors had a negative viewpoint about the location, the lack of retail development promised, the low demand in prospect traffic and an unclear understanding of what the community was about apart from being home to the golf hall of fame. Research among prospects/rejectors to the community revealed similar issues, including a perception that "no one was there." One respondent put it best: "It looks like a ghost town," a daunting indictment for any residential community.

Conventional wisdom suggested that a project with the World Golf Hall of Fame and two golf courses, including the only collaborated Jack Nicklaus/Arnold Palmer design, should be marketed to golf "purists." But this golf intensive, male-focused posture had led to slow sales and a stalled project.

The agency elected to move away from the obvious. "We targeted women, upscale boomers versus empty nesters or retirees. We knew from past research that women are the primary decision makers when selecting the community. They typically identify and gravitate to the more emotional values of a community, which were identified as the primary barriers to World Golf Village."

Research indicated that the female target group disdained the "golf only" perspective that had been communicated about the development. Many did not understand or value the Nicklaus/Palmer collaboration. While they valued the premium nuances of such a select development, they wanted to see a well-rounded, thriving community. Even the "pioneer" buyers—mostly empty nesters—wanted to see a broader age mix, particularly families.

According to the agency, "Our creative strategy moved away from the obvious and known—that this development was about golf—and positioned it as the premiere world-class village that the developers had originally intended." Their message became: "The people you see everyday at World Golf Village are as unique and special as the golf."

The agency sought to shift the positioning of this upscale development to a fashionable, stylish, even aspirational place to live. As a premium, gated community it was important to communicate an exclusive, yet approachable attitude. Their approach was to sell "personality" versus product (golf, homes) as the introduction to the community. Golf was known and a given, but we did use icons and the Hall of Fame logo as a reinforcement to the stature and prestige of the community."

Executionally, the agency chose black- and white visuals to separate its client from the competition, while creating a fashionable air.

In addition, target research by their media group indicated the need to promote outside the local market in order to fulfill sales absorption goals and realize the potential for this community.

To reach this target and amplify the creative positioning, the media plan called for lifestyle publications as the primary medium, whereas the original program had been primarily local and regional retail newspaper. Business reply cards were inserted to qualify prospects and measure individual publication effectiveness.

Other communications programs included open house events, out-of-town packages, collateral, partner direct mail and a presence on the Bloomberg Intranet.

The results have been exceptional: Sales revenue for 2004 was well above the planned goal; sales over the past two years are up 170 percent. Traffic has grown, but more in qualified leads, as opposed to simply raw traffic. In simpler terms, the Guest Relations program has attracted the right kinds of people. Along with strong sales growth, significant positive changes have occurred in attitudes and perceptions about World Golf Village: Overall "excellent" opinion of the community is up 127 percent over the past two years.

This campaign was awarded a Silver EFFIE in 2005 by the American Marketing Association. It was the highest award for any real estate campaign nationally.

THE PERFECT HOME WHEN YOU HAVE CHAMPAGNE TASTE, AND, FORTUNATELY, A CHAMPAGNE BUDGET.

THE ESTATES OF WORLD GOLF VILLAGE

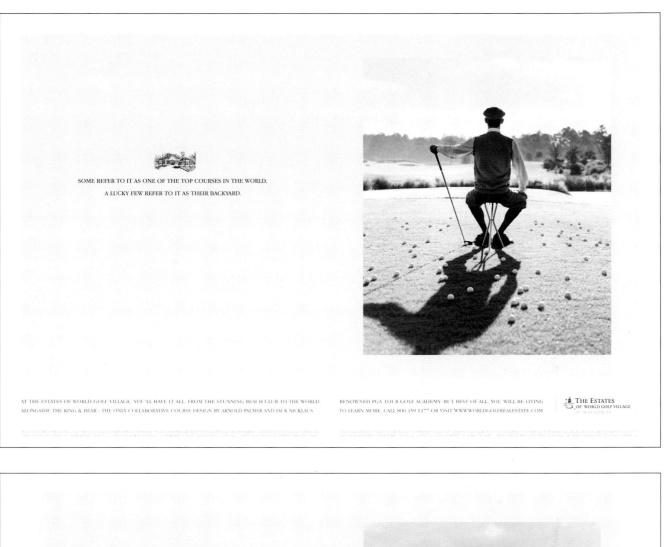

SOME REFER TO IT AS ONE OF THE TOP COURSES IN THE WORLD.

A LUCKY FEW REFER TO IT AS THEIR BACKYARD.

AT THE ESTATES OF WORLD GOLF VILLAGE, YOU'LL HAVE IT ALL. FROM THE STUNNING BEACH CLUB TO THE WORLD
ALONGSIDE THE KING & BEAR - THE ONLY COLLABORATIVE COURSE DESIGN BY ARNOLD PALMER AND JACK NICKLAUS.

RENOWNED PGA TOUR GOLF ACADEMY. BUT BEST OF ALL, YOU WILL BE LIVING
TO LEARN MORE, CALL 800.459.1177 OR VISIT WWW.WORLDGOLFREALESTATE.COM

THE ESTATES
OF WORLD GOLF VILLAGE

DRIVING THROUGH OUR COMMUNITY, YOU'LL REALIZE YOU HAVE ARRIVED

LONG BEFORE YOU PULL INTO YOUR DRIVEWAY.

WHAT MAKES OUR COMMUNITY SO EXQUISITE? IS IT THE STONEWORK OF OUR WINDMILL? OR THE STUNNING BEACH CLUB AND PGA TOUR GOLF ACADEMY? OF COURSE, YOU ALSO CAN'T FORGET ABOUT
THE KING & BEAR - THE ONLY COLLABORATIVE DESIGN BY PALMER AND NICKLAUS. TRUTH IS, THE ANSWER IS ALL OF THE ABOVE. TO LEARN MORE, CALL 904.940.4715 OR VISIT WWW.WORLDGOLFREALESTATE.COM

THE ESTATES
OF WORLD GOLF VILLAGE

CASE STUDY: Mauna Lani Resort

Mauna Lani Resort, in Hawaii, was just over 20 years old and had initially enjoyed a top-tier perception. But over the years, the property had failed to make certain upgrades in both product and communications. Research showed that Mauna Lani was viewed as a "dated" property by many in the group and trade business; resulting key sales numbers were trending down on a year-to-year basis.

The client replaced their agency without a review and hired Guest Relations based on its category experience and on initial insights the agency offered to the resort.

Examining research and the competitive set, the agency discovered a key insight: What separates the resort is its natural connection to the environment, in literally all aspects of the resort.

"We discovered that the natural environment Mauna Lani enjoys fits what we've learned from our past research as well as our own knowledge of the target market: Consumers want a connection to the culture or heritage of the places they visit. They desire a more experiential visit. Mauna Lani, with its vast environmental and cultural points, can deliver on these perceptions and be an obvious destination point."

Based on this insight, the agency formulated a new brand position: The Place to Experience the True Culture of Hawaii. The agency wanted to create the perception that Mauna Lani was the destination point to experience the real flavor or heritage of Hawaii.

Sublimating the usual resort amenities under the "natural adventures" communications platform would truly make Mauna Lani a considered destination point. Travelers would learn that Mauna Lani is not a spartan, environmentally pristine property, or just a golf and spa resort that casually promotes the local culture. And it isn't a luxury hotel set in a resort location. It's a casual, elegant blend of activities, local culture and unique natural experiences that make Mauna Lani a destination point for natural adventures.

To deliver this message, the agency chose a variety of tactical approaches, including shifting to lifestyle books and away from Hawaii/travel-only publications. They also worked with the publications to create unique events at Mauna Lani.

Beyond publication exposure, a new collateral package was created that romanced the brand and included separate pieces for higher ticket business (weddings, bungalows and groups). With the Internet growth and importance in travel, Guest Relations created a daily blog on the website with interesting stories and key event notices about the resort. The agency also added an online newsletter that tells the stories of Mauna Lani. And, the authenticity of Hawaiian culture is expanded upon a separate website, www.maunalaniculture.org.

Internal marketing is key to the guest experience and with that a turndown program was developed to provide guests with new ways to discover Mauna Lani's 3,200 acres.

Results have been gratifying for both agency and client, showing a strong shift from negative trends to positive year to year growth in occupancy levels, average room rate and RevPar, since the launch of this program.

Further, creative and media placement strategies have led to an increase in press and editorial coverage, further enhancing overall branding results.

Music (Hawaiian and otherwise) to a client's ears.

....

A. Cover and inside spread of brochure

B. Magazine ad

A

B

La Agencia de Orcí & Asociados

Delivering Latino Share of Heart™

Founded in 1986

11620 Wilshire Blvd.
Suite 600
Los Angeles, CA 90025
(310) 622-4600
www.laagencia.com

KEY NEW BUSINESS CONTACT:
Dilys Tosteson García, (310) 444-7300

AGENCY PRINCIPALS:
Héctor Orcí – Chair
Dilys Tosteson García – CEO & President

CLIENTS: Allstate Insurance Company, American Honda Motor Company, Georgia Pacific (Brawny, Angel Soft), McNeil Consumer Pharmaceutical Nutritionals (Splenda, Lactaid), CASA (National Court Appointed Special Advocates), Verizon Communications

FULL-TIME EMPLOYEES: 100

La Agencia de Orcí

"Share of Heart.™" It isn't every day that you find those words in an agency creative brief or strategy statement. Unless, of course, the agency happens to be La Agencia de Orcí & Asociados. One of America's leading national Hispanic agencies, La Agencia de Orcí has built its clients' successes on what the agency calls its Share of Heart™ philosophy: Touch the consumer with emotionally and culturally relevant messages.

As agency CEO & President Dilys Tosteson García puts it: "Advertising is an emotional experience. Our work doesn't just inform or educate the consumers, it engages and inspires them, it moves them culturally—it establishes a relationship with them. Change is constant and culture, dynamic. So is our consumer.

"We live in a world where emotions drive actions; this is why our Share of Heart™ philosophy is more relevant than ever. There is an emotional connection to the Latinos in the U.S. that the agency strongly upholds as a responsibility and we love creating great work. Our agency passion is dedicated to connecting the vibrant Latino consumer with brands in a meaningful and long-lasting way. We deliver positive results by engaging the Latino consumer with a message that is captivating, relevant and insightful. This is how Share of Heart™ becomes share of market—and results become profits for our clients."

For agency co-founders Héctor and Norma Orcí, making brands part of the

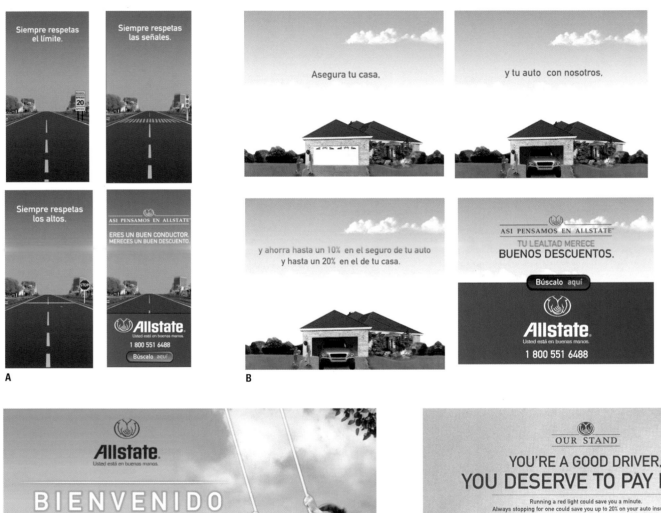

A

B

C

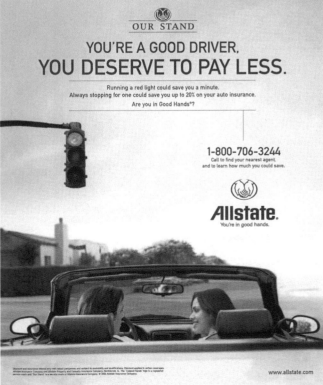

D

U.S. Latino consumer's heart began in 1981, when McCann Erickson brought the Orcí team from Mexico to create La Agencia de McCann Erickson, the agency's U.S. Hispanic arm. Their client list included an impressive roster of brands, among them, Disneyland®, General Motors, El Pollo Loco and Coca-Cola®. The agency's success as a market pioneer provided impetus for the Orcís to separate from McCann and found La Agencia de Orcí & Asociados as their own independent agency in 1986.

Developing ideas that resonate culturally with Hispanics has helped the agency transform brands unknown in the Hispanic market into leading brands. Observes Ricardo Cárdenas, Executive Creative Director, "Our Share of Heart™ philosophy moves beyond a :30 spot, it's in everything we do. We use it to do best-in-class work across all disciplines, using an integrated communications approach."

For La Agencia, getting to that place they call Share of Heart™ is a three-stage process that begins by gaining a clear understanding of the marketplace. This starts with a market audit to evaluate the competition, and with learning the environment and social business factors related to the category and brand.

The next step is getting to the essence of the brand itself. The agency asks: What does it do? What is inherent in the brand? What does it do for people? Does it move people? In the case of a car, is it a smart,

A. Allstate — Banner ad "You're a good driver. You deserve a good discount."

C. Allstate — Banner ad "Your loyalty deserves good discounts."

C. Allstate — Online landing page "Welcome to Allstate" for banner ad campaign.

D. Allstate — English-language ad for Hispanic publications.

E. Acura — Magazine ad for the Miami market. Tagline reads "The best part of setting goals is surpassing them."

F. Acura — TV "Both Worlds" :30 spot for the Miami market.

E

F

quality vehicle that people rely on?

The final, and equally important stage, is understanding the Hispanic people. The agency sets out to understand where they live, work and play, and to learn what they feel. What is happening in the environment around them? What factors from Latin America have an impact on their view of the U.S.? What factors in U.S. society affect them? Using street smarts as a tool, La Agencia goes into the community to observe and understand Latinos in the U.S.

This could be in the form of ethnography, or as simple as spending time at the dealership, retail store or bar. In today's marketplace, the Latino consumer is more complex than ever with increased media outlets, technology, and in using a language when and how they choose.

Clearly, the agency's approach yields impressive results, as exemplified by its work for Lactaid®.

As Margarita Fitzpatrick, Account Director for Lactaid, tells it: "The target

was Hispanic families. Our challenge was to educate the consumer about lactose intolerance, as Hispanics are more prone to suffer from it. We needed to make them aware of Lactaid as a truly beneficial, lactose-free alternative to milk."

The agency's insight was to realize that word-of-mouth is a highly effective tool for marketing to Hispanics, primarily because of the English-Spanish language barrier and the strong community ties that characterize Hispanic groups. "We were

A

B

A. **Lactaid** — TV "Pass it on" :30 spot.

B. **Lactaid** — Banner ad "Enjoy the pleasure of lactose-free milk. With Lactaid."

C. **Splenda** — Banner ad "Subscribe to the Splenda Recipe Club."

D. **Splenda** — TV "Sweet Moments" :30 spot.

able to use that insight to create the right campaign for our audience. We created milk moments for sharing with friends and family, showcasing usage occasions and product benefits.

"'Pásala bien'" (Pass it on without problems) became a metaphor to create word-of-mouth about how milk could be enjoyed without stomach problems; Lactaid became a way for families to share great moments they couldn't share before."

The result of the campaign? The Lactaid TV and print ads beat all previous Hispanic standards set by ASI. Awareness measures were brought to an all-time high and sales grew over 20 percent.

The agency is quick to point out that knowing the heart of its consumers can also work through creative public relations, not just TV. Case in point is their client, Cazadores®, a tequila that's part of the Bacardi USA portfolio.

The challenge for the brand was not only to reach its audience culturally, but also to overcome the barrier to television advertising.

Stephen Chávez, VP Director for Public Relations, comments, "In response, we created a cultural exchange program around the brand by bringing ten representatives from Mexico to create an 'edutainment' experience for the brand through public relations. Cazadores received complete television and print media coverage in both Spanish- and English-language media. The media coverage lifted the brand's presence in that highly competitive category, generating media value that was over three times the investment."

So how does the agency's philosophy of emotional connection to consumers translate into its own culture and environment?

"Come to our office and you'll see," says Dilys Tosteson García with a smile. "You'll find it in our work, and in our people; you'll see shows of affection among the staff and clients; you'll meet community leaders in our lobby. Wherever you go here, there's the hustle and bustle of music, and the smell of food, accompanied by fun, healthy conflict and inspiration."

Community leadership and involvement also remain a strong focus for the agency, a way to stay in touch with Hispanic consumers that can't be replaced.

Notes García: "Orcí is a strong leader in our community, our industry and with the consumers we serve. The agency has received leadership awards from numerous leading Hispanic organizations. Orcí management and staff serve on community boards supporting educational opportunity, access to capital, political participation and other causes important to the progress of Latinos in this country. Through our activism we lead clients into the community arena, which is so important to our market's aspirations. On the educational front, Orcí teaches an annual course of UCLA's Extension program on Hispanic Marketing, now in its 19th year.

"The Orcí vision is to make the world a better place for Latinos. Our vision guides us to build strong relationships between brands and Latino consumers. We are committed to our consumers on their journey, keeping a pulse on the culture with relevant insights that go beyond language.

"Orcí cultivates a comprehensive perspective of our consumers' world as they move back and forth between Hispanic and non-Hispanic aspects of their lives—family, friends, work, entertainment, play—blending the best of cultures and languages into new experiences. In five years, we hope to service a thoroughly multicultural mainstream market."

C

D

CASE STUDY: Verizon®

Richer. Deeper. Broader. Words to grow by for Verizon. But how could they be translated into a campaign that would resonate with Hispanics?

According to Orlando Zambrano, Group Account Director, it began with solid strategic groundwork.

"When Bell Atlantic, our client, merged with GTE in 2000, they asked us to help them position the new company, Verizon Communications, in the Hispanic market. By 2005, their positioning had evolved in response to a changing marketplace." This meant adapting their national "richer, deeper, broader" campaign in a way that resonated with Hispanics. "We knew we needed to define the target group opportunities by drilling deeper into the Hispanic target dynamic. Only by doing that could we find a germane theme to mirror the national campaign tagline; a tagline broad enough to be a long-term brand campaign claim."

Following these first steps, the agency set about determining what was needed to make the campaign relevant from the Share of Heart™ perspective. "Through consumer research, we identified which, if any, cultural cues could be imbued into the mass campaign to make it culturally meaningful." It was also important, the agency points out, to ensure that all elements were consistent with the mass-market strategy, i.e., one brand, one voice.

"Through our findings, we learned which spots could be tailored to the Hispanic market. We also recommended original creative that brought broadband to a level that our consumers (primarily 18-24, early adopters, young progressives, mostly single, with household incomes less than $40K) could truly relate to."

Original creative demonstrated how the benefits of broadband deliver a richer, deeper, broader experience to consumers, "a todo lo que da," or "to the max," and pushed Verizon's credibility as a broadband provider, while making broadband more tangible and relevant to its consumer.

Two mass-market TV spots were adapted. "In" was modified to better accommodate preferred Hispanic music genres, while minimizing the African-American and urban feel. "Adrenaline" called for a Hispanic voiceover. Additionally, four :30 testimonial commercials were created to reflect key Hispanic passions that could be intimately tied to broadband: music, soccer, wrestling and home improvement. These spots were grounded in how Hispanic consumers use broadband. New creative

A

was developed for radio, print, interactive and numerous product integrations.

Close attention was paid to selective media as well. Explains Teddy Hayes, VP, Media Services: "In order to obtain high reach and frequency, and to emphasize Verizon's transition to broadband services, we used local media support to efficiently reach Hispanics in key Verizon markets."

B

C

We also chose select environments that appeal to early adopters of technology and the late majority segment of entertainment, music, gaming, technology, news and sports. We delivered the "a todo lo que da" experience via customized media sponsorships to demonstrate the real-time benefits of broadband." The agency also used alternative media, including dot-com video lounges and digital banners on Fox Sports en Español.

As a result of the agency's efforts among Hispanics, Verizon's broadband cue increased by 26 percent, its entertainment cue by 66 percent, and its banner campaign achieved an above-average response. Both client and agency are pleased with the results, says Dilys Tosteson García.

"The campaign results are right in line with what the client was hoping to achieve: results were consistent with the overall strategy while forging much needed relevancy and affinity with the Hispanic consumer."

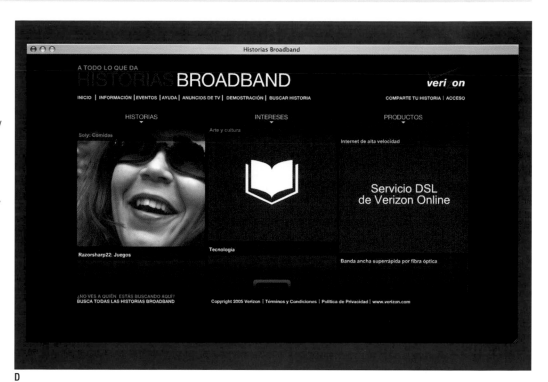

D

E

A. **Banner ad** — "Music transforms me."

B. **Magazine ad** — "Soccer Fan."

C. **Magazine ad** — "Barista."

D. **Website** — "www.historiasbroadband.com."

E. **TV** — "DJ" :30 spot.

F. **Banner ad** — "The good thing about online soccer is that fouls don't leave bruises."

F

CASE STUDY: **American Honda Motor Company**

To put it simply, in 1988, Honda was not on many U.S. Hispanics' shopping lists. Understanding that it needed to establish a relationship with this growing market, the company conducted a review of agencies and awarded the job to La Agencia de Orcí. The agency's charge? Create brand awareness and purchase intent among U.S. Hispanics.

Once again, the agency turned to its Share of Heart ™ philosophy. First on its agenda was in-depth research into the market and consumer relationships with automotive brands. They conducted a competitive review to determine what messages were being communicated to the market, and studied lifestyles of target consumers to learn what roles vehicles played in their daily lives. Using the research, La Agencia de Orcí went about creating work based on the lifestyle of its target, Hispanic adults 18-54 (with narrower targets for each vehicle segment). Robert Santiago, Group Account Director, explains: "We knew that only by understanding the lives of our target, could we create relationships with the American Honda brand."

The agency says that it began by earning the right to sell Honda vehicles to Hispanics. "We didn't enter the market with a sales message. It was important to demonstrate to U.S. Hispanics that Honda understood the market and wanted to establish a

B

long-term, mutually beneficial relationship."

Before any car advertising began, the agency began that relationship by associating Honda with community events and organizations that were important to consumers. "We created a campaign for Hispanics in which Honda urged them to register for the Census. We helped Honda bring the Ballet Folklórico de Mexico to the U.S. for a nationwide tour, and we developed an association with soccer for Honda.

"Once Honda was established as a friend in the community, we began product advertising tailored to the Hispanic consumers based on primary research." Integrated marketing campaigns included TV, radio, print and online components, while

community events and sponsorships continued. Alternative media, including use of websites, product integration and high-profile sponsorships, were also part of the agency's efforts.

And how has Honda's share of the Hispanic consumer's heart changed?

"American Honda is now consistently in the top three for brand awareness and purchase consideration, and sales have continued to increase for over a decade. Today, almost all U.S. Hispanics consider Honda when making an automotive purchase."

....

A. **Magazine ad** — "15 Minutes" spread.

B. **Website** — "www.tuchicacivic.com."

C. **TV** — "Tu Chica Civic" :30 spot.

B

C

Lopez Negrete Communications, Inc

Where Passion Goes to Work

Founded in 1985

3336 Richmond Avenue
Suite 200
Houston, Texas 77098
713-877-8777, 888-398-0657
Fax: 713-877-8796
www.lopeznegrete.com

KEY NEW BUSINESS CONTACT:
Alex López Negrete, President/CEO/CCO
832-295-2112

SENIOR MANAGEMENT:
Alex López Negrete, President/CEO/CCO
Cathy López Negrete, Executive Vice President/CFO/COO

CLIENTS: Wal-Mart Stores, Inc., Bank of America Corporation, Visa USA, Tyson Foods, Domino's Pizza, Azteca Milling/MASECA, Reliant Energy, Microsoft Corporation, Sonic Drive-Ins, Novartis Pharmaceuticals, ConAgra Foods

Lopez Negrete Communications, Inc.

Truth, reality and relevancy. For agencies and clients alike, they're the Holy Grail, the often-elusive keys to the consumer psyche.

For Lopez Negrete Communications, finding these keys to the Hispanic consumer's psyche has earned them respect not only as one of the most creative Hispanic agencies in the nation, but also one of the most strategic.

Ask the agency to give one major reason for its continued success and the answer is clear: They've stayed strongly focused on bridging the gap between corporate America and the Hispanic community, on establishing a dialogue between the two that empowers each to reach their goals.

Cathy and Alex López Negrete started that dialogue in 1985, under the name of Third Coast Marketing. With all their savings and dreams invested, and two clients on their roster, they began their agency from a small townhouse in Houston. By then, the Hispanic market was growing quickly, with companies and marketing agencies eager to connect. And, connect they did.

In fact, the agency's Hispanic work for its clients was so successful, it grew beyond what even Cathy and Alex might have dreamed. Not only had they added key clients like Warner-Lambert and Foley's Department Stores to their roster, they'd also built an impressive agency reel of major national clients through their general market agencies, including Shell Oil and Veragon Corporation.

A

B

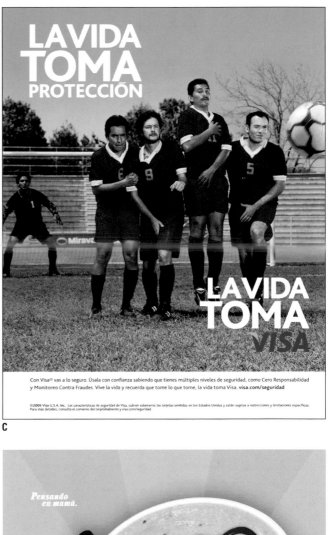

C

D

Buoyed by their success, the agency decided to focus solely on marketing to Hispanics and, in 1990, changed its name to Lopez Negrete Communications. It was a way, the agency says, to better reflect the culture, purpose and direction of the company. Unquestionably, that direction has been the right one. The agency has continued to broaden its account base, as well as its menu of services, by adding major national accounts, including Wal-Mart Stores, Azteca Milling/MASECA,

Visa USA, Microsoft Corporation, Tyson Foods, Novartis Pharmaceuticals, Domino's Pizza, Sonic Drive-Ins, Bank of America and ConAgra Foods.

A particular source of pride for the agency, and one that defines its strengths and branding philosophy, is its relationship with its clients.

"It is our mission to be a client's most visionary and insightful partner, with a unique and unsurpassed understanding of the Hispanic consumer. We are aware that

success for our clients comes from creating fully integrated communications programs, not just ads. That's why we refer to ourselves as a Hispanic marketing agency," said Alex López Negrete.

"We believe the way to accomplish our clients' goals is by communicating with the Hispanic consumer in the most respectful and impactful way possible, translating knowledge and insight into relevance and action," he continued.

For Lopez Negrete Communications,

E

F

G

Lopez Negrete Communications, Inc.

dialogue with clients always begins with, "How do we create a relationship with your Hispanic customer?" rather than, "What ads or campaigns will we produce for you this year?" For this reason, the agency works from the inside out—working on making the products, services and brand relevant to the Hispanic consumer and making sure their clients are ready to deliver on the promises made through the communications first. Only then do they move on to the creation of communications.

"What sets us apart is our ability to create a deep and meaningful bond between the brand and the Hispanic consumer," added López Negrete. "We build relationships by creating a true understanding of what the client has to offer, along with a sense of trust, value and community. This takes a brand from unknown to tried and from preferred to loved. This is what we helped Wal-Mart to achieve."

From the beginning of its relationship with Wal-Mart, the agency was true to its philosophy. It spent almost the entire first year of its relationship touring store after store, market after market, talking to hundreds of Hispanic associates and customers about relationships they had, or felt they could have, with Wal-Mart and the role that Wal-Mart played in their lives.

"What it came to was a deep understanding of what it would take for Wal-Mart to become their mass retailer of choice, across all categories, for generations to come. This gave us the freedom

A

B

C

D

to create work that spoke to—and continues to speak to—Hispanic truths, realities and relevancies."

Today, Wal-Mart is, by far, the indisputable retail leader among Latinos. But there's more to the company's relationship than sales, according to López Negrete. Perhaps the greatest reward for Wal-Mart and its agency has come from the Hispanic community itself. The agency has successfully helped put Wal-Mart firmly at the center of that community with outreach programs and various initiatives.

Another relationship the agency is especially proud of is its long-standing association with Bank of America. Once again, Lopez Negrete's ability to touch Hispanic consumers in an effective, lasting way is bringing its client positive, measurable results. But the agency sees teamwork in developing strategies as equally critical.

"Our team is deeply involved in creating long-term strategies side-by-side with our client," said López Negrete. "That's how strong working relationships are built. Having a place at the strategic table is critical, and I think it's been the key to the extraordinarily long relationships we've enjoyed with clients, most of which are more than a decade long."

For Bank of America the agency's strategy goes far beyond advertising, running the gamut of direct marketing, governmental relations, public relations and, once again, community relations. The result? The creation of what is, today, the most coveted and recognized financial services brand by Hispanics. Lopez Negrete's positioning statement for the brand, "Superación Constante," has record recall in the category. Added Cathy López Negrete: "It speaks to Hispanics' desire for constant improvement, hope and upward mobility, and the role the bank plays in that quest as their partner."

Speaking to Hispanics' desires and culture is, for Lopez Negrete, also a way of life at the agency.

"When a stranger walks through the agency, he or she is transported," observed Cathy López Negrete with a smile. "Beyond the music playing and beyond the constant flow of English and Spanish through the halls, there is no question that this is an agency that lives in the world of Latino culture, history and emotion. The energy is always up; there's nothing subtle about us! Colors are big, emotions are big, opinions are big. And best of all, our sense of family is big."

Walking into Lopez Negrete is indeed like walking into a large Latin family home. All 40,000-plus square feet of it.

"Some companies put lots of effort into making their environments these kinds of museums for their work and awards," explained Alex López Negrete. "Our workspace is made to stimulate creativity and connectivity with Latin culture. Have we won awards? Yes, plenty of them. And they're nice to have, because it says that our peers see our work as noteworthy and creative. But ultimately, it's not about the crystal you take home from a gala once or twice a year. It's about making a difference to the bottom line and achieving mutually agreed-upon business objectives. One client once paid us the ultimate compliment: 'I hired your agency because you were a unique collection of exceptional people. I knew I could learn from you. You were different than all the other agencies. You were the un-agency agency.'"

It's this passion for the Hispanic consumer, for their clients, and for truth, reality and relevancy, that translates into success for Lopez Negrete Communications and their clients. The Holy Grail, indeed.

E

F

A. **Goya** — Magazine ad

B. **MASECA** — Magazine ad

C. **Goya** — Magazine ad

D. **Azteca Milling** — Magazine ad

E. **Microsoft** — Magazine spread

F. **Houston Astros** — Outdoor billboard

Which came first, the chicken or the egg? For Tyson Foods, chicken was first . . . the absolute mainstay of the company. But in 2001, Tyson acquired IBP—one of the nation's largest beef and pork processing companies. No longer just a chicken company, the poultry powerhouse had now become the world's largest provider of protein. Among Tyson's marketing challenges was to create a new brand platform that would take them beyond a chicken company to a manufacturer of branded protein products. That meant creating a new corporate brand vision, which became "Tyson, Proudly Powering America." That vision gave birth to a new advertising slogan: "Powered by Tyson." Unfortunately, none of this added up to sales within the Hispanic market, which was ripe for Tyson.

Statistics show that 64% of Hispanic food expenditures go toward food at home—versus 57% for non-Hispanics—and 33% of these expenditures are on protein—versus 27% of non-Hispanics.

Ironically though, Hispanics have a lower awareness of protein as a powerful source of energy. So not only was Lopez Negrete charged with educating the Hispanic community about the energy-related benefits of protein, they had to leverage Tyson's own segmentation research and

communication platform to uncover the drivers that brought "powering" to life in the Hispanic market, and then build a 360-degree Hispanic campaign.

The agency learned that the literal word "power" created confusion. Hispanics have a more "nurturing" attitude toward food, and a vigorous word such as "power" had some negative connotations. Alternate words like "energy" and "nourishment" connected more emotionally, so the Spanish phrase "Alimentado por Tyson" was launched to communicate the spirit of the message with real meaning, relevance and effectiveness. "Alimentado" is multidimensional and encompasses meanings such as "nourished," "nurtured" and "energized."

The integrated campaign featured a series of humorous television commercials depicting outrageous feats of strength attributed to Tyson protein. The campaign went on to win "Best Of Show" at the American Advertising Federation ADDY® Awards in Houston. In conjunction with the television push was spot radio featuring Hispanic-relevant products in tiered markets, national magazines to target segment lifestyles, and an online campaign with a Spanish transcreation of the English language website and recipe-focused online banners.

Lopez Negrete complemented their advertising campaign with other integrated disciplines such as public relations and promotional activities. One of the most popular ideas Lopez Negrete hatched was using Hispanic celebrity and entertainer Chef Pepín as Tyson's Brand Ambassador. This colorful character was utilized across multiple channels, ranging from online promotions to point-of-sale to retail and community grassroots events. You could say they were taking protein to the people—and the people responded in a big way. For example, in about a year and a half, loyalty to Tyson pork shot up 107%, top-of-mind awareness for chicken jumped 150% with unaided awareness up 128%, and the beef brand purchased in the last 30 days showed a staggering 400% increase for Tyson. The icing on the cake came in 2005 when the American Advertising Federation honored the campaign at the national level with its prestigious Mosaic Media Usage Award, as the year's most successful integrated multicultural marketing and diversity effort that demonstrated the spirit of AAF's Mosaic principle.

The chicken or the egg? For Lopez Negrete, their clients and their clients' customers always come first.

¿Has comido proteína hoy?
Dale energía a tu familia con el pollo fresco de *Tyson*®. Deliciosas y tiernas pechugas de pollo llenas de proteína y sabor, en las que puedes confiar para preparar los platillos como a ti te gustan y como tu familia adora.

¿Has comido proteína hoy?
Dale energía a tu familia con los Chicken Nuggets de Tyson. Sabrosos "nuggets" de pollo llenos de proteína, calidad y sabor en los que puedes confiar cuando buscas algo rápido, rico y nutritivo para tus niños.

Alimentada por **Tyson**

Alimentada por **Tyson**

¿Has comido proteína hoy?
Dale energía a tu familia con
el tocino precocinado de Tyson.
Irresistibles tiritas con sabor a
"Hickory" y llenas de energía.
sabor y calidad, ideales para
darles a tus platillos un sabor
muy especial en sólo minutos.

¿Has comido proteína hoy?
Dale energía a tu familia con los *Beef Steak
Strips* de *Tyson*®. Deliciosas tiritas de carne
de res precocidas y llenas de proteína.
En pocos minutos tú y tu familia recibirán
la nutrición, la calidad y el sabor que más
les gusta.

Alimentado por **Tyson**

CASE STUDY: Visa USA

Will that be cash or charge? If you're Hispanic, the typical answer has long been, "Cash, por favor." That's because less than 50% of U.S. Hispanics own a credit card compared with 72% of the general market population. The market is certainly affluent enough. More than 20% of the Hispanic population has household incomes in excess of $50,000; 15% earn between $35,000 and $50,000. Another 15%, between $25,000 and $35,000.

So what's the problem? Fear of debt and fraud. Culturally, Hispanics tend to shy away from debt because many feel it's dishonorable to owe money or to be in debt. Plus, they know it is "easy to get in trouble." As for fraud, many Latinos with limited knowledge of financial products feel uneasy with these unfamiliar methods of payment. All that complicated fine print in English translates to the potential of someone taking advantage of them, so cash tends to be king. Hispanics simply prefer cash as a better and easier way to manage their money.

For Visa USA, the challenge was to change Hispanic attitudes about credit card usage in general while driving Visa brand preference and loyalty specifically. So, Lopez Negrete developed a communications platform to promote Visa as the most secure way to pay, especially when compared to cash, implicitly educating Hispanic consumers as to Visa's security features and directly promoting usage by setting their minds at ease.

A highly targeted mass media campaign was launched that included cable and network television commercials, radio spots, online banners and print advertising in national Hispanic consumer magazines, all homing in on seasonal usage periods. Recognizing that people will needlessly go to extreme measures to protect their money, Lopez Negrete's effective and exceptionally relevant message was that they need not bother, because "Visa has you covered" ("Con Visa vas a lo seguro"). The campaign utilized humor and showcased exaggerated scenarios to illustrate people going to "extreme measures" to protect their money. The message was clear: Visa's security features make it the safest way to pay, especially compared to cash. And not only was net security message recall up 6% in only three months into the campaign, but Visa outperformed the competition with regard to relevance, uniqueness and familiarity, strongly supporting equity brand attributes. Cash or charge? Now, it's Visa, por favor.

Martin|Williams

Great Partnerships = Great Work

Founded in 1947

60 South 6th St.
Suite 2800
Minneapolis, MN 55402
612-340-0800
www.martinwilliams.com

KEY NEW BUSINESS CONTACTS:
Mike Gray, President/Chief Marketing Officer, 612-342-9623
Erika Collins, New Business Manager, 612-342-9858

SENIOR MANAGEMENT:
Mike Gray, President/Chief Marketing Officer
Tim Frojd, Chairman/Chief Financial Officer
Tom Moudry, CEO/Chief Creative Officer
Lannie Dawson, EVP/Media Services Director
Jim Henderson, EVP/Group Creative Director

CLIENTS: Anhueser-Busch (Michelob), Boy Scouts of America, Cargill, Lincoln Financial Group, Mahogany Bay, Marvin Windows and Doors, Mediawise, NewPage Corp., Payless Shoe Source, Pfizer Animal Health, Revlon Haircare, Shakers Vodka, Steelcase, Syngenta, 3M Dental & Commercial Graphics

FULLTIME EMPLOYEES: 210

Martin|Williams

In many respects the growth and success of Martin|Williams mirrors the development of Minneapolis/St. Paul over the past 25 years, as a diverse, nationally recognized arts and creative mecca, yet still grounded in a Midwest sensibility.

What makes Martin|Williams unique is its easy-to-get-along-with operating style, along with the creative edge that comes from over two decades of consistently producing outstanding work across a broad cross-section of cate-gories for brands as diverse as Target, 3M, US Bank, L.L.Bean, Syngenta, Staples, E*TRADE, Payless Shoes, Revlon, and others.

"We understand the competitive challenge of retail in our gut," says President/CMO Mike Gray. "Considering how fast business moves today, a retail point-of-view is especially valuable in other categories as well." The agency brings a decisive, intuitive, action-oriented style to getting results, and by no means do they claim to do it alone. According to Gray, "*Great Partnerships = Great Work, and great work drives results.* Client partnerships evolve out of honest, direct dialog, valuing creative instinct and strong results."

At Martin|Williams, "partnership" isn't some kind of fuzzy ideal. Partnership is how they work internally and with their clients. An air of creative partnership permeates the agency. From "idea centers" throughout the company

A

B

C

that allow folks to get together at any time without a formal reservation, to larger, casual conference rooms with soft seating arrangements that force people to have conversations about work and ideas, rather than meetings.

In fact, you can't walk into the agency without seeing that they really mean what they say, because written right on the lobby wall across from the first ad the agency ever created are the four simple rules for working at Martin|Williams:

• Be a partner with our clients
• Treat others well
• Do great work
• No running

According to CEO/Chief Creative Officer, Tom Moudry, "that's basically everything anyone needs to know about us. Clients want what we want—a big idea—that they can wrap their brand around—and together, we get them there. We take the complex and make it simple. We are grounded and easy to do business with. We stay focused on the problem and do the right thing."

Take for example the story of L.L.Bean. The company was experiencing declining sales and new customer files were not growing. The reality was that they were mailing more and more catalogs to the same older customers. Martin|Williams helped them shift dollars and messaging to channels aimed at younger prospects. The agency also helped L.L.Bean see the possibilities of

D

Traditional Wool Cruiser Jacket from $159

Hunting Wabbits?

For all things classic or new, call 1-800-231-4321 or shop llbean.com

L.L.Bean DIRECT FROM FREEPORT, MAINE™

E

Classic Adirondack Chair $159

Even men get conversational in chairs like this.

For all things classic or new, call 1-800-231-4321 or shop llbean.com

L.L.Bean DIRECT FROM FREEPORT, MAINE™

F

Hunter's Boat and Tote® from $19

For anyone who wants to sneak up on a picnic.

For all things classic or new, call 1-800-231-4321 or shop llbean.com

L.L.Bean DIRECT FROM FREEPORT, MAINE™

A-C. L.L.Bean — magazine ads

D-F. L.L.Bean — small-space magazine ads

G. L.L.Bean — TV spot, "Fireflies"

G

giving the brand a contemporary appeal by using the power and authenticity of their 90-year old name. The campaign helped L.L.Bean achieve significant growth through the Internet channel, and it positioned the brand as a more "contemporary" retailer. The work won a Gold EFFIE for business effectiveness.

Agency leadership believes the business of creating compelling work can be simpler than many people make it out to be. "We owe much of that philosophy to the type of clients we've attracted and retained, in particular large retailers, who haven't the time or patience for excess hierarchy or the hollow promise of a 'secret ingredient' strategic process," says Gray. If you start with the right mindset, right people, and a shared understanding of the challenge, then getting to a 20-ton idea is more straight-forward than often portrayed.

At Martin|Williams, getting to and supporting a 20-ton idea starts with small strategic brand teams that address four basic process questions designed to get the group's collective mindset onto an idea as quickly as possible.

"We don't neglect research if it is required. But we don't wait for a research hand-off to get creative thinking started," says Moudry. "With an idea, research can be used to evaluate it, expand on it, support it or discard it."

"We use a number of success yardsticks like sales, share gain, customer

A

A. **Payless Shoe Source** — TV spot, "Favorite Aunt"

B. **Payless Shoe Source** — TV spot, "Party to Party"

B

traffic count, awards, web metrics, awareness and attitude shifts. Every client is different in terms of what they value and how they frame success. We take our lead from our client," says Moudry.

"However, because of our retail experience, we are most interested in sales and business growth. Retailers don't wait three months for results from an awareness study to make a judgment; they have to face the tyranny of daily num-bers. While advertising can't be solely responsible for sales, there is something direct and honest about sales growth that appeals to our Midwest sensibility."

Payless Shoes came to Martin|Williams following a three year decline in sales. The brand was losing its critical young-adult women customer group to other shoe discounters and mass merchants. Honest dialog identified that the brand had neglected to capitalize on the strong emotional appeal of shoes. The BOGO offer (Buy one, get one for half price), dominated promotional advertising and really positioned the brand. Payless was known narrowly for cheap shoes, when in fact, the brand helped young women experience "fun fashion possibilities." The Martin|Williams team brought a fashion spirit and emotional appeal to the brand and helped grow same-store sales in a very difficult retail category.

And while retail successes line the agency's case history files they are just part of Martin|Williams' client repertoire. Take, for example, the case of Revlon. Faced with increased competition from L'Oreal, Clairol and salons, Revlon wanted to turn up the heat on its hair color line.

Revlon admitted that the agency was a long shot at the beginning of the review because Martin|Williams lacked health & beauty experience, and because Revlon didn't stray far from its midtown Manhattan headquarters. However, the agency's selling ideas and no-bull style convinced the New York-based company to hire the shop.

Martin|Williams has built an outstanding national creative reputation with a vast array of clients and creative challenges. Their creative has won numerous national awards for effectiveness in the marketplace, as well as for sheer creativity within individual categories. They are a strong, highly strategic group of experienced individuals who are open, genuine and results-oriented.

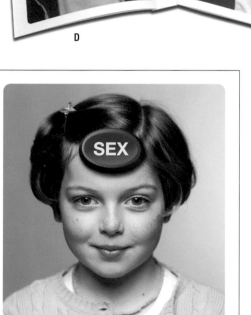

C

C-F. Mediawise (National Institute on Media and the Family) — (C) transtop, (D) brochure, (E) bus ad, (F) print.

D

F

E

CASE STUDY: Cargill, Inc.

How can you change a strongly held perception among business leaders in the food industry to convince them that your company isn't simply a cost-efficient commodity supplier?

Well, if you're Cargill, the largest privately held company in the U.S. and have over $70 billion in annual revenues, 90-plus individual business units—operating in over 70 countries and employing 84,000 people—you turn to the superior branding talents of Martin|Williams.

For over 130 years, Cargill had been proud to be known as the most advanced and efficient supplier of commodities in the world. At the same time, Cargill's customers were consolidating and becoming more sophisticated, and pressure on commodity prices were fraying the relationships Cargill had established.

Research with global customers revealed current perceptions of the company were transaction-focused and were best summed up by the words of a customer heard in research: *"When Cargill says it believes in a win/win, they mean Cargill wins twice."* Ouch.

Cargill understood that it needed to move beyond its traditional strengths in trading and low-cost processing, to leverage its capabilities in supply chain management, food applications and health and nutrition.

Cargill's challenge was to become more customer-focused, innovative and collaborative with customers. Thus Cargill underwent significant internal changes to better meet customer expectations and to change from a transaction focus to a relationship focus.

Martin|Williams needed to help define how to communicate these changes, as well as coordinate corporate brand messaging with the communication efforts of the more than 90 individual Cargill business units throughout the world.

The complexity of the communications challenge involved contacting a hard-to-reach and time-pressed target audience to address the strongly held "commodity-only" perception built up over 70-plus years. Simply saying "Cargill is more than commodities" in a clever way was not enough. Brand communications needed to prove that Cargill can, and does, go beyond selling

A

commodities.

To capture this communication, the brand strategy *"Collaborate>Create>Succeed"* was created. To make this believable, Martin|Williams told corporate folk stories about how Cargill uses its size, scope and expertise all along the food chain to help customers solve real business problems. These stories revolved around one of the customer's three key challenges: delivering growth from new products, simplifying complex supply chains or improving the health and nutrition of their products.

A comprehensive media strategy that addressed the specific habits of their time-pressed target audience was implemented. It integrated a variety of media including print advertising in high-profile general business and vertical food trade publications; online advertising in high-traffic business news sites such as *WSJ Online, MarketWatch.com* and daily food industry news aggregators like *SmartBrief;* and national cable television including CNBC *Squawkbox,* CNN and Fox News. High-reach events like the Olympics and golf were also included.

Martin|Williams created *CargillCreates.com* as a destination for readers and viewers to turn to find out more information on a specific case study and to request additional information from Cargill. Each print, broadcast and online ad included the call to action to visit this site.

The *"Collaborate>Create>Succeed"* brand strategy helped focus this giant company internally and instilled employee pride, which in turn motivated better work with customers. The communications were also coordinated to ensure that the promise made in external communications was delivered in actual customer engagements.

Since the *"Collaborate> Create>Succeed"* brand strategy was implemented as a rallying cry for the Cargill brand, it has had a galvanizing effect throughout the Cargill organization. This message has transcended the corporate advertising effort and is now the basis for almost every piece of internal and external communications, ranging from annual reports, corporate recruiting, independent business unit advertising and collateral, as well as all corporate brand advertising.

B

WE FOUND A WAY
TO REMOVE THE SUGAR WITHOUT
REMOVING THE TEMPTATION.

Cargill

C

WE KNEW WE HAD TO HAVE THE
CHOPS TO HANG WITH THIS CROWD.

www.cargillcreates.com

Cargill

D

An annual Awareness and Attitude Study among the target audience measures progress towards the awareness and perception change goals revealed:

- Significant* increase in perception as "the best agri-food company to work with for the most innovative solutions" (117 Index).
- Significant* increase in willingness to "pay a premium price for Cargill products and services" (121 Index).
- A critical factor in changing the perception has been the integrated advertising effort as the brand has experienced a significant increase in Ad Awareness (122 Index).
- CargillCreates.com had over 50,000 visits during the first 120 days following its launch.
- Cargill experienced double-digit sales and profits growth for the year ending May 2005, this for the second consecutive year since the campaign started in 2003.

Significant at the 90% Confidence Interval

As a result of the campaign by Martin|Williams, the target audience now significantly views Cargill as a partner with innovative solutions and is now more willing to pay more for Cargill products.

A. **Magazine ad**

B. **TV spot** — "Florence"

C-D. **Magazine ads**

E. **Website** — cargillcreates.com

E

CASE STUDY: Lincoln Financial Group

When Lincoln Financial decided to become a national advertiser for the first time in 40 years, they searched for an agency that had the experience and reputation for powerful branding.

In 1999, Martin|Williams was hired to lead the effort to create a coordinated brand campaign for Lincoln. As the lead strategic agency, Martin|Williams' challenge was to focus the efforts of seven other communications entities on a long term strategic brand message, increase brand name awareness, create positive brand associations among very affluent consumers, as well as with financial intermediaries, a critical trade audience.

Through extensive account planning, that incorporated in-depth interviews with LFG executive management and financial advisors in local offices, Martin|Williams felt the wisest course was to focus the marketing campaign on the affluent segment of the U.S. population.

A key insight was that the affluent are motivated and driven by the chance to collect one-of-a-kind life experiences. Their increasing net worth enables them to do things with their lives that the majority of Americans can't.

During the initial six years, Martin|Williams effectively built their original campaign called "Clear Solutions" around enabling this core motivation and letting the affluent know that Lincoln Financial understands exactly what drives them.

Not content to stay still, in 2004, Martin|Williams led a strategic initiative that identified a major mind-set shift that was taking place among affluent Baby Boomers in the financial services industry. This shift required that they reframe the Lincoln Financial brand to keep it relevant with the growing ranks of the super affluent.

Baby Boomers were essentially redefining retirement. No longer is it considered a stopping point, but rather, a turning point full of potential and possibilities.

With this insight, Martin|Williams led the development of a fully integrated campaign aimed at owning "the optimism of the future." To convey this notion, they created the positioning tagline, "Hello future."

They leveraged this insight in an integrated effort against both consumer and financial trade audiences, with a foundation of business, news and finance programming and editorial. With Lincoln Financial Group, they created four spectacular entitlements and media sponsorships to add plan reach and elevate brand perceptions:

• Lincoln Financial NBC Sports Report

A

B

• Lincoln Financial Battle at The Bridges (ABC Sports Primetime golf special featuring Tiger Woods)
• Lincoln Financial Field (home of the Philadelphia Eagles)
• Lincoln Financial 100th Anniversary

The "Hello future" campaign is just beginning to gather positive results in the marketplace. However, initial results show in 2005, brand awareness among the target audience increased to an impressive 49% from 39% in 2003, a 26% change. Even more importantly, among the extremely desirable super-affluent audience (those with IPA of $500K+), brand awareness surged to a record 60%.

....

A. **Magazine ad** — Consumer print

B. **Poster** — Battle of the Bridges Golf Tournament Sponsorship

C. **TV spot** — "Skiier"

C

mcgarrybowen

Founded in 2002

601 West 26th St.
New York, NY 10001
212-598-2900
fax: 212-598-2996
www.mcgarrybowen.com

NEW BUSINESS CONTACT:
Adrian Keevil, 212-598-2907

SENIOR MANAGEMENT:
John McGarry, Chief Executive Officer
Gordon Bowen, Chief Creative Officer
Stewart Owen, Chief Strategic Officer
Jonathan Buckley, Chief Operating Officer
Adrian Keevil, Director of Business Development
Eric Vukmirovich, Chief Financial Officer

CLIENTS: Verizon, Marriott, InBev, Crayola, Chase, Reebok, Kraft,
Century 21, Disney, Wall Street Journal, Learning Leaders, USOC

FULL-TIME EMPLOYEES: 200

mcgarrybowen

Founded in 2002, mcgarrybowen is an independent marketing communications agency envisioned by four principals with over 100 years of experience working with some of the world's biggest and most admired brands. Together they've built an organization devoid of the distractions of politics and bureaucracy, and dedicated to focusing on what they know works: client leadership, strategic insight, and creative innovation. mcgarrybowen services include traditional advertising, re-branding and

logo design, interactive advertising, event management, retail design, and even product design.

mcgarrybowen's first assignment began with a question—what should Verizon do for the first anniversary of 9/11? That company had given itself to New York on that day to keep the telephones running. Everyone, including Ivan Seidenberg, the company's CEO, who started 30 years ago at Verizon as a splicer, helped repair lines around Ground Zero; they also lost a

major building to the attacks.

The partners presented a concept that would become a prayer of optimism for tomorrow and a message of thanks to the people of Verizon and others who served on the tragic day. The spot featured an unprecedented collaboration between megaproducer David Foster, music executive Brian Avnet, popular singers Josh Groban and Jewl Anguay, and director Leslie Dektor, all of whom donated their time to the project. The

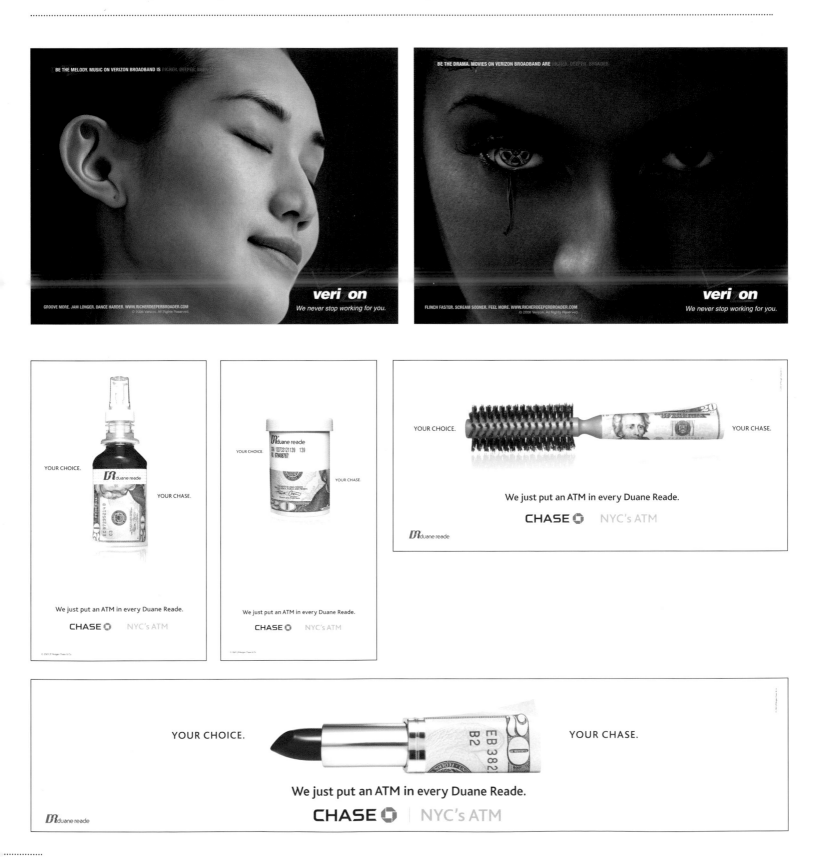

agency wrote, shot, and completed the commercial in just three weeks. The resulting piece, "Lady Liberty," aired on 9/11/2002 and mcgarrybowen was born.

After the success of "Lady Liberty," mcgarrybowen went on to become the lead brand agency for Verizon. Marriott Hotels came next, and within three years they have partnered as lead agency for some of the world's greatest corporations and brands: Crayola, Pfizer, InBev, Reebok, Century 21, Kraft, Disney, Dow

Jones' Wall Street Journal, and the U.S. Olympic Committee.

"What separates mcgarrybowen from other agencies is, first and most important, that the partners work on clients' businesses every day," says CEO John McGarry. "We have created a model where our most senior people manage accounts with the strongest, most competitive, and most intelligent people in the business reporting to them. We have been fortunate enough to be able to create

a model from scratch that reflects the way clients want their businesses to be run in today's world."

"Our strategic and creative platform is based on the concept of the Big Idea and Organizing Idea," adds executive creative director, Gordon Bowen. "Any idea that comes out of this agency has to be a big idea, rooted in the brand and strategic fundamentals. An idea that you hear once and it hits you. They also have to be organizing ideas. Ideas that drive a full

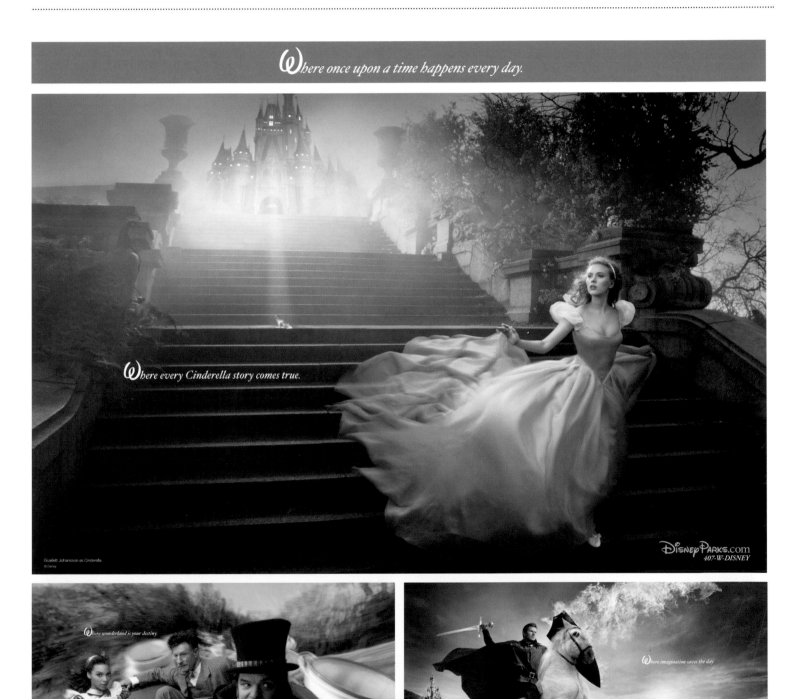

communications plan. Ideas that inform the entire company and brand. Ideas that work as well in a million dollar TV production as they do on a napkin."

When Kraft approached mcgarrybowen, the food giant was experiencing the "disappearing middle" for its enhancers brands (salad dressing, mayo, and barbecue sauce). On the low end of the market, store brands had improved significantly in quality and package appearance. On the high end a number of relatively inexpensive premium brands were stealing share from Kraft. mcgarrybowen needed to create an engagement platform to excite the consumer to discover the Kraft difference.

The Big Idea and Organizing Idea came from a simple observation rooted in quantitative research—the Gen X mom was a much different woman than advertisers gave her credit for. More than ever, top-tier design was available to her on a mass scale. She shopped at places like Target and Crate and Barrel and, when she couldn't afford those places, she would go there for ideas and then try to find similar items at less expensive retailers. What to make for dinner is cited as the one of the most stressful things modern moms face. The line, "Kraft your Salad" is meant to inspire Gen X moms to express themselves in the kitchen and have a little fun—to experiment with new and interesting ingredients. As the most trusted brand in the category, Kraft was perceived as the permission to try something different—the glue that held it all together.

One of the greatest things about a Big Idea and Organizing Idea is that it works across all media. mcgarrybowen presented in-store programs such as stickers on unexpected ingredients in the produce section, floor tiles, and parking lot cooking stations. They created an interactive campaign and website where one could input all the spare ingredients one had and the site would suggest interesting recipe ideas. They wanted to surround the consumer and encourage her to Kraft her world.

mcgarrybowen has a branding philosophy that's focused on ensuring that what they do is compelling, unique, and business building. That philosophy is based on a few consistent tenets:

Information-driven: They want to get as much information as possible and get it as soon as possible. Rest assured, if you don't already have it in place, they will recommend research against your target audience.

Information source agnostic: mcgarrybowen looks at every client on an individual basis. They're experienced and comfortable across a wide range of original and secondary research techniques, from the most rigorous quantitative studies to in-depth ethnographies. They'll recommend what's right for the problem, not simply what they already know how to do.

Contextually-based: They are always mindful of the larger business and marketing context.

People as People, not just People as Consumers: The best ideas usually come from a broader understanding of what matters to people; their hopes, dreams, fears, and desires, not just as consumers, but as people.

Values-based: Today it is increasingly difficult to create sustainable differ-

entiation based on functional, or even benefit-driven, attributes. Even in the pharmaceutical category, where companies invest billions to create functional differences, it's becoming increasingly rare.

Some say mcgarrybowen is the most successful start-up agency in history. In four years, mcgarrybowen has become the largest independent agency in New York, with billings approaching $2 Billion. In an industry wowed by the latest buzz words, this agency is proof that demand for serious client service, coupled with outstanding creative, not only still exists, but is valued by companies that understand the importance of branding.

While any ad agency can promise you great branding, mcgarrybowen will deliver media neutral big ideas, face-to-face, day-in and day-out, right from the top.

CASE STUDY: Reebok

"I got my MBA from Marcy Projects."
–Shawn Carter

i am what i am

When the mcgarrybowen team first met with Reebok's then CMO, Dennis Baldwin, he summed up the brand's problem in one sentence. "Ask 10 people at Reebok what we stand for and you will get 10 different answers." If the people at the company weren't sure, the consumer had no idea. The problem was one of relevance and consideration.

With Reebok, mcgarrybowen first looked to the past, to see what they had to work with. They found a rich history and history with a point of view. Whether it was inventing the first track spike in 1895 (the same shoes worn by the famously hard-headed track stars of the English team in the 1924 Olympic Games, made famous by the film "Chariots of Fire"), revolutionizing gym work-outs by introducing the world to Step Aerobics, redefining fit with PUMP, creating the athletic lifestyle/classics category, embracing a star like Allen Iverson to speak for the brand when no one else would touch him, or being the first company to market an athletic shoe endorsed by musicians (Jay-Z and 50 Cent), Reebok has always been about doing things their own way, blazing new trails, and celebrating the individual.

But somewhere along the way Reebok had lost its voice. By the end of the 1990s, the traditionally strong Reebok brand had fallen to third place behind both Nike and Adidas. And they were heading for fourth fast.

Reebok needed to recapture the essence of what Reebok stood for as a brand and the role their brand plays in the lives of young people.

mcgarrybowen believes there are two ways to fix a problem in advertising. One is to impose a personality onto a brand. The other is to find the personality of the brand.

Reebok at its core was, and always had been, about celebrating and empowering individuality and individual achievement, about challenging the paradigm.

The best part about it was this inherent brand POV was both different from the competitors and uniquely relevant to their target. Every young person struggles to answer the same basic question—"who am I?"—and we know that brands play a role in helping kids answer this question and express to the world who they are. mcgarrybowen wanted to encourage kids to embrace their individuality and not be afraid to be who they were. "We felt we were on to something," said John McGarry, mcgarrybowen CEO.

Next they went out and talked with kids. And listened. The word on the street is different from a focus group room in Stamford. Kids said they often saw the world as us versus them. As big conglomerate versus the little guy. As power versus powerlessness.

mcgarrybowen found that they admired—indeed, strived for—individuality. Being who you are. Reebok supports those who stay true to themselves, the ones who do it their way. They celebrate their irreverence, imperfection, and humanity. The ones who are comfortable enough in their own skins to say: I am what I am.

I Am What I Am [IAWIA]. mcgarrybowen and Reebok decided to extend an invitation (not a command) to the young. An invitation into a brand and a club that celebrated individuality.

It was executed with traditional and non-traditional media ranging from TV, print, and OOH, to video games integration, PSP, and iPod downloads.

In 2005, Reebok spent about 80M globally in a variety of media, much of it unconventional, such as:

- Unlockable video game content.
- Downloadable content for PSP and iPods
- Street teams handing out posters and DVDs with commercials at events, and concerts
- Underground release of a mix CD with G-Unit
- Interactive TV
- Video on Demand

IAWIA was represented in TV & print by strong individuals like Allen Iverson, Jay-Z, Amelie Mauresmo, Christina Ricci, and many more.

(Music)
(Various different NBA players practicing)

ALLEN IVERSON VOICE OVER: A jump shot can get you...

a shoe deal...

a supermodel...

(Music)

a big house...

fancy cars...

a bunch of "yes" men...

and a Swiss bank account.

But none of these things...

can get you a jump shot.

(Fade out)

When mcgarrybowen first spoke with the Marriott marketing group, the travel industry had been hit hard by the economic downturn and travel lag that followed 9/11. The need to increase occupancy had driven Marriott and its competitors to rely heavily on promotional and price-driven marketing tactics.

The time had come for Marriott to rise above the din of price and promotion and associate itself with a set of values and emotional brand benefits.

Six months later, in February 2004, mcgarrybowen and Marriott launched the "Big Story," a fully integrated campaign that unified Marriott's loyalty program brand and eight lodging brands under a single banner of "It's the Marriott Way." The objectives of the campaign were three-fold: to elevate Marriott to the status of icon brand in the hotel category, to create meaning and differentiation for each individual sub-brand, to lift the image of the by-Marriott brands through their association with the Marriott brand.

By late 2004, Marriott Hotels & Resorts (MHR) were in the process of rolling out thousands of new beds and fresh, white bedding to enhance their guest's experience. mcgarrybowen proposed launching Marriott's new bed package to conumers as part of a new "Revive Collection" of services and amenities. The target was the achievement-oriented frequent business traveler, with a creative bulls-eye on Gen X (ages 25-39).

In contrast to the competitive clutter, mcgarrybowen's team decided to associate Marriott's new bed with the true end benefit of a great night's sleep: a great next day.

Revive.

A simple-but-powerful message that encapsulated the consumer-end benefit in a single word. The ads featured revived, rejuvenated achievers using their beds as a launching pad. Instead of trying to own the night, Marriott was positioned to own the next day and the infinite possibilities of a new beginning. The print ads represented the bed as hero and the guest as heroic.

During creative development, focus groups strongly confirmed the campaign's stopping power, ability to communicate the main message, and memorability among Gen X and Boomer business travelers.

Given that 75% of MHR's frequent business travelers travel by air, mcgarrybowen tailored a strategy to "surround the air traveler."

At the core of the media plan was a dramatic presence in twelve key airports. This was supplemented by a national print effort and a robust plan online, with high-impact placements including page takeovers on business, news and money sections, and interactive peelbacks.

Unexpectedly high excitement among the international marketing network at Marriott resulted in the company's first-ever simultaneous campaign launch in 16 countries on five continents.

Actual spending on the launch of the campaign cannot be disclosed, however, Forbes Magazine estimated spending at $90MM—far beyond the actual budget.

Marriott's "Revive" campaign was recognized as outstanding and received: JC Decaux's 2005 award for "Innovation and Impact in Airport Advertising;" Two Gold awards and "Best of Show" at the 2005 Mobius Awards; Multiple HSMAI Adrian Awards (for "creative brilliance and best practices in hospitality, travel, and tourism-related marketing"); Multiple SIAA Awards (recognizing "achievements of the service industry in marketing and advertising").

Only four months into the "Revive" campaign, a significant increase was seen in consumer perceptions of Marriott Hotels & Resorts as "innovative" (+7pts) and "stylish" (+5pts)—both key drivers of loyalty and preference.

Within six quarters of the "Big Story" campaign's launch, Marriott's RevPAR (a key industry metric) had increased 9.2% VYA and their stock price (MAR) had increased 55% (from $44.55/share to $68.99/share).

Business results continue to be outstanding. Marriott Hotels & Resorts has continued to maintain its 3:2 lead in 1st-choice preference over Hilton, its closest competitor.

Merkley + Partners

Great Thinking Memorably Expressed

Founded in 1993

200 Varick Street,
12th Floor,
New York, NY 10014
212-366-3500
Fax: 212-366-3637
www.merkleyandpartners.com

HOLDING COMPANY:
The Omnicom Group

KEY NEW BUSINESS CONTACT:
Morgan Shorey, 212-366-3870

SENIOR MANAGEMENT:
Alex Gellert, CEO
Andy Hirsch, ECD
Randy Saitta, ECD

CLIENTS: The Ad Council, Arby's, Aunt Jemima, AXA Equitable, Citigroup, Cold-EEZE, Duncan Hines, E-LOAN, Ferrero Rocher, Mercedes-Benz, Mrs. Butterworth's, Novartis, Pfizer, PSEG, Starwood Resorts & Hotels Worldwide, TAP Pharmaceuticals

FULL-TIME EMPLOYEES: 212

Merkley + Partners

"A lasting relationship of mutual respect between a consumer and a brand. That is ultimately what we aim to build." For Executive Creative Directors Andy Hirsch and Randy Saitta, the strategies, the media and the executions may vary, but the end goal is always the same. "We get tactical when we have to get tactical. But long-standing connections between our clients and the people they need to reach is really where we earn our success."

Founded in 1993 with just over 40

people and $55mm in billings, Merkley + Partners now has over half a billion dollars in billings and more than 200 employees.

In the past 10 years, they have grown beyond their general advertising roots to become a full-service agency specializing in general advertising, healthcare, and direct relationship marketing. The company, part of the Omnicom Group, excels at building brands with relevant, well-placed messaging and exceptional creative execution.

But it didn't all happen by accident. Long known for its insightful strategic thinking, the agency approaches every challenge from the broadest possible perspective. "The first thing we do is address the business opportunity; the last thing we do is make ads," says CEO Alex Gellert. "We believe most markets and brands follow a predictable pattern. We call it the 'Big Fat S'—a variation on the classic business school model."

As dominant brands reach their peaks

A

B

C   D

A-B. AXA Equitable —TV and print campaign: Planning your financial future…For most of us, it's the 800lb gorilla in the room.

C-D: Cold-EEZE — Some things are easier to get over than others. Poster aimed at college students extols the benefits of taking Cold-EEZE to cut a cold in half.

and begin to decline, the category landscape changes. Smart marketers challenge themselves to invent the next S-curve, thereby changing the competitive playing field to their advantage. Merkley works with clients to successfully navigate the current S-curve and define the next one.

To understand a brand, its evolution and its relevance to a marketplace, Merkley reviews and employs category, company and consumer research to reveal insights that provide the basis of the brand's strategy. Once a strategy is in place, testing and refinement lead to the next step of the process, the Governing Brand Idea, or GBI, which will lead to the future S-curve.

The GBI is the very essence of the brand and defines its relevance to prospects and customers. More than "just" a strategy or a creative idea, the GBI allows successful brands to deploy consistent messaging across multiple touch points to magnify and solidify their appeal. "We believe that an effective GBI must be consumer-informed, idea-led, and brand-neutral," says Executive Planning Director Stacey Lesser. "Only then will we produce extraordinary campaigns and consistent perceptions across the entire brand experience."

"We work side-by-side with our clients and elicit their participation throughout the process. Not only do we not have all the answers, the pace and complexity of our clients' businesses require up-to-date

E

F

G

E-G. Citigroup — Global brand campaign for Citigroup Corporate and Investment Banking targets the C-suite at multi-national and top-tier regional companies around the world.

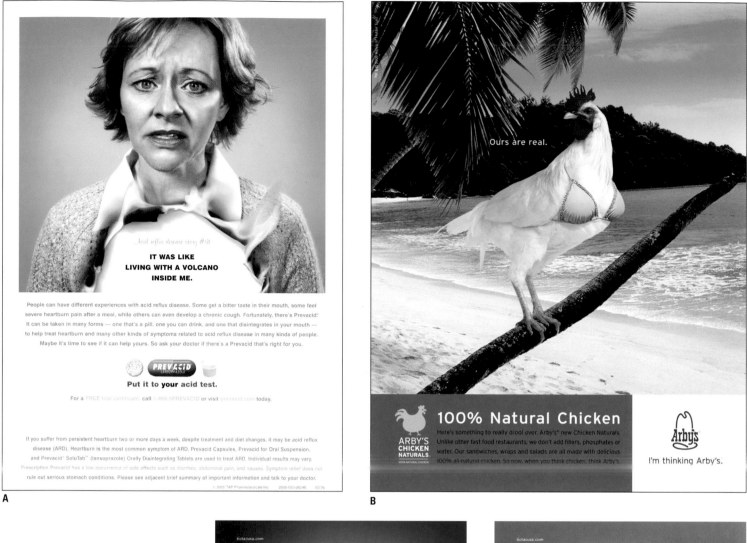

A

B

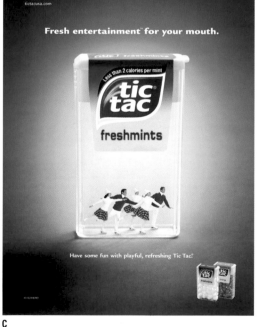

C

D

A. Prevacid — General awareness DTC print ad.

B: Arby's — Launch of Arby's Chicken Naturals in Sports Illustrated Swimsuit Edition.

C-D: Tic-Tac — In a cluttered category of sameness, work for Tic-Tac uses a fresh metaphorical approach replacing the tiny mints with what they actually represent: fun!

and active client contributions to help drive knowledge and insight."

As media channels continue to proliferate, and individuals gain more and more control over how they consume information, Merkley believes that brands must abandon traditional "siloed" disciplines and adopt new, integrated marketing techniques. Merkley iD is a communications planning department established to connect brands to consumers in the most effective manner possible by combining three separate disciplines into one integrated department.

Merkley iD delivers 3-dimensional communications plans that leverage both contact and content in pursuit of their client's goals.

"Our in-depth understanding of both the brand and the target prospects gives us the ability to add value to any communication program," says Mathilde Bennington, General Manager of Merkley iD. "We employ a media planning process called Action Targeting at both the national and local levels. This differs significantly from traditional media in that we do not define target audiences in terms of broad demographic segments. Instead, we use a variety of proprietary and

secondary research to gauge predictive consumer behavior and its direct link to media consumption."

This model delivers customized plans based on evidence that past consumer behavior is the most precise indicator of future response. Because they are targeting people based on their actions, they effectively shift their media goals away from delivering bulk impressions and towards delivering actual customers. As a result, they are always accountable to real world client success. Because they do not target broad, homogeneous audiences, their solutions are inherently media-neutral and often involve nontraditional communications programs.

"When all is said and done, we deliver creative that works," says Executive Creative Director Andy Hirsch. "Effective, media-agnostic, and uniquely ownable for our clients."

While they'd agree that their creative reputation is best viewed as an aspect of their clients' success, they recognize that prospective clients may look to awards as a sign of excellence. In the last four years, Merkley and its clients have been recognized with more than fifty awards at the Clios, One Show, Emmys, Kellys,

AICP, Cannes, and London International. They're most proud that the AdCouncil has chosen Merkley from among forty agencies to receive its Gold Bell for Creative Excellence in 2003 for its Housing Discrimination campaign.

If that isn't enough, Merkley was the first agency to set up an in-house digital print production facility. Plus, understanding the quick turnaround times and localization involved in retail advertising, Merkley utilizes a web-based technology that allows the agency to communicate, revise and proof ads in real time with both clients and printers.

For Mercedes-Benz Independent Dealer Groups, the web portal has allowed them to choose imagery and taglines for customization on events and promotions with same-day turnaround, a critical component in the retail arena. On average, Merkley releases ninety retail ads per day.

Whether it's a multifaceted campaign for Arby's, the launch of a new drug for Novartis, or coordinating a retail sales event for Mercedes-Benz Dealers, one look at the work and you'll agree when it comes to great branding, the one thing they all have in common is the agency Merkley + Partners.

E

F

E-G: Mercedes-Benz — Security, performance and exhilaration "Unlike any other". Powerful visual metaphors help illustrate the values of the Mercedes-Benz brand.

G

CASE STUDY: Mercedes-Benz

For decades it was the unchallenged leader in automotive luxury. But a handful of newly formed, heavily financed and flashy brands took to the road in the late 1990s and Mercedes-Benz found its sales slowing and its lead position under attack.

Merkley + Partners looked in depth at the problem. They applied their proprietary Manifesto Conflict research technique to pinpointing consumer attitudes. And then came up with an idea designed to polish the three-pointed star of Mercedes so it would blind the competition and demonstrate the world's love of the brand.

The strategy was strikingly simple. Research showed a lack of deep, loyal relationships between competitor owners and many of the younger, pretender brands such as Lexus and Infiniti, and less substantive brands such as Audi and BMW. If it had one thing, Mercedes had a legacy of trust among owners who had stayed true to the brand year in, year out. It quickly became imperative to build on that trust, and demonstrate the real connection between car and owner, between the kind of people who truly love cars, and the kind of cars—Mercedes—that inspire true love. Boomer owners would react with respect and pride; Gen Xers could begin to see a brand capable of inspiring emotional connection. In short, when it comes to category leadership, a brand should show, not tell.

Fast forward to February 2004 and phase one of the campaign: recruitment communications. Or, eliciting some of those special owner connections. Merkley designed and placed a newspaper print ad in *USA Today* asking Mercedes owners to submit photographs of themselves and their cars. A special feature icon was added to the Mercedes website, www.mbusa/lovemercedes.com, introducing owners to the campaign concept. Both tactics instantly demonstrated to non-owners the special kind of relationship Mercedes owners have with their cars and planted seeds for the future. Banner ads appeared on high traffic media websites such as the *Wall Street Journal* and *USA Today* soliciting photo submissions, and a direct call to current owners was engineered through Mercedes owner publications and outbound e-newsletters.

Word spread. People talked—and responded. Hundreds of photographs poured in to the submission office and phase two of the campaign was switched into high gear.

The result? The "Portraits" campaign: a series of beautifully edited montages of owner images, snapshots of automotive moments in time. People on the hoods of their cars, behind the wheels, longhaired in the 1970s, faded and proper in the fifties. Different versions played to Boomer and Gen X audiences to tremendous reception. With the campaign in full swing, the Mercedes website became a rapidly growing family album showcasing owners and inviting potential customer prospects to a special Mercedes event, The Love Mercedes Brand Tour ride-and-drive event.

This concept event raced across 12 major metropolitan cities, giving potential customers the opportunity to get behind the wheel of a new Mercedes without any sales pressure. Dealerships across the nation received Portraits campaign collateral and information packs, and the Mercedes PR machine rolled into action to add momentum.

For anyone who says it can be hard to quantify short-term marketing success, think again. In a category where a sales percentage point can reap huge financial dividends, Mercedes saw brand preference soar and the all-important Gen X consumer get on board. Overall brand consideration rose 11 percent between the second and third quarters in 2004, a two-year high that moved Mercedes to the top of the competitive set. Gen X attitudes improved dramatically with potential buyers showing a 9 percent increase in perception of Mercedes as a brand with momentum, and a 5 percent spike in Gen X belief that Mercedes could be a brand for them.

Today the brand is not only intact, but stronger than ever.

A-B: Mercedes-Benz — "Portraits" campaign: Real people with a real emotional connection to their cars. The "Portraits" campaign documented this undeniably strong bond in both television and print.

A

B

In an age of monster trucks,
a gentle giant.

THE NEW, FULL-SIZED 7-PASSENGER GL. *If it were just large, it would be no big deal. Instead, it is the only full-sized luxury SUV engineered like a Mercedes-Benz.*

It all starts with a sedan-like driving experience. Like our luxury sedans, the GL features unit-body construction and a smooth-shifting 7-speed automatic transmission that create responsive, precise ride and handling.

In addition, 4MATIC® permanent 4-wheel drive continually monitors each wheel for slippage, resulting in a secure, confident ride on all kinds of road surfaces, in all kinds of weather.

The GL's over 80 cu.ft. interior features a leather steering wheel, an 11-speaker sound system and

heated 8-way power front seats. Extra-thick windows and sound-dampening materials in critical areas quiet wind noise. There's even a 3rd-row see-through roof panel that lets everyone enjoy light and sky.

Most importantly, the GL relies on brains as well as brawn to protect its passengers. In fact, it has the most safety features of any full-sized SUV. For instance, there's 12-way protection from 8 air bags, as well as our front-row active head restraint technology.

Add to this a 335-horsepower V-8 that produces 339 lb-ft of torque and a 7,500-lb towing capacity, and you see why, to put it gently, the Mercedes-Benz GL is engineered like no other truck in the world. And why it's more Mercedes to love.

Starting at $55,675*

Unlike any other.

Mercedes-Benz

MBUSA.com

C

At our best when things
are at their worst.

AFTER MORE THAN 65 YEARS OF SAFETY FIRSTS,
WE KNOW WHAT'S NEEDED IS MORE THAN JUST ANOTHER INNOVATION.

That's rooted in an idea so powerful it will change what is possible.

Unlike any other.

Mercedes-Benz

MBUSA.com

D

The word "engineering" means
different things to different people.

TO STUDY THE EXTERIOR LINES OF THE 2007 SL-CLASS IS TO STUDY A WORK OF ART.

THIS IS THE 2007 SL-CLASS. *Awe-inspiring beauty. Both above the hood and beneath it. To us, that is engineering.*

Unlike any other.

Mercedes-Benz

E

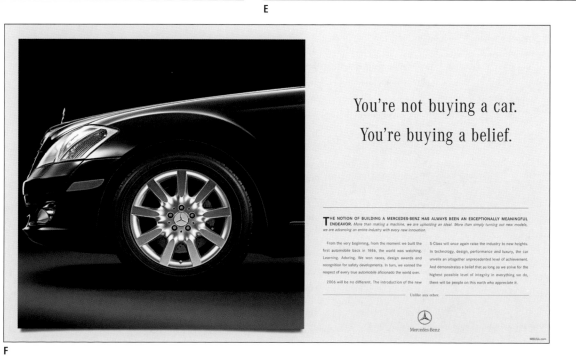

You're not buying a car.
You're buying a belief.

THE NOTION OF BUILDING A MERCEDES-BENZ HAS ALWAYS BEEN AN EXCEPTIONALLY MEANINGFUL ENDEAVOR. *More than making a machine, we are upholding an ideal. More than simply turning out new models, we are advancing an entire industry with every new innovation.*

From the very beginning, from the moment we built the first automobile back in 1886, the world was watching. Learning. Adoring. We won races, design awards and recognition for safety developments. In turn, we earned the respect of every true automobile aficionado the world over.

2006 will be no different. The introduction of the new

S-Class will once again raise the industry to new heights. In technology, design, performance and luxury, the car unveils an altogether unprecedented level of achievement. And demonstrates a belief that as long as we strive for the highest possible level of integrity in everything we do, there will be people on this earth who appreciate it.

Unlike any other.

Mercedes-Benz

MBUSA.com

F

C-F: "Leadership" campaign — The philosophy of a true leader. This campaign reasserts the unique beliefs that elevate the Mercedes-Benz brand above its would-be competitors.

CASE STUDY: Arby's

We're all just animals. Get hungry, got to eat, got to get it right now. The folks at Merkley + Partners know that better than most. Just ask the Arby's creative team, charged in 2004 with giving consumers a renewed and carnivorous appetite for the beloved roast beef brand beginning to lose its flavor with customers.

Once iconic, the neon ten-gallon attracted customers to Arby's restaurants across the country and had them lining up for the signature roast beef. But times change, and without the new currency of burgers, pizzas and tacos to trade, Arby's had found itself short-changed and overspent with promotional dollars outstripping return at an alarming rate of 5 to 1. Clearly, an answer was needed and fast.

Many strategy sessions and fast-food working lunches later, they had it. Merkley's defining insight, culled down from hours of analysis, was designed to address Arby's stale and tired reputation with customers, while driving those same customers back to the hundreds of Arby's franchisees facing an increasingly uncertain financial future.

The idea? Let's call it The Urge. Boiled down, when it comes to food, consumers follow their guts; they feed the urge. They saddle it up in the passenger seat to drive out of their way; they drop everything to drag it across town. So when a craving kicks in, consumers know what they want and do anything to get it.

Armed with that insight, creative for a new campaign to relaunch the brand began immediately, governed by the principle that the way into people's wallets is through their irrational urges, their craving or hankering for a particular kind of food, rather than through their rational minds. And, the creatives took it one step further. They used the advertising to demonstrate that once the craving for Arby's food sets in, it is so distracting that it gets in the way of all other thought.

There can be few people who haven't seen the results. 250 commercials produced in just 18 months redefined the brand for consumers and reacquainted Arby's customers with their animal urge. A new ten-gallon icon became the symbol of that urge, popping overhead like an idea light bulb every time an office cube worker, a guy doing construction, or anyone stopped thinking and let their stomachs do the talking. The campaign's tagline "I'm thinking Arby's" has now slipped into the national lexicon and Merkley has continued the brand re-engineering through FSIs, point of purchase materials, restaurant staff uniform upgrades, and new packaging featuring a more modern, earthier tone and visuals.

Originally playing to the brand's heritage in the roast beef sandwich, the campaign has gone on to convince consumers that whatever they crave, Arby's has the answer. Chicken, salads, and other menu items have all ridden the wave to a successful comeback. Arby's sales immediately soared more than 7 percent over the previous year and have continued to climb by 3 percent a year since then. The average spend-per-customer-ticket is up, and franchisees across the country have embraced the new creative and branding.

It's enough to make one pause, tilt back the ten-gallon and take a long look at what's turning out to be a satisfying horizon for business and brand.

I'm thinking Arby's.

A

B

C

A: **Arby's** — In-store window banners created for Arby's Fish promotion.

B-C: **"I'm thinking Arby's"** — TV Campaign.

Mullen

Relentless Creativity

Founded in 1970

Wenham, MA
Winston-Salem, NC
Pittsburgh, PA
Detroit, MI
www.mullen.com

KEY NEW BUSINESS CONTACT:
Melissa Lea, EVP, Director of Business Development, 978-468-8553

SENIOR MANAGEMENT:
Joe Grimaldi, President and CEO
Edward Boches, Chief Creative Officer
John Fitzgerald, President, Winston-Salem
Bob Bernardini, President, Pittsburgh
Keith Ulrich, SVP, Detroit

CLIENTS: General Motors, Wachovia, XM Satellite Radio, LendingTree, Turner Broadcasting System, The Stanley Works, Four Seasons Hotels & Resorts, Department of Defense, 3Com, Stride Rite, Progress Energy, match.com, Grain Foods Foundation, Highmark BlueCross BlueShield, PPG Industries, Sealy/Stearns & Foster, R.L. Winston Rod Co., Royal Ahold, T.J. Maxx, MassMutual, Panera Bread

Mullen

While Mullen operates out of a sprawling country estate on several bucolic acres just outside Boston, MA, the venue isn't meant to be one of those "look how hip we are" ad agency affectations.

Rather, the agency chiefs prefer the location, as opposed to being in an office building in the middle of downtown, because they want as few distractions as possible that might take their employees' minds off building the brands of their clients.

"We felt that being away from the city gives us a different way of looking at things," said agency president and CEO Joe Grimaldi. "Our way, branding isn't something you create with a pad of paper or a storyboard. It's what you are. Your beliefs. Your values. All that adds up to what others can reliably expect of you. We've always believed in being a brand, not just building one for our clients."

One way that Mullen sharpens its people's focus on the clients' needs is by

not following the practice of designating the various agency disciplines (advertising, strategic planning, media, public relations, direct marketing, interactive marketing, design, events, retail marketing, etc.) as freestanding profit centers. This eliminates interdepartmental turf wars over the client dollar.

"We've never had profit centers, and in the last couple of years, we've reallocated office space within the company so there's more of a cross-pollination between

A

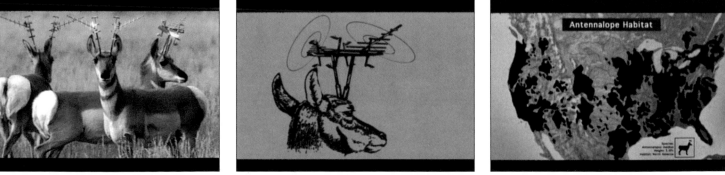

B

[disciplines]," said Edward Boches, chief creative officer with the agency. "The idea is to get people in the room and do what's best for the client without being discipline-centric."

By doing business in that fashion, in a place that is off the beaten path, Mullen officials feel they can put more energy into being attentive brand stewards. And if that is a shopworn descriptor, it is also a monumental responsibility, since the agency defines the term "brand" as the intersection point(s) between the company and the consumer.

"A brand is every single encounter a product has with the consumer," Grimaldi said. "And we have to make sure [the client's] message is seamlessly integrated, no matter how it's delivered—broadcast, outdoor, interactive, etc. We don't go into a project with a predetermined toolbox of how we're going to find a solution.

"We strongly believe that a brand today should spend less time talking about what it makes and why you should buy it, and instead express what it stands for and invite you to share those beliefs. The best brands are defined by their customers' beliefs and values, as well as their own, and strive to build a community that unites the two."

As such, the agency's philosophy on branding and its use of multiple communication disciplines can yield a solution that goes beyond the obvious. For Stride Rite Children's Group, the

C

A. GM Card — Bureau
For GM, the agency helped define the card, distinguish it from other reward cards, acquire customers and launch sub-brands.

B. Nextel — Antennalope
For seven years, the agency guided Nextel from a start-up two-way radio company to the leading wireless provider to businesses with clever and surprising spots like this one using antennalopes to introduce Nextel's coast-to-coast walkie-talkie.

C. Monster.com — When I Grow Up
Mullen launched both the dot-com craze and this storied brand with what has been hailed as one of the most popular Super Bowl spots of all time.

D. Four Seasons — Paris
Known for its stunning print work, Mullen has for years understood that an image can, in and of itself, help define a brand.

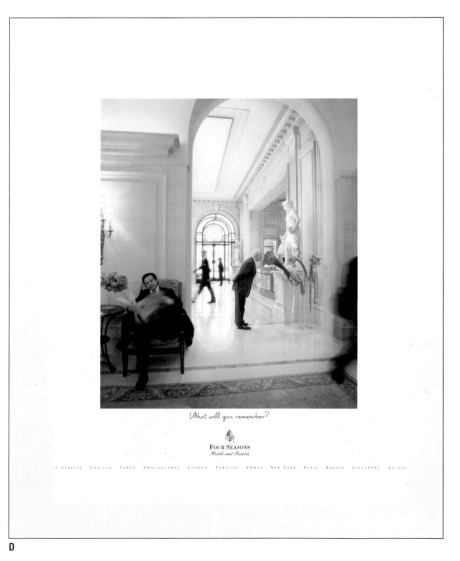

D

agency had to get consumers (parents) to think of kids' shoes beyond the normal fit-and-durability criteria.

In the recent campaign—themed "Life's waiting. Let's go."—the agency's approach was to tap into the desire parents have for their children's self-confidence to grow as the kids themselves grow. The campaign let parents understand that Stride Rite sees their kids as they do, rather than as another set of little feet to make a sale on.

"We have a long history as the premier maker of children's footwear," said Pam Salkovitz, president of Stride Rite. "Yet most parents think of us in purely rational terms such as fit and quality. That's enviable, but not powerful enough emotionally. Mullen helped us stay true to our product benefit by elevating it to a more provocative promise."

And to the point that the agency's no-profit-center approach doesn't stifle the use of any discipline, the advertising campaign "achieved its full expression,"

according to Boches, by incorporating direct mail, in-store posters and packaging into the traditional media mix.

Likewise, Mullen has had success building other clients' brands by not tying everything around the conventional advertising model:

• The agency dropped bags of Smartfood popcorn out of helicopters and transformed popcorn from a commodity into a #1 brand in three years.

• They launched a 40-market

A. Stride Rite — Pink Dress
Mullen helped reinvigorate this famous children's shoe brand by eschewing the rational benefits of fit and comfort for the emotional benefit of confidence, all summed up in four words: "Life's waiting. Let's go."

B. Smartfood — Babies
It was nearly 15 years ago when the agency redefined brand advertising for snack foods and beer. Prior to Smartfood, all advertising was about what went inside the bag or bottle, not what happened outside of it.

C. Swiss Army — Bottle Opener
With this viral poster campaign for Swiss Army, the agency helped reinvigorate the brand by creating a new way to look at the knife with lots of blades: one blade at a time.

D. Oxygen — I Am Baby
Mullen's launch of the Oxygen network is considered one of the most successful media brand launches of all time. They positioned the network as a brand that recognized, celebrated and harnessed the power and energy of women.

A

Swiss Army Equipped Tour in partnership with National Geographic and Outward Bound to bring the "equipped" brand positioning to life.

• On behalf of Eddie Bauer, they negotiated a national sponsorship of the IMAX film, *Lewis and Clark;* secured the apparel sponsorship of Jim Whittaker's Return to Everest trek; and developed a partnership with legendary broadcaster Charles Osgood to promote the Lewis and Clark sponsorship.

• For XM Satellite Radio, they worked with the producers of the hit FX show *Nip/Tuck* and not only secured title sponsorship to the commercial-free season premiere, but also wove XM into the actual story lines. They also got $5 million worth of promotional activity above and beyond the media buy, integration into *Nip/Tuck's* Web site and live appearances on XM by the show's stars.

In the case of LendingTree, the agency realized that the company does more than give consumers a place to seek out a good rate on a mortgage or home equity loan. The agency found the connecting point between the service offered and the resulting consumer empowerment, and came up with the tag line: "When banks compete, you win."

Mullen's branding philosophy—for itself as well as its clients—and its "remote" facility also serve to make staffing decisions easier. Not every person wanting to work at a big agency wants to

B

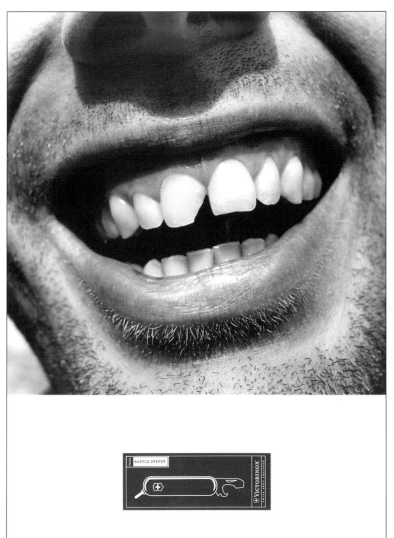

C

D

do so in a small town. Not every ad professional can handle an environment in which all the disciplines are brought together under one roof.

"When you're hired at Mullen, you join a group of people who really want to accomplish something," said Grimaldi.

"There is a certain kind of person that thrives in this model," said Steve Calder, agency executive media director. "They are very intense. They are curious people. They are people who have a strong point of view, but can check their ego for other points of view."

Those points of view have allowed the agency, founded in a two-room apartment in 1970, to become one of the nation's top 25 agencies. And the culture of Mullen allowed the agency to survive in 1987 when its former HQ burned to the ground and everything was lost. Not only did the agency survive under adverse circumstances, but it grew by 74 percent the following year.

As the agency's credentials material boasts: "People who come to work at Mullen don't just want to be in advertising; they want to be in business at Mullen."

"You don't wait for permission around here," Boches concluded.

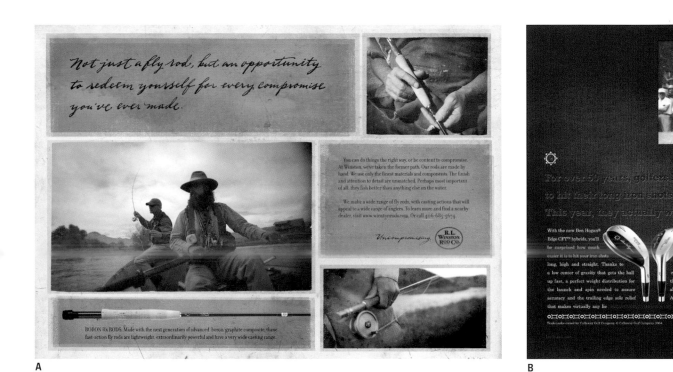

A

B

C

A. R.L. Winston Rod Co. — Compromise
The agency has a long history of creating and defining outdoor brands: Timberland, L.L.Bean, Outdoor Life Network, Simms Fishing and R. L. Winston Rod Co., to name a few.

B. Ben Hogan — Fifty Years
In the hands of Mullen, one of the great brands in golf grew nearly 300 percent in sales in just two years. Proof that the tag line is possible on and off the course.

C. Eddie Bauer — Seattle Suede
From a "me-too" khaki retailer, Mullen positioned Eddie Bauer as the authentically American outdoor apparel brand. For the first time in 40 months, the retailer posted positive results.

CASE STUDY: LendingTree

The genesis for LendingTree took place when a graduate student named Doug Lebda was trying to buy a condo and was frustrated by the process. And he found he wasn't alone.

Most consumers think of applying for a loan as an intimidating and paperwork-laden process, one where some large institution holds sway over their needs and dreams.

"Getting a loan was harder than it had to be because the process was of benefit to the lending institutions," said Jim Hartrich, EVP/group director on the LendingTree business at Mullen. "Consumers felt they were having to beg them to take their business."

Lebda created a model that would appeal to both sides. Lenders would want to participate because they'd get solid, prequalified leads. Consumers would benefit because they would have institutions competing for their business.

However, if the concept was sound, the landscape presented obstacles. Launching in 1999, the world was in the throes of the dot-com boom. There were already sites offering loans; indeed, so many that consumers were already looking at them the way they looked at the plethora of land-based banking choices—as commodities with no personalities.

After researching the marketplace, the agency determined that the heart and soul of the brand was consumer empowerment. Mullen took that passion and harnessed it to position LendingTree as the place where the consumer is in charge. Instead of sweating the loan process, which consumers hated with a passion, the advertising campaign would put loan-seekers in the decision-maker's seat. Or as the agency expressed it: "We put the wingtip on the other foot."

"We showed consumers how to stop being victims and use LendingTree to put themselves in control," said Hartrich. "We created a situation where they would be the ones to say yes or no, instead of the bank."

In one of the first television ads, a number of bankers in suits are seen cooling their heels while a casually clad couple gleefully put them through the interview ringer, driving home the message of the empowered consumer.

Another ad shows a man whose child has been accepted into an Ivy League school. In a daze, he begins thinking of the outrageous ways he'll need to make extra money to afford the tuition. That is, until he walks in on his wife overseeing a mob of lenders vying to give the couple a loan.

"LendingTree had the business concept," said agency president and CEO Joe Grimaldi. "What they needed from us was to create a brand for them that represented a powerful, unique promise for the consumer.

Part of what made the brand launch a success was a media strategy built upon continuous optimization. The brand team constantly adjusted the media plan, creating upwards of 50 plans per year in pursuit of generating increasing levels of response at decreasing cost. Using a proprietary optimization tool, Proof™, the agency was able to model the prospective impact on the business of changing creative rotations and product mix, extensive use of 15-second spots and network radio, and various mixes of network, cable and TV day-parts and then immediately put this learning into action.

In the four years the agency has had the business, it has increased total brand awareness from 25 percent to 73 percent—a 39-point edge over the closest competitor. Loan applications have gone up 294 percent, acquisition costs have been reduced 64 percent and $10.6 billion in closed loans have been generated.

Rejection

Ivy League

CASE STUDY: XM Satellite Radio

How does an agency help a client build a brand and sell something—radio—that consumers are used to getting for free?

This was the challenge when Mullen went to work for XM Satellite Radio. The service offers consumers commercial-free programming and has enough variety to satisfy any listener's need. However, to get XM service, consumers have to buy a receiver as well as pay a monthly subscription fee.

XM launched in the last half of 2001 and after a strong beginning, awareness leveled off. Mullen was hired in May of 2003.

"This was the classic case of moving from early adopters to mainstream consumers," said Tom Jump, EVP/managing partner on the XM business. "It's like crossing a chasm, and our challenge was to get people over the barrier of why they should pay for something they've been getting for free."

After a great deal of market research, and speaking to hundreds upon hundreds of XM users, the agency decided the strongest approach was to go at consumers with an emotional appeal.

"The average person was disappointed with terrestrial radio," said Jump. "They hated the tremendous amount of commercials they had to sit through. Our goal was to ignite the passion consumers had for radio by highlighting what they love best about the medium. XM offers consumers more of what they like, and its breadth of programming means they can always find something that they will enjoy."

The television ads for XM didn't spend time talking about all the choices, but played to the emotional connection one would make with the service. One ad showed a man enjoying his XM car radio so much while he's driving to work that instead of leaving the car outside, he drives into his office building and parks by his desk. Only then does he shut the car off and move the XM unit to a desk docking station.

"There's a lot of information about XM that you can't cover in 30 seconds, so we tried to create a buzz and interest," Jump said.

The agency built the XM brand with television and print ads as well as with other innovative methods. For example, the client was the presenting sponsor for the premiere of the provocative FX series *Nip/Tuck,* offering it commercial-free. The agency worked directly with *Nip/Tuck's* writers and directors to seamlessly immerse XM's products into the show, while the media group negotiated a multimillion-dollar tune-in campaign.

The next challenge for Mullen will be to get people thinking about XM as a portable music device, much like an MP3 player.

"XM wants to be seen as a content-delivery system," Jump said. "There are so many places [its service] can be delivered, it doesn't take much of a crystal ball to see that you could put XM into a variety of applications."

Band

Truce

Lost

Osborn & Barr Communications

···

We Create Belief That Creates Results™

Founded in 1988

1 North Brentwood Boulevard
St. Louis, MO 63105
888-BELIEF-2
fax: 314-726-6350
www.osborn-barr.com

NEW BUSINESS CONTACT:
Steve Kunkel, VP of Client Services
St. Louis, 314-236-6900

SENIOR MANAGEMENT:
Joe Osborn, President
Steve Barr, CEO

CLIENTS: Agraturf Equipment Services, Department of Interior, Elsevier, Environmental Protection Agency, FBA East, FCS Financial, Foxboro Conference Center, General Services Administration, Goldline Controls, Hayward Pool Products, Inc., ICL Performance Products LP, Interstate Seed Company, Intervet, Inc., Iowa Farm Bureau Federation, Iron Solutions, John Deere U.S. & Can., Michelin U.S. & Can., Monsanto, Na-Churs Alpine Solutions, National Parks Service, National Pork Board, Native American Management Services, NCBA, NORDYNE, Propane Education & Research Council, QUALISOY, RFD-TV, Smith, Bucklin & Associates, The Solae Company, Solutia, Inc., Specialty Fertilizer Products, Spiderworks, United Soybean Board, US Potato Board, USDA

FULL-TIME EMPLOYEES: 140

Osborn & Barr Communications

When it comes to cultivating great ideas, especially for companies in the agricultural business, nobody does it like Osborn & Barr Communications.

Founded in 1988, O&B began with just four employees and a single client, Monsanto.

The agency grew quickly, acquiring additional prominent agricultural brands. Over the years, it has continued its track record of consistent growth, branching out to new clients, new regions and new disciplines. Today, O&B is one of the largest agri-rural marketing communications firms in North America. Its founders, Joe Osborn and Steve Barr, oversee an international, full-service marketing communications agency with more than 140 employees and more than 35 clients. Some of the most important and influential businesses in North America entrust O&B with their brands, including John Deere, Monsanto and Michelin.

Osborn & Barr's unique passion for its clients' specialized businesses and markets enables it to provide communication campaigns and branding based on extensive knowledge of each segment. This specific market intelligence is a key competitive advantage for O&B. "Our employees live, work and play in the markets we specialize in and provide deep insight into the opportunities and challenges marketers face," says Joe Osborn, president.

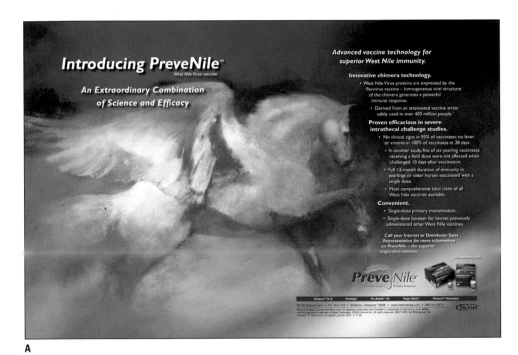

A

A. PreveNile

B. USDA National Agricultural Statistics Survey

C. National Cattlemen's Beef Association

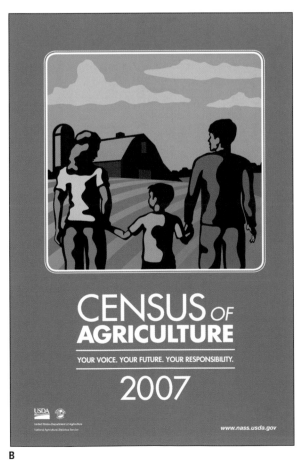

B

C

This firsthand knowledge has helped O&B provide clients such as the Iowa Farm Bureau Federation, the state's largest grassroots organization, with the understanding and strategic thinking necessary to reposition the organization and reach its more than 152,000 members with a meaningful message. The theme "People. Progress. Pride." rang true to the Farm Bureau's target in research. However, before it was introduced to the entire membership,

O&B recognized that for the rebranding to be successful, the new theme first had to be accepted and communicated to the Farm Bureau staff. O&B instituted "Living the Brand" training. Just as the O&B staff knows their clients' businesses inside and out, "Living the Brand" training made the Farm Bureau staff an integral part of communicating the brand message. This informative training helped reinforce the campaign and aided in its success.

"We pride ourselves on our ability to cultivate long-standing relationships with clients," says Steve Barr, CEO. "Osborn & Barr has experienced continued growth by being a strategic partner that clients can count on to understand their business and create resourceful methods of communicating their message to targeted audiences."

As its experience and knowledge of the B2B communications environment grew in the agricultural sector, O&B

D

E

D. National Pork Board

E. United Soybean Board

F. Michelin Profit More at the Biltmore event

F

Osborn & Barr Communications

was able to extend its services into other industries and markets that could benefit from its expertise.

One such opportunity was working with Hayward Pool Products, Inc.

Hayward had built strong relationships with pool builders; however, new pool installations are only part of their market. Existing industry trends indicated that pool owners only thought about pool equipment when it broke, and then they just wanted to get their pools up and running again quickly, so they simply replaced what was broken. Hayward challenged O&B to help them reach the untapped "I want to improve my pool" market. The result was the "Improve My Pool" store within a store: a broad set of point-of-purchase materials, including window clings, floor stickers, hang tags, counter cards, product coupons and store signage, all designed to identify products that could improve the pool environment and drive people to an information kiosk. The kiosk included a booklet customers could flip through to get descriptions of all the options available to improve their pool experience. It also contained an "advertorial" booklet with success stories and ideas ranging from increasing energy efficiency to pool safety tips.

After two years, the largest pool retailer in the United States reported a dramatic increase in sales above projections for Hayward equipment since integrating the Hayward Improve My Pool store within a store.

In a business where many clients frequently change ad agencies looking for new and different ideas, O&B constantly pushes itself to provide its clients with powerful ideas. That's a testament to the in-depth market knowledge O&B prides itself on. As a full-service agency, O&B provides integrated creative solutions no matter what the marketing challenge.

If you ask Joe Osborn what sets O&B apart, he'll tell you it's their market focus. "By specializing in a few core markets, we're able to bring more to our clients than just communication skills. Our people bring firsthand knowledge and insight that allow us to create branding that's more meaningful, more powerful in reaching the target audience." And since O&B has been fortunate in attracting and retaining major blue chip clients, the agency's clients, large and small, benefit from innovative cross-promotions that O&B

creates to help each client maximize its marketing budget.

Steve Barr adds, "Our work is more than what we do, it's a snapshot of who we are and where we've been."

As Osborn & Barr Communications moves into its 19th year of business, it will continue its deep-rooted passion for focusing on cultivating business in its core markets.

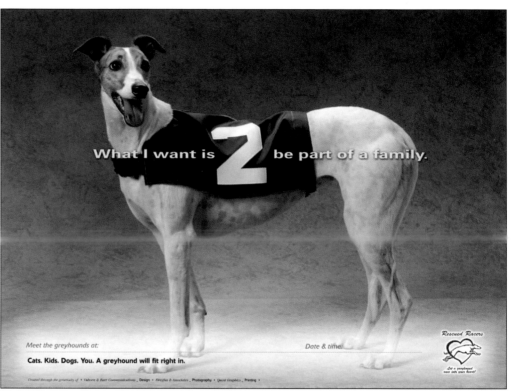

A

B

C

D

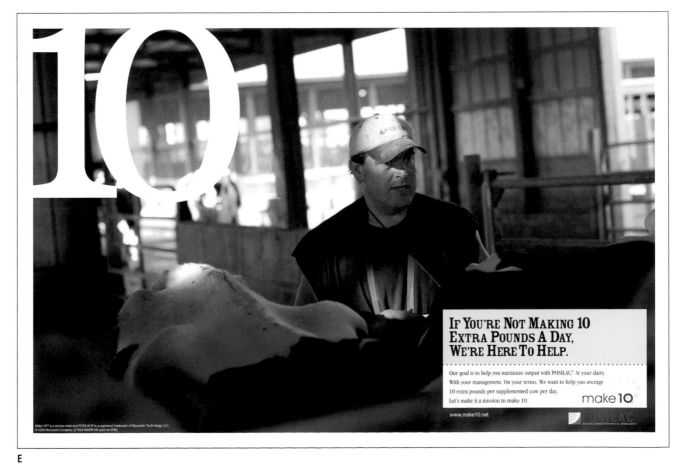

E

CASE STUDY: USDA Rural Development

When USDA Rural Development searched for an advertising agency that understood rural America from the ground up, they found it in Osborn & Barr.

USDA Rural Development (USDA RD) is a government organization committed to increasing economic opportunities and improving the quality of life for people in rural America. In a typical year, their programs create or preserve more than 300,000 rural jobs, enable 40,000 to 50,000 rural Americans to buy homes and help 450,000 low-income rural citizens rent apartments or other housing.

However, USDA Rural Development had a major challenge. It had gone through numerous name changes during the past several decades—evolving from Farmers Home Administration, Rural Electrification Administration, Rural Development Administration, and Rural Economic and Community Development. While the Farmers Home Administration was a very recognizable brand with offices in more than 1,700 of the 3,000 counties in America, there was little to no awareness of USDA Rural Development, which only had 800 offices and had little to no signage while being located within existing USDA Service Centers.

Osborn & Barr recommended the development of a new brand identity for the organization to increase the internal and external awareness of the valuable programs and services USDA Rural Development offers to rural communities.

O&B conducted research with USDA Rural Development employees to assess their understanding of the brand. Based on the preliminary research, various brand positions were developed and tested with external and internal target audiences.

From those results, a single position was chosen, and O&B developed a logo for USDA Rural Development to convey the positioning: a typical rural landscape—the distinct water tower and the mix of buildings (homes, storefronts and factories), all nestled in the rolling green hillside (the USDA logo baseline).

While a consistent brand identity is essential for greater awareness, proper brand management is more than the development of a logo and tagline. In order to bring the brand identity to life, the brand promise must be lived consistently by all employees. Extensive training was needed to ensure all internal employees were communicating the same message to rural residents, business owners and community leaders across the country.

Immediately following the brand launch, O&B conducted training sessions focused on media training, media relations and how to "live the brand" on a daily basis. For USDA Rural Development's 47 public information coordinators, O&B provided training on how to develop a communications plan, how to deal appropriately with media and how to conduct a good interview. A guide on brand strategy was developed, as well as a step-by-step manual on how to properly and consistently use the new logo and tagline. Communication kits that provided templates for key marketing tactics were also provided.

These efforts have been very well received among USDA Rural Development employees as well as within USDA as a whole. In a recent market research effort targeting internal USDA Rural Development staff, 96 percent were more connected or just as connected overall to rural development than before the launch. In addition, ratings for USDA Rural Development employee commitment to rural communities, and its mission as an agency, were high. On a 10-point scale, the average rating among all employees surveyed was 8.6. While work remains, USDA Rural Development has made significant progress toward its goal of communicating its mission to its employees and to the nation.

....

A. Rebranded USDA Rural Development logo

B. USDA Rural Development general public service announcement

C. USDA Rural Development healthcare public service announcement

D. USDA Rural Development general public service announcement

E. USDA Rural Development healthcare public service announcement

F. USDA Rural Development general public service announcement

USDA
Rural
Development
Committed to the future of rural communities.

A

Emily inherited her father's smile. Thanks to USDA Rural Development, she can inherit the family business.

Across the country, USDA Rural Development has been a valuable resource for guaranteed business loans and other programs that help people build stronger rural communities and brighter futures. For more information, contact your local USDA Rural Development office or visit www.rurdev.usda.gov.

USDA Rural Development
Committed to the future of rural communities.

USDA is an equal opportunity provider and employer.

B

Ann's treatment meant travel to a modern medical center. Because of USDA Rural Development, it was a 10-minute drive.

When Ted & Ann got married, the nearest advanced medical care was over 100 miles away. But today, thanks to USDA Rural Development, it's a different story. We're helping local medical centers get the technology they need to provide the best healthcare possible. And for some, it's making the difference of a lifetime.

To learn more, contact your local USDA Rural Development office or visit www.rurdev.usda.gov.

USDA is an equal opportunity provider and employer.

C

College gave Derek a reason to leave his hometown. USDA Rural Development is giving him a reason to come back.

For millions of rural Americans, USDA Rural Development has meant a brighter future for their communities with programs to help keep businesses strong and opportunities plentiful. For more information, contact your local USDA Rural Development office or visit www.rurdev.usda.gov.

USDA is an equal opportunity provider and employer.

D

There are 973 people in this town. With USDA Rural Development, advanced healthcare is there for all of them.

Too often, small towns miss out on big advances. At USDA Rural Development, we believe everyone deserves access to modern healthcare. Because whether the population is millions or hundreds, everyone counts. To learn more, contact your local USDA Rural Development office or visit www.rurdev.usda.gov.

USDA is an equal opportunity provider and employer.

E

With the right tools, Hal can work miracles. At USDA Rural Development, we understand completely.

There's pride in doing things yourself, knowing that what you've created is uniquely yours. So USDA Rural Development provides guaranteed business loans, housing and infrastructure improvement programs and other services to empower rural communities to find their own futures. For more information, contact your local USDA Rural Development office or visit www.rurdev.usda.gov.

USDA is an equal opportunity provider and employer.

F

CASE STUDY: United Soybean Board

A

B

You've got to know beans about soybeans to help the United Soybean Board create a campaign to support their number one market. And Osborn & Barr Communications knows beans and the farmers who grow them. That's why the United Soybean Board (USB), a nonprofit, farmer-led, quasi-governmental organization administered by the USDA, looked to O&B for help.

The domestic animal agriculture market is crucial to U.S. soybean farmers, with 94 percent of domestically used soybean meal going to U.S. livestock and poultry feed. In addition, 40 million bushels of soybeans were exported as poultry, and just over 15 million bushels of soybeans were exported as pork in 2004. Success for domestic animal agriculture is success for soybean farmers. But poultry and livestock producers who use a great deal of soybean meal face a number of pressures, not only from regulations and activist groups, but also from community opposition and negative images.

The farmer-led United Soybean Board and its 64 farmer-directors invest in more than 350 marketing and research projects annually, and this was an issue of major importance to them. To support their number one market for soybean meal, USB together with O&B developed the Animal Agriculture Initiative to inform U.S. soybean farmers how valuable livestock and

poultry are to their soybean operation. In crafting the appropriate message to reach the essential audiences for USB, O&B created local magazine and newspaper advertising, as well as outdoor display boards, radio advertising and Web site marketing. The precise messages varied depending on the specific Qualified State Soybean Board (QSSB) that was delivering the message.

O&B developed two different campaigns, one focusing on the economic impact of livestock producers to a state, the other focusing on the social impact of livestock producers on their local communities. Working with the QSSBs, O&B tailored the most appropriate message, delivered through the most appropriate media, for each state.

Since this is a new ongoing campaign, many of the projects are still being implemented. However, according to USB's semiannual Soybean Producer Attitude Survey, the number of soybean farmers who could correctly state that over 90 percent of domestically used soybean meal goes to livestock rose from 2 percent in 2004 to 10 percent in 2005.

A. United Soybean Board All-You-Can-Eat campaign

B. United Soybean Board Animal Ag campaign

The Pere Partnership

Every brand has a problem.
Every problem has a solution.

Founded in 1988

1 Penn Plaza
New York, NY 10119
212-279-9300
Fax: 212-279-9308
www.perepartnership.com

SENIOR MANAGEMENT:
Glenn Pere
David Atlas

CLIENTS: HBO, A&E, AMC, TBS, TCM, DirectTV, Biography Channel,
Fox Sports Net, Cinemax, TNT, Project ALS

The Pere Partnership

The name says it all. The Pere Partnership, as Glenn Pere, President and Chief Creative Officer says, "We're partners with everyone we work with, whether a client or supplier, we're all in this together."

Who do you call when you want to advertise the greatest fight of the century? How about one of the greatest comedies or dramas of all time? How about a once-in-a-lifetime Rolling Stones or Springsteen concert? Well, if you're a network, you call the best in the business, the company that has come through for countless clients time after time—The Pere Partnership.

What makes The Pere Partnership unique isn't their offices overlooking New York City, or the ping pong table where they do some of their best thinking. It's their passion. Their intense desire to work harder, dig deeper, and go beyond the expected. One look at how this entertainment ad agency began and you'll understand why they never take the easy way out.

As Glenn Pere, President and Chief Creative Officer, tells it, "I was working at my dad's ad agency, doing general advertising; it was a great business. I remember going to work with him at the age of 5, then going in during school holidays, to working summers cleaning the stat machine, onto doing paste-ups and mechanicals, to eventually working there full time. Everything I learned in advertising, everything I learned creatively, I learned from my dad. Advertising was truly in our blood.

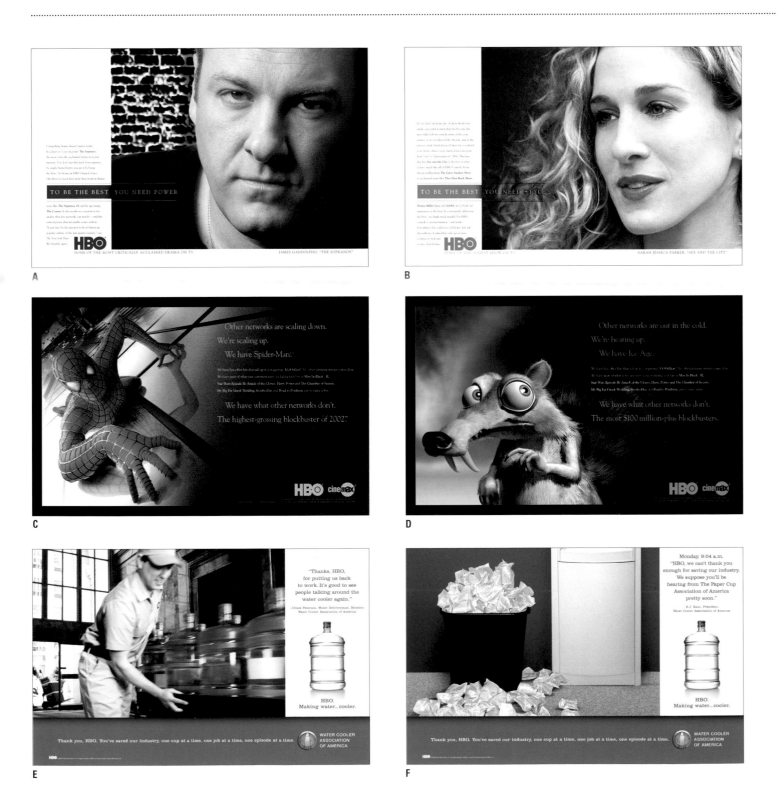

A

B

C

D

E

F

"Back to general advertising. I needed something sexier. I needed to see if I could start and operate my own agency. So, in 1988 I left the family business to follow my passion for entertainment advertising." And follow his dreams he did. Pere went after the largest, most prestigious clients in entertainment. Within weeks the agency had its first assignment from HBO, and today, twenty years later, HBO is still one of their top clients. "For almost 20 years we have been working closely with Pere.

I'm amazed at the consistent level of creativity that comes out of their shop. We trust our brand with them, they get it. They've been involved in so much of our creative from the early days of *Dream On*, to *The Sopranos*, to *Jerry Seinfeld, The Rolling Stones, Bill Maher,* our sports and boxing franchise, and so much more. Their work is fresh, topical, and often brilliant. They always deliver, they're a big part of our team," says Eric Kessler, President of Sales and Marketing at HBO.

With recognition like that other networks were soon to follow. AMC, IFC, TCM, Fox Sports, A&E, TBS and Cinemax to name a few. The Pere Partnership has worked with the biggest names in the business as well: Jerry Seinfeld, Bruce Springsteen, Oscar De La Hoya, Billy Crystal, Martin Scorsese, Ray Romano, Joe DiMaggio, Bill Maher, the Rolling Stones, and the list keeps going.

How does Pere explain the agency's success? "Great work comes from great

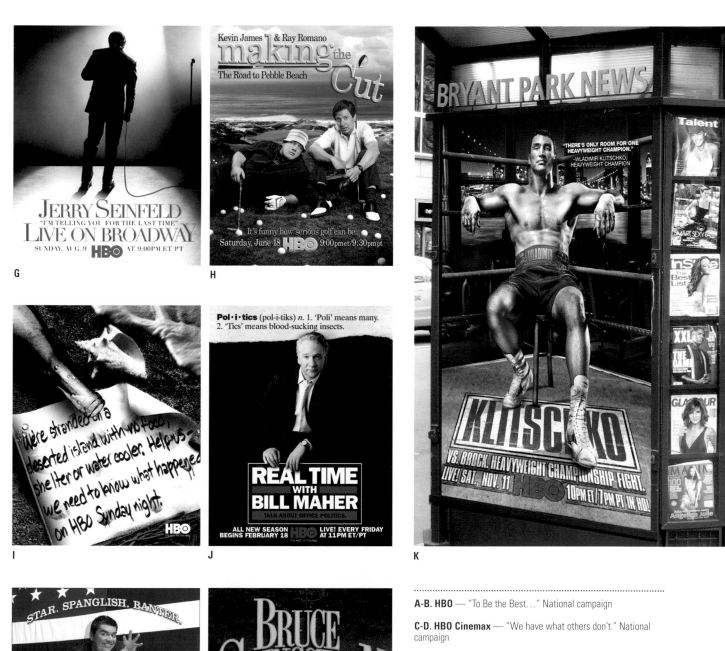

A-B. HBO — "To Be the Best…" National campaign

C-D. HBO Cinemax — "We have what others don't." National campaign

E-F. HBO — "Water Cooler." National trade campaign

G-M. HBO —Various individual and event national campaigns

desire. We don't settle for anything less than great work. We have high expectations for ourselves and everyone else we work with, and in the end, we always deliver beyond the expected. As Lori Peterzell, VP, Consumer Advertising A&E Network says, "I would be remiss if I didn't take the time to acknowledge the remarkable work that Pere has been doing on behalf of the A&E brand. My job is made more fulfilling by the very fact that you and your company have helped us achieve the highest level of creative and advertising communications in the industry. I believe you have helped make us the envy of our competitors. You keep raising the bar. It is truly a delight to receive and to see your professionalism carried through all the way to final product." Pere believes that as much as they'd like to believe that a show's success is all dependent on their work, in reality they know they are part of a great team. They rely greatly on their clients/partners to allow them to do work that garners comments from people such as Lori.

So, when it comes to creative, by no means does Glenn Pere just sit back and delegate assignments to the agency's "B" team. At The Pere Partnership there are no "B" or "C" teams. Everyone working there is a thinker and a doer giving their hearts, souls and brains to each and every assignment—including Pere, since he is involved in every assignment the agency takes on. Pere believes great communication and smart thinking happen when the complete team is involved, "It doesn't require a great deal of meetings to be successful. We get it. We're in the business of knowing our clients, our client's marketplace; then we go to work. Not just conceptually, but following through and making sure the execution delivers and is as visually stimulating and provocative as the concept itself. We have the opportunity to work with the most powerful brands in the industry and realize our work needs to be as powerful as the brands we work for," adds Pere.

"What makes entertainment advertising so unique is that today there over 500 channels, there are new movies breaking weekly, there are new DVDs hitting the shelves almost daily, there's the internet— all of which are competing for eyeballs. There are literally thousands of options a consumer has for their entertainment needs, and that's all in a half-hour time slot. I don't know of any other industry where there are so many options. Our communication needs to resonate, and needs to stay top-of-mind. Essentially, what we're asking for, with our messaging,

is that people put just about everything in life on hold to tune in. That's asking for an awful lot."

Just as The Pere Partnership has set the bar high for creative, they're continually exploring out-of-the box avenues beyond traditional media to reach their target. The company utilizes innovative integrated creative solutions that employ outdoor, guerilla marketing, public relations, and alternative media strategies.

Everyone likes to get awards. While The

Pere Partnership has received their share of them, along with honors and publicity on shows from *The O'Reilly Factor* to the *Evening News,* Glenn Pere believes there is simply one key indicator of a job well done. "When you look at the work you've done over the years, all the campaigns you were fortunate enough to work on, and you still wouldn't change anything, any copy, any layout, any font, anything. That's a job well done."

G

H

I

J

K   L

CASE STUDY: **Military History Channel**

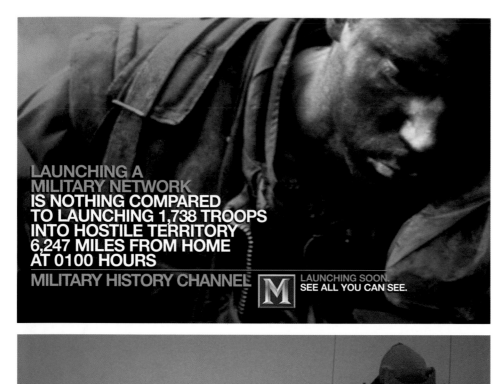

LAUNCHING A
MILITARY NETWORK
**IS NOTHING COMPARED
TO LAUNCHING 1,738 TROOPS
INTO HOSTILE TERRITORY
6,247 MILES FROM HOME
AT 0100 HOURS**
MILITARY HISTORY CHANNEL
LAUNCHING SOON.
SEE ALL YOU CAN SEE.

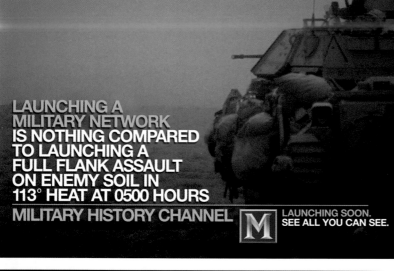

LAUNCHING A
MILITARY NETWORK
**IS NOTHING COMPARED
TO LAUNCHING A
FULL FLANK ASSAULT
ON ENEMY SOIL IN
113° HEAT AT 0500 HOURS**
MILITARY HISTORY CHANNEL
LAUNCHING SOON.
SEE ALL YOU CAN SEE.

LAUNCHING A
MILITARY NETWORK
**IS NOTHING COMPARED
TO LAUNCHING AN F-14
IN 30 FT. SEAS WITH
45MPH SUSTAINED WINDS
AT 0400 HOURS**
MILITARY HISTORY CHANNEL
LAUNCHING SOON.
SEE ALL YOU CAN SEE.

Based on the success of its military-related programming, the History Channel made a decision to launch a new channel that would interest military buffs, as well as everyone who ever had an interest in military affairs and strategies. And so the Military History Channel was born, a network devoted entirely to military-related subject matter. To ensure the new channel was a success, the network enlisted the help of The Pere Partnership.

While this expansion made sense from the point of view of programming, ratings and brand expansion, the national climate towards all things military was decidedly less-than-positive due to the situation in Iraq, a fact that had to be taken into account in creating the introduction.

The Pere Partnership's mission was clear. Create branding that positioned the launch as an event and the channel as a destination, while simultaneously showing due respect to our men and women in uniform, past and present.

Rather than take the traditional approach of treating the product or the benefit as the hero of the ad, Pere felt that the real heroes, and the true inspiration for the channel itself, were the men and women who have risked and given their lives throughout history, those who lived and inspired the stories the network would present.

"We felt it was important to create ads that highlight the challenges faced every day by those individuals who serve in the armed forces and show that launching a military channel is relatively easy compared to what our soldiers go through," says Glenn Pere, The Pere Partnership President & CEO. Just one look at the ads and one knows this channel is the real thing.

As the objective of the Military History Channel was to show all perspectives of war, from the front lines to behind enemy lines, the unfolding events in Iraq acted as an impetus to engage the public in the realities of war and the Military History Channel's commitment to authenticity.

Since this strategy developed by Pere and the team at the Military History Channel was about the dynamics of war, not the politics behind it, the Military History Channel's launch was an unequivocal victory for all.

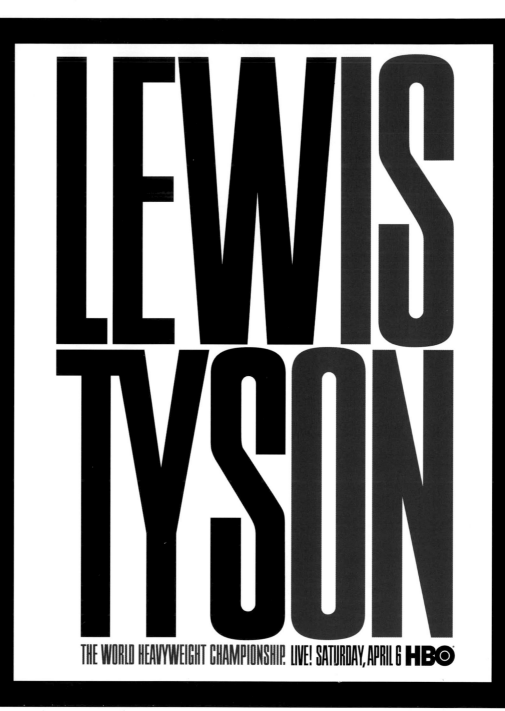

When boxing advertising comes to mind, it's usually associated with 'image driven' visuals of the fighters themselves—we've all seen the muscular physiques and intense expressions with copy that speaks to the boxing enthusiast. But when Mike Tyson and Lennox Lewis inked their deal to meet in the ring, it wasn't just for a fight, it was destined to be the greatest bout of all time, and HBO wanted the advertising for the pay-per-view event to be just as unconventional as the spectacular itself.

That's why HBO chose The Pere Partnership. Pere's goal was to brand the event and develop a campaign that would immediately communicate this wasn't just one of the most eagerly awaited bouts in the history of the boxing. It was one of the biggest events in the history of sports, with two of the greatest names in the sports world.

Glenn Pere, CEO and Creative Director, seized the opportunity and began working with his teams. They were determined to break away from the expected, and the result was a knockout campaign. "To this day, 5 years later, I still love this campaign, and love that it stands the test of time," Pere says.

Print ads and TV commercials were produced and began running months before the pay-per-view event aired. The advertising scored big by promoting the event, in addition to reinforcing the strategy of branding HBO as the premier network for continually bringing viewers the greatest series and events on television.

The final ad created by The Pere Partnership bears no resemblance to typical boxing ads. Using typography as the core messaging for a boxing match is, to say at the least, a departure from the genre. Yet, the simple and powerful elegance of the Lewis Tyson campaign created a bold graphic statement that was far more memorable than even the most dramatic photography. The agency's creative solution showed it understood the larger than life nature of this bout, and clinched it with two simple words, "Is On."

"As soon as the deal is done, the very first thing we do is focus on creating the name and the artwork for the fight. That name and that artwork create the first impression in the consumer's mind, and live forever in the annals of the sport once the fight is over," said Mark Taffet, HBO Sr. Vice President of Sports Operations & Pay-Per-View. "We need the best, and that's why for fights which are the biggest of the biggest, we turn to Glenn Pere and his agency, The Pere Partnership for their innovation and expertise. Lewis Tyson wasn't on until Glenn said it was on. As a result the Lewis Tyson fight was the largest grossing fight in boxing history."

Now The Pere Partnership is looking to break more records with their most recent fight campaign: "The World Awaits" De La Hoya Vs. Mayweather.

When Glenn Pere, Creative Director and CEO of The Pere Partnership, received a call from a good friend on the board of Project A.L.S. to develop PSAs, he knew it was time to face the fatal neuromuscular disease that took his mother's life in 1993 after she suffered with it since 1988.

"We didn't need anyone to brief us on this campaign, we didn't need focus groups, I was to be the focus group," said Pere. "I lived through the pain of watching my mother suffer every day. I've thought about it every waking moment. It's taken me 19 years to be able to stand up to ALS. Every single adult needs to know about A.L.S., and I knew exactly what I wanted to say."

The Pere Partnership went right to work on a campaign. Pere zeroed in on communicating the effects of the illness in the most provocative way possible. One campaign was presented to the Project A.L.S. Board; it was powerful and articulate. The tag, "ALS, a disease no one can live with" couldn't be more direct. Each ad grabs attention with dramatic type that forces one to read and react to Project A.L.S.'s call for help. Headlines like, "ALS. A disease that takes your breath away," "ALS. A disease that leaves you speechless," "ALS. A disease that's impossible to stand," and "ALS. A disease that's tough to swallow." All educate as well as engage the target audience with their deceptively simple frankness.

In addition to the initial print ads, The Pere Partnership is creating TV, radio, and web banners expanding the theme "ALS, a disease no one can live with" to surround the target and broaden the campaign's reach.

The campaign is getting a great deal of attention. Since it began, many people have been contacting Project A.L.S. with donations, as well as asking about other ways they can help.

"I've always wanted to do whatever I could to help eradicate the disease that took my mother's life," said Pere. "I'm finally able to make a difference."

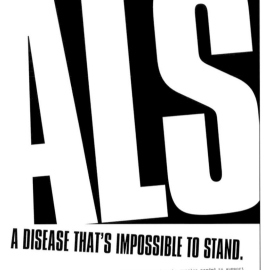

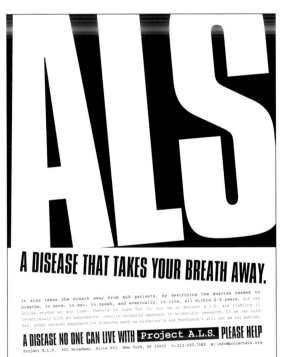

Richter7

....

Disrupt the Status Quo

Founded in 1971

280 South 400 West
Suite 200
Salt Lake City, UT
801-521-2903
www.richter7.com

SENIOR MANAGEMENT:
Scott Rockwood, CEO
Dave Newbold, President
Peggy Lander, EVP Client Services
Tim Brown, EVP, Public Relations

CLIENTS: Brigham Young University Athletic Dept., Back to Basics, Beneficial Financial Group, Biolase Technology, BD Medical, BSD Medical, CaseData, Christopherson Travel, Deseret Book, FranklinCovey, GBS Benefits, Get Away Today Vacations, Hogle Zoo, Lehi Roller Mills, Living Planet Aquarium, Medtronic, MountainStar Healthcare, Office of Utah Lt. Governor, Park City Chamber/Visitors Bureau, Parsons Behle & Latimer, Polynesian Cultural Center, Questar Gas, Salt Lake City Corporation, SonicScrubber, Tony Divino Toyota, Ultradent, Utah Hospitals & Health Systems Association, USANA, Workers Compensation Fund, Zions Bank

When potential clients and prospective employees walk into Richter7 in Salt Lake City, they'd best present their id at the door.

Not their I.D., as this has nothing to do with their legal drinking age. It's their id, that aspect of the human mind that [specific descriptor of Freud] Dr. Sigmund Freud determined was not under the sway of the rational neurons. Instead, it was under the control of instinct and emotion.

"Was Freud an ad man?" agency principal Scott Rockwood ponders. "According to Freud, the id was the unconscious force rooted in our passions, a force that deeply affects how people experience and interpret the world around them. He discovered that our emotional nature had a mind of its own and a power that transcends logic."

What Richter7 has done with the id is to recognize that much of what makes a brand successful is tied to emotions.

People will pay more for one brand over another regardless of the price, because they are confident in that product. That confidence often morphs into preference.

"People generally buy a particular brand because they like it," said agency principal Peggy Lander. "With 'like' being the pivotal, emotional word. Most of the advantages a strong brand has over its competitors can be traced back to strong emotional connections that have been made the with brand's target audience.

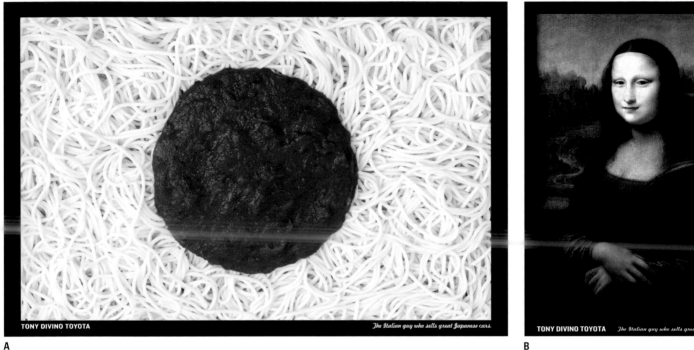

A

B

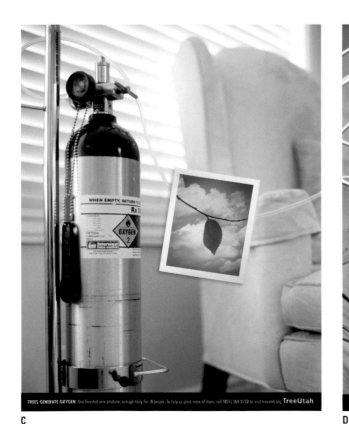

C

D

Branding is emotional imprinting."

"For years, most marketing strategies have been based primarily on the rational benefits, unique selling propositions and logical arguments of brand superiority," said agency principal Tim Brown. "The assumption is that most people are rational beings. The weakness in this approach is that we are first and foremost emotional beings. It is emotion, not intellect, that drives our behavior."

An ideal example of how this plays out is the Polynesian Cultural Center. The Center hired the agency in 1997 as it saw competition increasing and attendance dropping. Reason suggested people didn't understand exactly what it was. And those who did visit weren't making return trips.

As part of a major initiative to identify strategies to increase visitation and revenue at the Center, the agency conducted extensive research projects, including:

- Brand development, research and positioning;
- Visitation barriers;
- Pricing studies; and
- Travel-desk agent research.

"We discovered a number of things about the Center, but the most important were the factors impacting the brand positioning," said agency principal Dave Newbold. "We learned people would be emotionally attracted to an authentic destination, something very different

E

F

A-B. **Tony Divino Toyota** — Poster series

C-D. **Tree** Utah — Magazine ads

E-G. **Hogle Zoo** — Outdoor advertising

G

from the Waikiki tourist trap—so we focused our brand positioning on the Center's genuine Polynesian persona."

Those findings allowed the agency to forge ahead with a new print and television campaign focused on the "authentic Polynesia." The graphics and fonts were designed using the visual and textural elements of the Polynesian culture and landscape. The photos were not staged: they were real Polynesians performing everyday skills and talents. The headlines were culturally based and drew the reader into the ad for more details. Competitive Oahu attractions featured beaches, orange sunsets and hula dancers in their ads—the PCC advertising definitely stood out among the sea of "sameness."

The branding campaign launched in spring of 1998 and the Center's awareness, understanding, attendance and revenues all turned around. Today, the Center is still riding the crest of the wave generated by the agency's ability to tap the id of its audience.

What can an agency do with cheese? In 1998 Cache Valley Cheese came to Richter7. Its market share was dwindling; there was more competition and not enough of a distinct positioning for the product.

The agency burrowed down into the challenge by studying the competition, as well as identifying the most promising brand positioning strategy. Armed with that knowledge, Richter7, with close involvement from the client, created a strategy and a variety of creative executions based on the premise that Cache Valley was the only company that utilized "taste testers" to determine when the cheese had the perfect flavor.

Richter7 developed a humorous and engaging personality for the Cache Valley brand based on "cheese tasters" who ensured the cheese would always taste the way you expected. TV, radio and print campaigns were created with "cheese tasters."

One year after launching the campaign, market share came close to doubling, while unaided awareness went from 59 percent to 76 percent.

The formation of Richter7 was "predicated" when, in 1996, the distinguished creative journal *Communication Arts* featured side-by-side profiles of two Salt Lake City agencies—FJCandN and Williams and Rockwood.

The pairing of the two in the magazine segued into reality that same year, as the two shops combined under the FJCandN aegis.

Four years later in late 2000, the agency was bought by four of its senior employees—Scott Rockwood, Dave Newbold, Peggy Lander and Tim Brown. After much discussion, the agency was renamed Richter7 to represent the agency's eagerness to shake things up for its client the way an earthquake rearranges patio furniture.

"Disrupt the status quo," said Lander. "That's not our motto or some bite-sized slogan to us. It's our mission."

"Unless messages interrupt routine thought patterns, they're wasted," Rockwood added. "They won't connect simply because they won't be seen, heard or felt.

"Let's face it, people aren't naturally inclined to embrace advertising. The status quo is to shun it. Even abhor it."

Ask to see the creative department in most agencies and you'll be led to a specific area of the shop. Posit the same question at Richter7 and you won't have to go far.

A. Polynesian Cultural Center — Magazine ad

B. John Laing Homes — Billboard

A

B

"All our departments are creative departments," said Newbold. "To avoid confusion we call some of them media, public relations, account management, account planning and so on. But we don't consider creativity a gimmick. It's not long hair, nose rings and black ties. But we don't create by playing it safe."

And the willingness to intelligently take risks for clients has paid off. The agency has brought home gold from CA, The One Show, the New York Art Director's Club, the Obies, the Mercury Awards and the New York International Advertising Festival, among others. Richter7 is the most honored ad agency in the Mountain West region.

"A recent national study concluded that award-winning work is four to five times more likely to reach client goals than non-award-winning work," said Newbold. "We believe awards are merely a bonus for doing our job right in the first place, which is selling our clients' goods and services. It just so happens that the application of intelligent creativity is how that happens best.

"Otherwise messages are not noticed, and brands are not built."

Freud couldn't have said it any better.

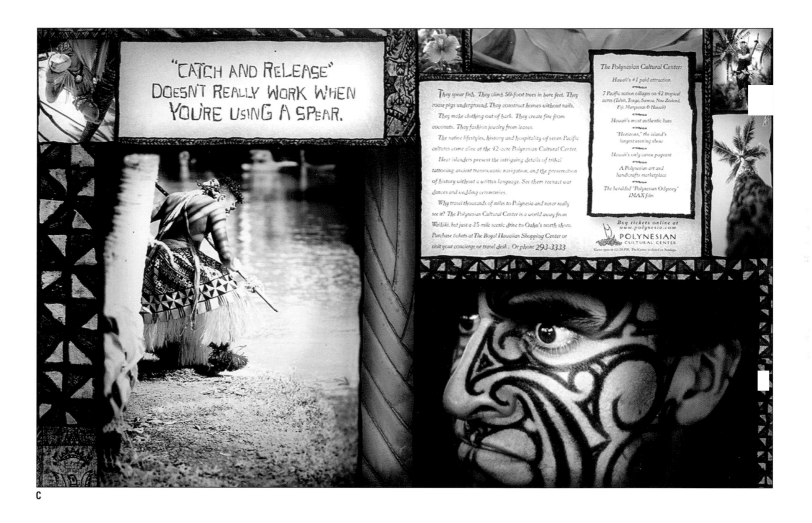

C

D

C. **Polynesian Cultural Center** — Magazine ad

D. **Workers' Compensation Fund** — Billboard

Prior to 1986, and before Richter7 won the Jackson Hole Mountain Resort business, a former Richter7 partner, who loved the resort and spent lots of time there, noticed the uniquely Western atmosphere taking a turn toward a Swiss chalet resort town. He felt the need to intervene and redirect the resort's marketing efforts. He saw the benefits of using genuine, natural ambience to bolster the resort's authentic Western brand. This thought process captivated Jackson Hole's leaders.

A

Richter7 won the business. The agency was brought in to build "skier days" and re-position the resort brand, all on a very limited budget.

At the time, the resort was lacking a strong brand identity and experiencing very little growth. Competition, along with a host of negative perceptions, kept it from making the very important, short-list of destinations for most skiers. Adding to that, political and practical realities prevented Jackson's owners from regularly updating the mountain with adequate ski lifts, restaurants and other basics.

It's a given that Jackson Hole offers some of the most spectacular scenery in the world—but as Richter7's extensive research revealed, Jackson Hole was known primarily as a summer destination, whose winter/skiing image was definitely not the envy of any competitor. Most skiers perceived the resort as being too cold, too difficult and too remote. Plus, the resort's modest advertising budget meant its direct competitors were outspending Jackson Hole by as much as 7-1.

Obviously, the challenges were daunting, requiring "disrupt the status quo," "out-of-the-box" strategic thinking.

One way Richter7 set about solving the dilemma was by utilizing one of its major creative credos—fresh, intelligent messages, by which a client can successfully leverage their marketing monies, increase market share, secure mind share, and above all, enhance their brand.

To achieve what the client (and the agency) wanted, Richter7

wrapped its branding philosophy—"creativity is all about generating an emotional response"—(and its award-winning advertising strategy) tightly around the client's needs.

Because every ski resort offers great skiing, it was key for the agency to position Jackson Hole in a niche so unique that no other resort could make the same claim. Taking advantage of Jackson's authentic Western heritage seemed the most natural position, and the one that the agency concentrated on in getting the message to prospective visitors—"Jackson Hole is the only resort that offers a genuine Old West adventure."

As Richter7 president Dave Newbold explains, "Very few ski resorts have actually gone through the process of creating a distinctive market niche. The Western image sets Jackson Hole apart. The resort can truly own that niche. Thus, in every message sent, regardless of the medium, the essence of the resort's brand is reinforced."

The agency went after the resort's target; i.e., predominantly male (70%), 35+, income of $50,000+; upper intermediate-to-advanced skier.

According to on-mountain research, this group is aggressive, naturally adventuresome, seeking an escape from everyday life, and maverick-like in their style. They dream about ski vacations at certain resorts, and often have a key 'short-list' of places they'd like to visit.

When it came to Jackson Hole, Richter7 conquered a huge marketing challenge and successfully met the resort's goals, reaching the desired audience by focusing primarily on the winter product through winter ski vertical and on-line ski sites.

The ad campaign, over the course of a decade, has reflected Jackson's Old West heritage by featuring sepia-toned photography, rustic border treatments, and Western-style typography. Elements of the resort's environment have often been photographically included in the advertising's design—river rocks, barn wood, elk antlers, pine fences, etc. Headlines took a rebellious, macho tone that appealed to the renegade attitude of the target audience.

"Each ad, each year, had to feel absolutely true to the brand's essence," Newbold stated. "It became very easy for a reader of a ski publication to pick out the Jackson ad. Even if we hadn't put a logo on the page, readers would still have guessed who paid for the ad just by the look, emotion and verbal tone of the message. In the process, we tried to create a

B

yearning to escape to this relatively undiscovered and wild locale."

Growth in "skier days" is one critically important measure of success for a resort. While the rest of the U.S. ski industry has reportedly experienced less than 1% growth over the past ten years, Jackson Hole's skier days have grown from 195,000, when Richter7's rebranding effort began, to a record 104% increase of 397,500 in 2005.

D

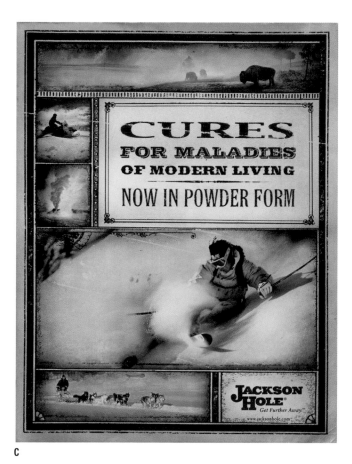

C

....

A. Direct mail

B. Poster

C-D. Magazine ads

E. Web home page

E

Nothing can produce as much anxiety as a long-time client announcing a merger. But often anxiety produces innovative thinking.

Richter7 had been Zions First National Bank's advertising/marketing/public relations agency since 1991. Seven years later, Zions and another bank, First Security, announced plans to merge, forming what would have been the Intermountain West's second largest bank.

To keep the business, Richter7 kicked in the turbo-chargers and went to work defending their end of the business. The agency performed extensive market research, from which it drew some new insights and strategies. In the end, the merger fell through, but the new set of branding tools—forged from its research and work on the request-for-proposals (RFP)—gave Richter7 a better way to help their client.

"Flashing back to 1998 when we did the study, we created a brand position that simply acknowledged the client knows and understands that it's their customer's money that keeps them in business, and those customers want and deserve access to this money," explained Richter7 CEO Scott Rockwood. "Our philosophy for moving our clients' businesses forward is based on creating brands based on strong emotional connections with the target audience. It's the breadth and depth of this connection that separates a dominant brand from weaker ones within the respective business category. We know that to achieve this, you don't just stumble upon these emotional drives."

As result of the research, the agency crafted a new tagline for the bank that's become synonymous within its footprint—"We haven't forgotten who keeps us in business."

To successfully improve the bank's image with customers, Richter7 crafted positioning statements addressing customers' strong emotional concerns that came out of the original interviews.

Additionally, a branding plan focused on internal communications and external advertising was developed to identify specific opportunities to help bring the new brand to life.

Along with the advertising, the agency developed style guides and brand training recommendations, among other communications tools, to help Zions' employees embrace and execute the new brand. Richter7 frequently presented its marketing plans and efforts to various groups within the bank to aid employees in understanding the research and the Bank's vision.

Since the new brand launch, TV has represented the bulk of the advertising dollars Zion has spent to reach customers and prospects in Utah and Idaho. Spots show examples of how Zions' bankers make their retail and business clients feel important by taking ownership of their problems and/or by providing the most appropriate solutions to their financial challenges.

Newspaper ads were incorporated to help deliver its promotional/campaign message, while reinforcing the brand essence of customer convenience, affordability and services. Radio figures into the branding mix, primarily due to cost-effectiveness in reaching the bank's target rural listeners.

The agency also helped Zions grow beyond its existing 35+ audience. Employing alternative media, as well as new products and services to appeal to the younger, technologically minded banking prospects, Richter7 worked to give the client a relevant face with college students and younger adults. The effort was dubbed "Code/Green."

"Code/Green was launched with a viral micro site," says Rockwood. "Showcasing product benefits in a way that would instantly captivate the target viewer, the site featured a rap song with animated caricatures of the bank's mar-

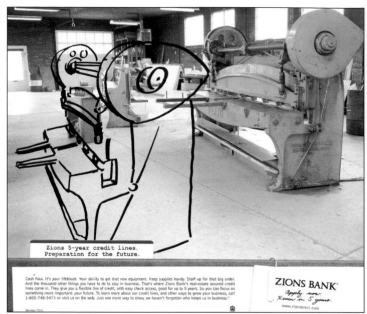

Zions 5-year credit lines.
Preparation for the future.

ZIONS BANK

Maybe our IRA rates are too generous.

The new Gold MarketPlus™ IRA.

ZIONS BANK

keting team. An added tactic of the 'media buy' included copying posters for students to 'wild post' on campus/dorm bulletin boards, etc. The bottom of each poster featured the little tear-out slips normally seen in a college setting; the only copy on the tear-out was the Codegreen URL."

The new brand position and execution at all levels has brought tremendous success for Zions Bank. According to recent research, more than 90% of Zions' customers felt the bank met their expectations; Zions has the highest ad recall of any financial institution within the category; perhaps most important, loans and deposits have generally increased by double-digits annually since the brand was launched.

Today, Zions Bank has the largest market share of any Utah bank, and in spite of having a relatively low branch penetration in Idaho, the institution ranks #6 in market share.

....

A-C. Magazine ads

DON'T JUST PLAN ON IT, PLAN FOR IT.
The complete, confidential, cost-free way to prepare for your financial future.

ZIONS BANK®
WE HAVEN'T FORGOTTEN WHO KEEPS US IN BUSINESS.

A
....

Sedgwick Rd.

The Agency Alternative

Founded in 1960

1741 1st Ave. South
Seattle, WA 98134
206-971-4200
www.sedgwickrd.com

HOLDING COMPANY:
Interpublic Group (IPG)

KEY NEW BUSINESS CONTACT:
Ray Vincenzo, 206-971-4278

SENIOR MANAGEMENT:
Jim Walker, President
Zach Hitner, VP/Creative Director
Forrest Healy, VP/Creative Director
Carolyn Yasui, VP/Media Director
Melissa Nelson, Account Director

CLIENTS: 21st Century Insurance, ArtsFund, Converse, Digeo, FruitStorm, Krispy Kreme/ICON LLC, Nintendo, Redhook, Seattle Art Museum, Seattle Repertory Theatre, Tower Records, WNBA Seattle Storm

Sedgwick Rd.

Where can you find the intersection of pop culture and powerful strategies?

Just follow Sedgwick Rd. and you're sure to get there.

In fact, the agency likes to refer to itself as a journey and a destination, where the scenery is always changing and there are no speed limits, rest stops or signposts. It's one continuous passing lane, where you can go as fast and as far and as brilliantly as you think you can. You're even likely to meet Frankenstein along the way.

That's the name of the central meeting area, and major hub of activity, at the agency's offices. It's a space featuring six moveable walls that can be reconfigured for different meeting purposes, a visible demonstration of the agency's conviction that creativity is never constrained.

Where did the road to Sedgwick Rd. begin?

With the dawn of the Web, Seattle and the entire West Coast became a region that worked on internet time. Entrepre-

neurialism, ideas and originality became Seattle's currency. In order to better trade in that currency, 40-year-old McCann Seattle became Sedgwick Rd. The name was taken from a picturesque rural road outside Seattle and alludes to Edie Sedgwick and Andy Warhol's "Idea Factory." It was the perfect name for an independent-minded agency that could meet the unique needs of challenger brands seeking to change the world.

Even though it was spawned from

A

B

C

D

A. **Krispy Kreme** — Chocolate Fling van wrap

B. **Krispy Kreme** — Chocolate Fling logo

C. **Moxi.com** — Pizza box

D. **Moxi.com** — Billboard

E-F. **Nintendo** — E3 print ads

G. **Nintendo** — Magazine execution

H. **Nintendo** — "Start Mayhem" microsite

venerable McCann Erickson and has been growing in Seattle for more than four decades, Sedgwick Rd. considers itself a new sort of agency, founded in the 21st century. Their approach to brand advertising and marketing recognizes that while the internet bubble may have burst, the impact of events leading up to the bubble have truly changed the advertising world.

To address these fundamental changes, Sedgwick Rd. focuses on being nimble, looking far outside the boundaries of traditional advertising for solutions that help clients build brands, while creating category-changing work that taps into the pop culture, dreams and emotions of consumers.

Adeptness at synthesizing current cultural trends and bottom-line business objectives is one of the agency's signature qualities. Sedgwick Rd. has become known as a unique place capable of tapping into pop culture to develop branding strategies that make traditional and non-traditional advertising more powerful, more relevant and more effective. This use of pop culture to create brand-building/category-changing work is clearly evident in the work Sedgwick Rd. has done for clients like Tower Records, Converse, Redhook, Nintendo, Washington Mutual, the WNBA Seattle Storm and others.

Says Sedgwick Rd. President Jim Walker, "At the core of our philosophy is

E

F

G

H

the understanding that we're communicating with people, not targets, not audiences, not market segments. Our work is successful because we recognize we're talking to people with busy lives, needs and desires. We leverage simple human truths to speak to consumers, allowing them to emotionally connect with the brand's promise."

The agency is particularly proud of how it did exactly that kind of work for Washington Mutual (fondly referred to as

WaMu), with whom Sedgwick Rd. worked for over 14 years. When WaMu began its run with Sedgwick Rd. in the early '90s, the bank was a Washington-only thrift with plans to become a financial services force on a national scale.

The branding work for WaMu was category changing, giving life and emotion to an industry typically thought of as boring. The bank launched into a series of new markets, each with new levels of success, culminating in the New

York launch that featured "subway station domination" advertising, media saturation around Wall Street and the buying out of Times Square theaters for 30,000 local teachers. The bank grew, becoming the nation's sixth largest financial institution. Brad Davis, former CMO of Washington Mutual, sums up the agency's performance this way:

"Sedgwick Rd. helped me to do the impossible at Washington Mutual: create a cultural revolution in banking. From

A

B

C

A-B. **Washington Mutual** — Billboards from the "Fear Not" campaign

C. **Washington Mutual** — Life-size cave buildout in Chicago

D-E. **Washington Mutual** — Times Square spectacular, day and night

F-G. **Washington Mutual** — Award-winning "Paul" TV spot

H. **Seattle Art Museum** — Mesmerizing billboard for Frida Kahlo exhibit

D

E

F

G

H

the front cover of BrandWeek to the Retail Advertising Hall of Fame, this post-modern approach to brand marketing was recognized as a driving factor in WaMu's remarkable growth from $30 to $300 billion in assets."

"It's all about making brands cultural phenomenons. When you change behavior, you get results. And clients want more than awareness, they want results. Awards, accolades and press coverage make us feel great and validate the creativity of our work among peers, but we live in a service business, meaning our efforts must deliver concrete results. We know we've done good work when our clients report that their employees, business partners and customers love the work. We're thrilled when it's gotten them energized and moved the needle," observes Walker.

In addition to pop culture, the arts are also an important influence on Sedgwick Rd.'s work. Its president, creative director and many of the agency's team members have backgrounds in the arts. The arts are a touchstone for how it portrays ideas visually, according to the agency, which continually renews its artistic wellspring through its work with Seattle Art Museum, ArtsFund, the Seattle International Film Festival and the Seattle Repertory Theater.

Even the agency's space is a crossroad where pop culture, the arts and functioning ideas connect. Its unique architecture has been featured in Interior Design, Frame Magazine and BMW Magazine. The offices, designed for constant communication, have no walled offices. Everyone from the president to summer interns works in open cubicles. Why?

Because, Sedgwick Rd. believes, good ideas don't happen behind closed doors. They occur in a vibrant, dynamic environment where everyone on the staff continuously gathers, debates and develops original ideas.

So where does Sedgwick Rd. see itself headed? In the direction it's been headed since its inception: toward questioning the status quo, toward boldness, honesty and intelligence, powered by a mantra taken from the words of Mahatma Gandhi: "Be the change you wish to see in the world."

To get there, be sure to take Sedgwick Rd.

I

J

K

I. Washington State Department of Health — Viral Web site from "Gross" campaign

J-K. Washington State Department of Health — Secondhand smoke TV spot

Ninety-nine bottles of beer on the wall, and counting. In the overcrowded beer market, Redhook's sales were flat and the craft-brew industry's market share was shrinking. Where could it turn to re-invent and re-invigorate its brand?

For Redhook, the answer was Sedgwick Rd.

The agency immediately got to work identifying the market issues that Redhook faced. Through consumer research, Sedgwick Rd. sought to discover ways to challenge existing marketing conventions for beer, especially craft brews like Redhook.

They also asked two critical questions: How could the agency help Redhook brand itself as an alternative to craft brew competitors, imports and other adult beverages? How could they reach the consumers their client was most interested in: People who regularly drink beer and want to shake up their usual routine?

Sedgwick Rd. soon learned a key insight into the consumers Redhook wanted to reach: People wanted a "special" everyday beer. The agency found that beer drinkers frequently get an urge for something a bit different, a beer that's less ordinary. This insight led to a tagline that spoke to beer drinkers; that told them there was a great alternative to ho-hum beer choices: Defy Ordinary.

Armed with this new branding line, the agency mapped a course for Redhook that would inspire regular beer drinkers to seek an everyday beverage that defied ordinary. They used iconic imagery to demonstrate that the brand was different from typical beers. The imagery was used in billboards, print, in-stadium, and in-environment, including coasters, table tents, posters and t-shirts. Sedgwick Rd. also created radio spots that demonstrated how people could turn everyday occurrences into opportunities to Defy Ordinary.

Media was also key to the brand re-invigora-

A

tion strategy. Out-of-home and in-store media were put to effective use, inspiring consumers to try Redhook when they were in the process of making a beverage choice. Outdoor billboards in and around professional baseball parks were also an important component of the campaign, helping to generate awareness and boost sales among an avid, beer-drinking audience.

Sedgwick Rd.'s new campaign also helped their client look at its brand in an entirely new way, leading to a complete redesign of the Redhook bottle and packaging. Sales began to climb, and have been climbing steadily ever since. Proclaims Paul Shipman, CEO & Chairman of Redhook Ale Brewery, "The brand is on fire."

You won't see anyone from Sedgwick Rd. running to put it out.

B

C

D

E

F

G

A. Defy Ordinary poster

B. Coasters and table tents

C-G. Iconic Redhook posters

H. Defy Ordinary outdoor

I. Stadium poster

H

I

CASE STUDY: Tower Records

In October 2005, after an extensive review of leading West Coast agencies, Sedgwick Rd. was tapped by Tower Records to communicate the relevance of the retailer's brand in a world where many shoppers download music online or go to big-box chains for their entertainment fix. Tower also wanted to extend its brand beyond music, and hype its vast array of videogames, movies, books and other entertainment products.

Sedgwick Rd. began the formidable task by analyzing Tower's 2005 consumer research initiative. As a cultural icon, Tower has maintained a strong 35+ age group following. The only problem was that while the company wanted to continue its appeal to this group, it also wanted to raise its awareness and relevance to a younger group that not only enjoyed music and entertainment, but also lusted after an immersive retail and pop culture experience.

The strategy embraced development of the "when you're in, you're in" message, creating an inclusive message with an exclusive feel that reinforces Tower's authenticity and heritage. It also positions the store as the place to go to explore,

A

experience and discover. "This allowed us to appeal to consumers who not only enjoyed entertainment, but counted on entertainment to enrich their lives as a currency for communicating with others," says Zach Hitner, creative director at Sedgwick Rd.

Solidifying Tower as the destination for those "tuned in" to the best of the entertainment zeitgeist, the agency created the "Life Played Loud" campaign, utilizing an array of unique print, broadcast and outdoor executions. Hitner explains, "the entertainment experience isn't limited to one environment, so messages have to reach consumers at multiple touch-points throughout the day, everywhere they are."

Edgy TV spots, which hit home via speeches made up of movie lines and music lyrics, jabbed fun at the extent to which entertainment-mad consumers rely on music, movies, etc., to communicate with others.

The TV spots worked wonders. Some caused complaints, proving that "the mes-

sage cut through the clutter." Tower loved it. The "Blessing" spot was named one of *Adweek's* spots-of-the-month (October 2005), and the spots won two 2006 Telly Awards. Outdoor and print work leveraged Tower's assets by featuring Green Day, Napoleon Dynamite and Madonna engaging in the Tower experience—holding and being part of the store's gift card.

Sedgwick Rd.'s campaign hit the mark in significant ways, such as creating a heightened awareness with a younger audience. Because of the ongoing campaign, Tower has achieved its goals of connecting with younger consumers, while keeping its strong cultural connection with older fans who continue to recognize the retailer as more than just a store.

Right on Sedgwick Rd. Tower's groovy. Entertainment-philes are listening.

A. Eye-catching *Vibe* magazine spread

B. Green Day billboard

C. Award-winning "Blessing" TV spot

B

C

SS+K

Knock hard. Life is deaf

Founded in 1993

88 Pine Street
New York, NY 11211
212-274-9500
www.ssk.com

KEY NEW BUSINESS CONTACT:
Noelle Weaver, 212-419-3344

SENIOR MANAGEMENT:
Rob Shepardson
Lenny Stern
Mark Kaminsky
Marty Cooke
Joe Kessler

CLIENTS: [primary] Delta, Lance Armstrong Foundation, MSNBC.com, Starwood Hotels, Blue Cross Blue Shield Association, Bill & Melinda Gates Foundation, Anheuser-Busch, Citibank

FULLTIME EMPLOYEES: 100

Take everything you know about ad agencies, turn it upside down, inside out, and you still won't come close to the innovative, unique approach of SS+K.

This is an agency that lives by the saying "Knock hard. Life is deaf." An agency that's out to completely reinvent the business of brand communications. And it's not just talk. One look at SS+K's work for clients like Delta, Starwood Hotels, NY Knicks, MSNBC and the Lance Armstrong Foundation and you'll know that they see things from an entirely different perspective.

"We never subscribed to the traditional agency model. Probably because we didn't set out to create a traditional agency," says Lenny Stern, partner. "That model is ineffective, inflexible, insufficient and simply perpetuates uninspired, reactive, symmetrical thinking."

Symmetrical thinking is the reason SS+K believes that so much of today's communications looks familiar. "If it looks like you've seen it before, it's because you probably have," says Marty Cooke, partner, chief creative officer. He believes that most marketers (and their agencies) consciously or unconsciously imitate what their competitors are doing. "If they're doing it, by God, we'd better do it, too!'

SS+K avoids cookie-cutter strategies, copycat tactics and me-too executions. "We believe that the best, and perhaps the only way to generate big, honking

A

B

C

D

E

asymmetric ideas is to get a bunch of smart people from different disciplines to tackle the problem together" says partner Rob Shepardson. Former physicists, speechwriters, artists, political consultants, athletes, lawyers, drag queens, journalists, pollsters and ballerinas all bring different talents and experiences to the table.

SS+K practices what they've coined as Asymmetric Communications™: The art + science of building brands + opinion in a fractured world.

Advertising folk sit with PR folk. Digerati sit with planning and research experts. Public affairs people sit with marketers.

This combustible mix of expertise and personalities gives SS+K a unique DNA that's well-suited to creating new ways of thinking, new ways of communicating and new ways to forge relationships for their clients and consumers.

SS+K's non-hierarchical structure means that clients get the attention of senior-level executives on day-to-day issues. Every brand team at SS+K is multi-disciplinary, so clients have senior people from the fields of advertising, design, PR and research working together on each and every assignment.

"It's also what makes our ideas so damn powerful," says Mark Kaminsky, partner.

SS+K's approach to creating asymmetric communications means that they have

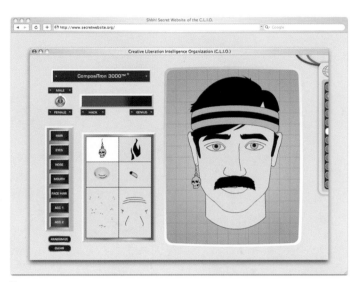

F

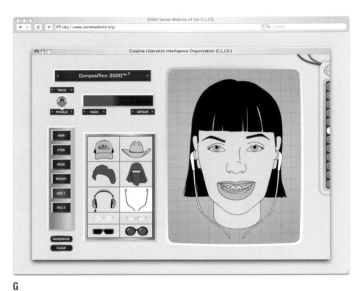

G

A. Asymmetric – Asymmetric. A flip book that showcases the atrocities of genocide and aims to build awareness of the issue.

B. Westin Hotels – Asymmetric. An art installation that counts clean breaths is projected in Westin lobbies.

C. ConQwest – Teenagers rush to start the big urban game

D. ConQwest – 20 ft. Inflatable animals are moved around the city as game pieces

E. ConQwest – Participant shooting a semacode with their Qwest cell phone

F-G. Clio Awards – Screen grabs from the Creative Liberation Intelligence Organization's [CLIO] secretwebsite.org

H. Clio Awards – Sticker blasts at leading agencies across the country

H

no bias to any particular medium. The ultimate answer may be a completely unexpected strategy, a big urban game, an advertising campaign, a public relations push, a music tour, a new identity or any combination of the above. It doesn't matter as long as it makes the brand or issue essential and inescapable.

Great brands used to be built with great stories that were advertised on TV, in print and on the radio. However, today's technology is changing how a story is told. It's splintering the audience. It's making people both harder to reach and easier to reach. They're not paying attention or they're paying too much attention.

For an idea to succeed in today's cultural soup, it not only has to be an amazing story, it has to be presented (or discovered) in a whole different way. At SS+K, today's best brand ideas tend to float free of any particular medium. They're more like butterflies; they can land anywhere. On the web, on the street, in a game, on TV, in a mall.

Whatever form they take, they engage people and convert them from passive recipients into active participants.

"We believe that asymmetric communications is an incredibly effective way to get brand stories into the culture. It's also an effective means to find the right way and right place to tell these stories," says Joe Kessler, partner. "Ideally, you want your brand's story to be where your target is and where your competition isn't."

For example: Client Qwest came to SS+K with the challenge of making their cell phones cool to teenagers.

Recognizing that currently cell phones were all about having the latest bells and whistles, SS+K needed to find a way for the teens to engage with the Qwest product and create a buzz. They needed to combat the competitor's 'bells and whistles.'

Then came the creative idea: To create and stage a big urban game in five of Qwest's cities.

Dubbed ConQwest, the game was a high-stakes urban treasure hunt where kids from five local high schools raced through the grid of the city streets to look for digital clues. By taking a picture of a new form of 3D Barcode technology called semacodes, the kids received text-message clues on their Qwest phones about where to move 20-foot tall inflatable game pieces towards the finish line to win $5,000 for their favorite charity and a concert by the band Yellowcard.

The games were an instant success.

The kids had fun. ConQwest created lots of noise and made lots of news. And due to its success, the event resulted in 6.5 million media impressions, massive local TV, radio and web coverage in all five markets and was mentioned on blogs as far away as Japan and Romania.

SS+K often breaks up a brand's story so as not to tell it all at one time and in one place. In this way people get to figure it out for themselves; they feel like they've discovered something, rather than feeling like they've been sold something. It flatters their intelligence. It turns them into co-conspirators and co-creators. It encourages them to share clues with their friends, which in turn creates communities of fans, believers and zealots. It also creates the ripple effect SS+K is known for.

While some may think that creating great asymmetric ideas simply happens by magic, there is a proven process behind the madness in producing them.

A. Time Warner – Cable TV. If pigs can fly, maybe a cable company can change

B. Time Warner – Cable TV. Use the pause button to stop and smell the roses

D. U.S. Fund for UNICEF – Print. Simple math make donations + change tangible

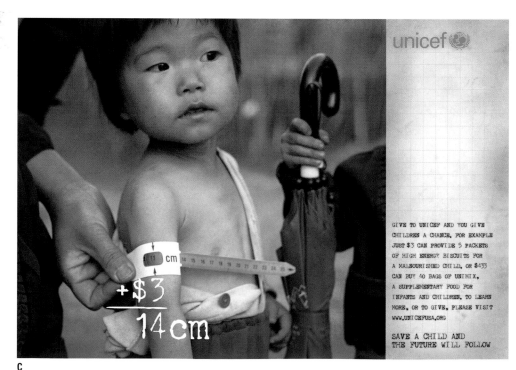

"You need to put your brand where the consumer is. Emotionally, psychologically, culturally and media-wise. We use every technique in the book, and then some, to get under their skin and define the key consumer truth," says Rebecca Matovic, the partner in charge of research and strategy.

The resulting work is unique, unexpected, effective and most importantly grounded in visible results.

In fact, client sales or measurable attitude shifts are how SS&K measures the value of their work. "We monitor all of our work and expect to see increases or whatever metrics are appropriate. In the real world that means inserting our clients brands and issues into the culture in a relevant way. Take, for example, how we helped our client Westin hotels become an industry leader with 'Breathe,' a smoke-free initiative for all of their hotels. Now others can only follow," says Mark Kaminsky.

That's the kind of innovative thinking you'll find throughout SS+K's case histories.

If you want safe, expected thinking go to an ordinary ad agency. If you want an agency that will knock hard no matter what the assignment, come to SS+K. You'll never have to worry about the world turning a deaf ear to your message.

D

E

F

D-E. New York Knicks – Newspaper. The actual ad + in context

F. New York Knicks – Outdoor. A first. Die-cut outdoor ads posted over existing ads

G. New York Knicks – Outdoor. The ultimate compliment. Fans ripping the cut-outs right off the walls

H-I. New York Knicks – TV. Spike Lee dining with a cut-out of Coach Larry Brown at Junior's Diner in Brooklyn

I. New York Knicks – TV. John McEnroe playing tennis with a cut-out of Quentin Richardson

G

H

I

CASE STUDY: Song Airlines

When Song Airlines, a division of Delta, set out to challenge JetBlue, Southwest, and the other established carriers, they knew they couldn't behave like a typical airline. So when it came to their advertising, they needed a firm that didn't act like a typical ad agency. In April 2005, Song awarded their business to SS+K.

Song's objectives were clear:
1. Raise brand awareness
2. Increase awareness of what makes Song unique—the choices and fun.
3. Increase load factors (percent of seats filled) in new and existing markets
4. Increase online bookings through flysong.com

The SS+K team reviewed Song's previous brand strategy of "Self Expression" and felt it to be an outward-facing notion about how you project yourself to others. Flying is not about perfecting an image. It's about a person's travel experience.

Song needed to find an asymmetric avenue — an entirely new way of looking at this proposition.

In an industry where long lines, delays and bad food have become the norm for the travel experience, consumer research showed that most people find the experience of flying impersonal and akin to riding in a cattle car.

According to Rebecca Matovic, SS+K partner in charge of strategy, "We quickly recognized that with all of the entertainment and food choices available on Song, each person's experience was as individual as they were."

SS+K realized people shouldn't have to sacrifice their individual tastes for a low airfare.

The Song experience was about "individuality—wrapped in joy."

The strategy was brought to life in the very un-airline-like "Row" campaign. In a playful and whimsical way, it demonstrated how Song could provide a unique lifestyle/experience for each passenger in every one of its 199 seats.

All consumer touch points were designed to reflect the Song experience. From ticket jackets to menu cards, even to onboard games for the kids, SS+K was instrumental in creating new products and branded merchandise to completely surround passengers with Song's joyful experiences.

Print, radio, billboard and TV ads were created with localized messages that helped to establish a relationship between the brand and consumer. Every piece of communications created incorporated flysong.com to drive more traffic to the website.

SS+K's also looked for opportunities to tweak competitors like jetBlue. For the JFK to LAX route launch, a chauffer was stationed in the baggage claim of the jetBlue Long Beach Airport terminal with a sign that read: "If you'd flown on Song, you'd be in LA by now." A Song "walk of fame" was created with gold stars on the floor of Song's JFK terminal. Each star highlighted a specific seat's individual food and entertainment choices.

So how did this unique approach work? Song quickly closed the gap with long-time category leader jetBlue. The campaign resulted in:
- 80% brand awareness (vs. goal of 70%) an increase of 22 points
- 55% brand + amenity familiarity, an increase of 17 points

star treatment
all the way to hollywood
JFK–LAX 7x/day
song
flysong.com

B

- 82% increase in load factors (percent of seats filled) exceeding forecast by 6 points
- 37% increase in online bookings, up 18% year-over-year with increases as much as 61% for specific route fare sales
- 4% of banner click-thrus led directly to ticket sales
- 93 million non-paid media impressions generated valued at $6.9 million over three months in local print and broadcast media

By all standards the campaign was an overwhelming success. Unfortunately, it was announced in December 2005 that due to Delta's bankruptcy, Song would be folded back into Delta, the mother brand. The SS+K team continued to work with both the Song and Delta brand teams to suggest ways that the best of Song could be injected back into Delta.

In April '06, Delta announced that based on its outstanding work for Song and its powerful strategic and creative thinking for the new Delta, SS+K would be the agency for all the advertising and rebranding of the airline.

1 *Leisure Travel Monitor* 2002

A

C

D

E

F

....

A. Asymmetric – A chauffer greets jetBlue passengers in Long Beach, CA "if you'd flown on Song you'd be in LA by now'

B. Asymmetric – The walk of fame at JFK for the LA route launch

C. TV – Song offers more food options

D. TV – Song offers more entertainment options

E. Outdoor – LA route launch. billboard in SoHo, New York

F. Print – Row Campaign. Un-airline advertising

CASE STUDY: Lance Armstrong Foundation

Ever wonder how all those yellow LIVESTRONG™ bracelets started appearing on the wrists of people all across the country? It was no accident. It was the coming together of Nike's original idea, the Lance Armstrong Foundation, a compelling story and SS+K's deft insight and orchestration.

Using their proven process of developing asymmetric ideas by first understanding consumer truths, SS+K learned that a little known sub-site buried in the main website called "LiveStrong" resonated with the audience. SS+K identified this phrase as the "big idea" for the brand.

This insight led SS+K to recommend focusing the brand and identity around the qualities of strength, knowledge, attitude and perseverance to lead the charge of making cancer a national priority. Importantly their insights and messaging helped shift the language people used from cancer 'victim' to cancer 'survivor'. And while the credit for inventing the wristband goes to Nike, based on these insights, it was SS+K's recommendation to place "LIVESTRONG™" on the now famous yellow wristband.

A

With the cultural success of the "LIVESTRONG™" yellow bracelet world-wide, SS+K created a campaign

B

in 2005—Unity is Strength—to translate the wristband phenomenon into a cultural movement by educating wristband wearers about cancer survivorship in an effort to make survivorship and research funding a higher priority.

The goal was to encourage people who wore the yellow band to band together and tell their story to others. The idea of millions of stories was simply represented by a series of yellow bands linked together and the tagline: 'Unity Is Strength'.

The 2005 campaign 'Share Your Story,' with its linked yellow bands, became part of daily culture by being posted in places where people take notice such as billboards, wall posters, on the sides of buses and in magazines. A :30 PSA was also created and ran on major broadcast stations and throughout the course of Lance's sixth winning of the Tour de France.

SS+K, together with their online partner BEAM, created a series of linked-band banner ads and viral emails that encouraged people to log on to livestrong.org and share their own story.

The results were astonishing, as of January 2006:
- Over 60 million LIVESTRONG™ yellow bracelets sold worldwide
- Thousands of hits to livestrong.org every day
- 93% of people link LIVESTRONG™ with Lance Armstrong Foundation
- 71% increase awareness of Lance Armstrong Foundation
- Yellow = cancer

While success comes a little easier when you're working with partners like Lance Armstrong and Nike, SS+K has played a key role in helping to steer this runaway phenomenon in a strategic direction that has put cancer on the national agenda and begun to raise awareness of the issue of survivorship.

D

UNITY IS STRENGTH

share your story at LIVESTRONG.ORG
LANCE ARMSTRONG FOUNDATION

C

A. Outdoor – Wrapping an entire building in New York

B. Cannes Invite – Enlisting the stars through seeding

C. Print – Banding together. Taking the band to another level

D. Transit – wrapping buses in yellow bands

Sullivan Higdon & Sink

We Hate Sheep

Founded in 1971

www.wehatesheep.com

SHS – Wichita
255 N. Mead Street
Wichita, KS 67202
316-263-0124

SHS – Kansas City
2000 Central
Kansas City, MO 64108
816-474-1333

SHS – Washington D.C.
6801 Whittier Ave., #301
McLean, VA 22101
703-752-7845

KEY NEW BUSINESS CONTACTS:
Tom Bertels, Managing Partner, 316-263-0124
Rand Mikulecky, Managing Partner, 816-474-1333

CLIENTS: Cargill Meat Solutions – a division of Cargill Inc., Cessna Aircraft – a Textron Company, Lycoming – a Textron Company, Pizza Hut, ITT Industries, SAIC, Rolls-Royce North America, Helzberg Diamonds, Kansas Health Foundation, UMB Financial Corporation, Delta Dental of Kansas, Jet Aviation North America and Spirit AeroSystems

FULLTIME EMPLOYEES: 95

Sullivan Higdon & Sink

All agencies strive to make a memorable first impression, but Sullivan Higdon & Sink takes it to a whole new level.

The first thing visitors notice upon arrival is a sheep head mounted on the wall. Its bloodshot eyes bulge from their sockets, and its twisted tongue dangles from its slack jaw. But what stands out the most is a rather severe looking arrow going all the way through the head, which might account for the look of surprise frozen on to the ewe's facial features.

So why the skewered sheep as a first impression?

Anyone working at SHS can answer that. The impaled ovine head means "we hate sheep," and it's displayed in a spot where staffers will see it as they walk in every morning. It's a daily reminder of job 1: separating each client's brand from the flock.

Differentiating brands in a

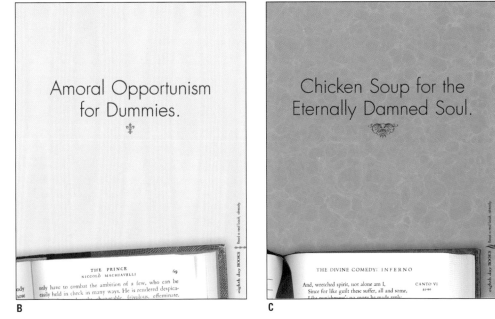

way that's meaningful and relevant is what it's all about at SHS. The sheep is featured on the agency's Web site and Visa cards, not to mention business cards, coffee mugs, and on much of the clothing its staffers wear to work. On any given day, dozens of SHS staffers show up in their "We hate sheep" regalia.

"Like most agencies, we counsel our clients not to try to be everything to everyone,"

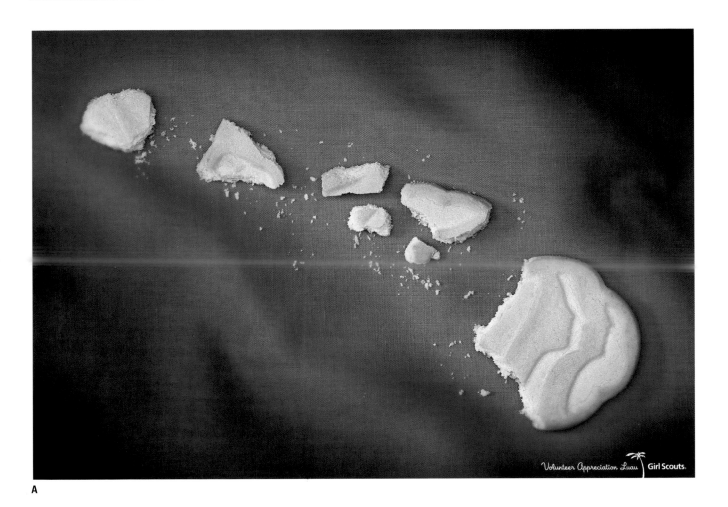

A

Amoral Opportunism for Dummies.

THE PRINCE
NICCOLÒ MACHIAVELLI

B

Chicken Soup for the Eternally Damned Soul.

THE DIVINE COMEDY: INFERNO

C

said Joe Norris, managing partner in the Wichita office. "Unlike most agencies, we've taken our own counsel. We've branded the agency in a way that defines and narrows our target audience. The whole 'we hate sheep' thing is just a little too weird for some prospective clients. Some have given us strange looks and started looking for the exit. But that's okay. If a prospect truly doesn't want work that stands out, then our relationship with them wouldn't have lasted anyway."

"Basically, it's the savvy prospects who recognize that 'we hate sheep' is actually a smart philosophy in a silly package," said Rand Mikulecky, managing partner in the Kansas City office. "Those prospects have not only embraced the philosophy, they've played it back to us. Instead of just calling us to tell us we've won the business, they get a little more inventive. One prospect notified us that we'd won their business by having a huge wooden crate delivered to the agency. Stenciled on the outside were

the words: 'Danger! Sheep Inside.' Inside the crate was a toy rifle with a tag reading, 'Congratulations, SHS. We're ready to kill some sheep.'"

While SHS adopted the "we hate sheep" brand positioning in 2001, the agency had been practicing it for years. To wit: the agency's brand building efforts for The Coleman Company and UMB Financial Corporation.

SHS helped Coleman launch a new brand of remote camping gear to the trade

D

A. **Girl Scouts** — Volunteer appreciation Luau poster

B. **Eighth Day Books** — Amoral opportunism ad

C. **Eighth Day Books** — Chicken soup ad

D. **Saint Mary College Soccer** — "Sore botch" poster

E. **Cargill** — Cowboy with calf ad

F. **Coleman Exponent** — Laundromat poster

DOING THE RIGHT THING ISN'T ALWAYS EASY.
BUT IT IS ALWAYS RIGHT.

E

F

Sullivan Higdon & Sink

by infesting downtown Salt Lake City with faux spiders and snakes. SHS's research had revealed that backpacking retailers were skeptical about Coleman's ability to produce the kind of compact, lightweight, high-tech gear their customers needed as they ventured off the marked trails and into the more remote areas where spiders and snakes lived. SHS met the challenge by developing a strategy to get the retailers buzzing about the new product line before they discovered that

Coleman was behind it.

Prior to the Outdoor Retailer Show in Salt Lake City, a box was mailed to all the key retailers. Inside was a coiled rubber snake and an invitation to "exit the beaten path" the following week, with no mention of Coleman. The snake theme continued when retailers arrived in the city and were greeted with huge images of that same snake, suspended from the side of office buildings near the convention center. On the first day of the show, retailers found

snakes everywhere, with a tag that read, "Exit the beaten path, Exhibit #526."

Buzz continued as everyone wondered who was behind the stunt. Arriving at Exhibit #526, visitors realized that the creepy crawlers they'd seen pre-show were the same critters featured on the packaging for Coleman's new Exponent brand—the company's new line of backpacking gear.

At bars after the show, retailers found that regular cardboard coasters had been replaced with die-cut Exponent "critter

A

THE OFFICIAL AIRLINE OF COUNTLESS HAPPY PASSENGERS.
AND THE OCCASIONAL KOMODO DRAGON.

B

C

A. **Big Rick's** — Pig POS

B. **Cessna Caravan** — Ad

C. **Cessna Caravan** — Postcard

D. **UMB** — "My Ugly Room" home improvement loan campaign

E. **Shatto Milk** — Packaging for milk & butter

coasters"—another innovative tool used to make them view Coleman and the new brand in a different way.

Even in so-called conservative marketing environments, such as banking, SHS is creating avenues for deeper customer involvement with the brand.

For UMB Financial Corporation, a super regional bank with operations in seven states, SHS has successfully implemented programs that involve social media and consumer-generated content.

SHS created the "My Ugly Room" promotion to help support the bank's home equity line of credit product. The promotion centered around a Web site where the public was invited to upload photos of their "ugly room" and fill out a profile that described what made the room awful (including how it smelled). Other visitors could "rate" how ugly the room was by clicking on the "Ugly Meter." The highest rated rooms were then placed in a drawing for prizes, including $10,000 to redeco-

rate. Along the way, all visitors were encouraged to "redecorate now" with a little help from UMB's products. SHS drove traffic to the Web site by utilizing traditional means, such as outdoor, and non-traditional means, such as ugly door hangers for people to give to their friends and redecorating select UMB Bank lobbies with ugly furniture and signage.

SHS was founded in 1971 by Wendell Sullivan and Al Higdon in Wichita, Kansas. Vaughn Sink joined the agency the

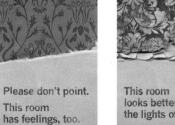

D

E

Sullivan Higdon & Sink

following year, and when he became a partner in 1979, the agency became Sullivan Higdon & Sink. The agency's first major client was Learjet.

SHS continued to grow and thrive for the next 14 years and, through its work for Learjet and other clients, the shop built up a formidable B2B practice with deep knowledge in the business aviation category.

In the late 1980s and early 1990s, SHS won five major new accounts, usually competing with much larger agencies in larger markets. Those included Cessna and the Coleman account, plus the national Pizza Hut print and POS business, and the largest banking network in the region—which later became a part of Bank of America.

After 20 years in B2B, SHS suddenly found itself with a significant amount of consumer work. The old departmental structure began to develop stress fractures as the team worked to balance the quick-turn demands of new retail clients with the longer-range requirements of existing B2B clients. It was decided that single departments weren't the best way to handle dual demands, and SHS restructured the entire agency.

Individual departments were done away with, replaced by more personalized, client-focused teams, with some teams focusing entirely on retail clients, others specializing in B2B.

When Vaughn Sink retired in 1997, the four new managing partners—Joe Norris, Rand Mikulecky, Sam Williams and Lynell Stucky—completed the acquisition of a small Kansas City agency, giving SHS its first office outside Wichita. One of the partners of that shop, Tom Bertels, later became the fifth managing partner. SHS now operates an office in Washington, D.C., as well.

In November 2005, SHS decided to celebrate a unique milestone—a third of a century in business. To mark its 33⅓ year anniversary, the agency operated its own radio station for 33⅓ hours, using a low-power FM transmitter.

"We wanted to play songs from 33⅓ LPs released in 1971, the year the agency was founded," Norris explained. "But we didn't want to be just another classic rock radio station. So the play list at Radio SHS was unique. It was just one song—T. Rex's 'Bang a Gong' from 1971. We played the same song over and over again for 33⅓ hours."

Quite a fitting way for a bunch of sheep-haters to celebrate their birthday.

A

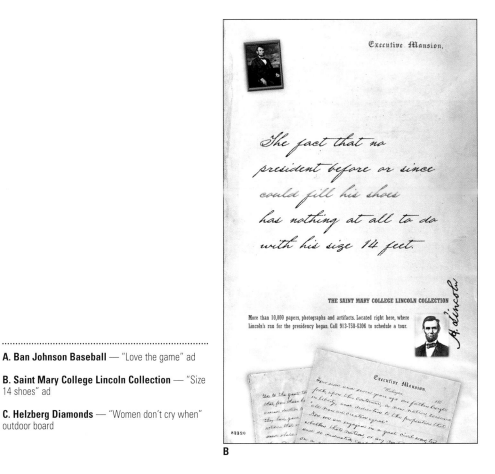

....

A. Ban Johnson Baseball — "Love the game" ad

B. Saint Mary College Lincoln Collection — "Size 14 shoes" ad

C. Helzberg Diamonds — "Women don't cry when" outdoor board

B

C

CASE STUDY: Cessna Citation

Cessna Aircraft Company debuted in 1927, but in the late 1960s Cessna found itself at a crossroads.

The company had been building single- and twin-engine propeller aircraft for almost half a century, and had more than 50 percent market share. But there was a significant and growing portion of the aviation business in which Cessna had no presence at all—the business jet arena.

That market was crowded with well-established competitors, and while Cessna's brand reputation was strong in the prop market, it was of no help to them in the business jet market. In fact, it was a hindrance. Who would want to buy a business jet from "those little propeller airplane guys"?

Cessna solved that problem by introducing a different kind of jet—the Cessna Citation. The first Citation neatly filled a gap in the market, between turboprops and jets. The new product was positioned as "the sensible Citation" —slower than every other jet on the market, but able to get in and out of shorter runways that faster jets couldn't.

By the time SHS became Cessna's AOR in 1987, the Citation line had grown to three models. By 1990, Cessna's reputation and broad base of Citation owners prompted the company to make a bold move: build a business jet that could outrun every other business jet in the sky. The business jet, which SHS helped Cessna launch, was called the Citation X.

How did "the little propeller airplane guys" convince the market that Cessna could build an aircraft so technologically advanced? By sticking close to Cessna's "sensible" roots.

While the Citation X was phenomenally fast, its speed also made a lot of business sense. Owners could literally have breakfast in L.A., lunch in New York and a business dinner in San Francisco. The Citation X wasn't just fast, it was sensible. The strategy was to position the Citation X as the next step in the Cessna evolution of the product line.

Because the Citation X was the proud, bad boy of the litter, ads had significantly more attitude and swagger than other Citation advertising. A headline touted, "Some opportunities knock. This one tears doors off hinges."

But sensibility and attitude weren't enough to ensure success. Bringing a new business jet to market is an enormously expensive undertaking for any manufacturer. Sales efforts and orders must begin years before the aircraft is delivered. Prospective buyers had to be convinced not just that Cessna could build the Citation X, but that Cessna *would* build it.

To generate the necessary advance orders, Cessna had to convince prospects that the Citation X was real, not just a "paper" airplane. The strategy developed was to allow prospects to "participate" in building the first Citation X to come off the production line. SHS created a series of oversized direct mailers, each containing one component of a Citation X scale model, allowing prospects to assemble a desktop model Citation X (in their offices) as the real aircraft was being assembled in the factory. For example, while the Citation X fuselage was being built, or the wing was being mated with fuselage, prospects were mailed scale models, to be attached. The strategy kept the prospects engaged over several months, while convincing them that Cessna was actually building the Citation X.

Today, Cessna Citations consistently outsell the competition by a wide margin and SHS ads for the Citation X continue to consistently outscore competitive ads in readership by focusing on the same three attributes—speed, speed and speed.

The same is true for Citation X direct mail programs. One mailer, which was designed to bypass corporate gatekeepers and hit the desks of hard-to-reach prospects, contained frozen ice-cream bars and was express-mailed to those prospects to illustrate the advantages of getting to a business destination quickly. Copy read, "Arrive too late and opportunities melt; sweet deals go soft." Cessna credits this program with opening doors and leading to at least one sale. And, when there's a $20-million product at stake, one sale covers lots of ice-cream.

Beats other business jets and steals their milk money.

Eat time zones for breakfast.

Wolf in wolf's clothing.

CASE STUDY: Westar Energy

This is the story about how the agency's unsheeplike philosophy moved a client far beyond the status quo. It's a tale about triumph of goodwill over scandal and greed. And the power of heroes in white hats riding to the rescue.

In the fall of 2003, Westar Energy, the largest electric-energy provider in Kansas, had been in full re-building mode for several months. An earlier, very public corporate scandal involving the mismanagement of funds by former executives had badly tarnished the electric utility's reputation among its 650,000 customers in the Kansas area.

The new executive team had some very formidable goals for restoring trust and good faith in the company, goals which included generating a hefty increase in an annual survey measuring public perception.

Herein was the dilemma for SHS: To move the numbers one must first move hearts and minds. But electricity is a commodity that's taken for granted; it's only thought about when the power goes out. And, who actually has warm, fuzzy feelings about an electric company anyway?

SHS decided that changing these perceptions had to be the foremost goal. Step #1: The agency conducted "man-on-the-street" intercept interviews. What came to pass out of all this "one-on-one" communication was lots of invaluable research, which yielded more than just a bit of curious, seemingly contradictory, insight into the minds of customers.

Regardless of the level of disdain for the past corporate corruption, these customers continued to regard Westar's rank-and-file service crews in heroic, almost mythical, esteem.

The takeaway strategy which the agency concentrated on was to recapture the hearts and minds of customers by continually reminding them of the tireless and endless dedication of the Westar employees who generate, maintain and restore the power that empowers everybody's take-it-for-granted way of life. The goal was to do all this by making the utility more human and approachable, just like the folks who now are running the company.

Step #2: SHS created a multimedia campaign for

Blow Dryer – SFX: Ambient bathroom tile echo.

SFX: Blow dryer clicks on, continues throughout

ANNCR: Every morning, in every home, it's a familiar sound.

ANNCR: Six hundred and fifty thousand Kansans taking their electricity for granted.

ANNCR: We wouldn't have it any other way.

ANNCR: Westar Energy. Doing whatever it takes to prevent bad hair days.

Westar, which intelligently, humanly and humorously nailed the strategy.

ACTION: A woman in front of the bathroom mirror, leisurely blow-drying her hair. The camera slowly pans across the scene.

VO: "Every morning, in every home, it's a familiar sound. 650,000 Kansans take their electricity for granted. We wouldn't have it any other way. Westar Energy. Doing whatever it takes to prevent bad hair days."

Additionally, newspaper readers found headlines such as "Heroes in white hats still ride to the rescue," positioned directly above the close-up of a white Westar hard hat resting on a lineman's head.

Did it all work? The answer is a resounding "Yes." After the first year of the campaign, Westar's customer satisfaction scores rose significantly beyond the company's aggressive annual goal. The following year, numbers continued their rapid ascent—exceeding expectations by an even wider margin.

Today, the story continues. Westar Energy remains one of SHS's most cherished clients. And the two companies continue working together to push Westar's customer satisfaction scores even higher.

TAXI

Doubt the conventional.
Create the exceptional.

Founded in 1992

TORONTO
495 Wellington Street West
Suite 102
Toronto, Ontario M5V 1E9
416-979-7001
www.taxi.ca

NEW YORK
11 Beach Street, 10th Floor
New York, NY 10013
212-414-8294
www.taxi-nyc.com

KEY NEW BUSINESS CONTACTS:
Canada: Jeremy Gayton
USA: Wylie Curtiss

SENIOR MANAGEMENT:
Paul Lavoie, Chairman/CCO
Jane Hope, EVP/Design CD
Rob Guenette, President/TAXI Toronto
Daniel Rabinowicz, President/TAXI Montreal
John Berg, President/TAXI New York
Zak Mroueh, VP/Executive CD/TAXI Canada
Steve Mykolyn, VP/Design & Interactive CD/TAXI Canada
Stephane Charier, CD/TAXI Montreal
Wayne Best, Executive CD/TAXI New York
Ron Wilson, VP/CFO

FULLTIME EMPLOYEES: 210

TAXI

If TAXI had a last name, there's no question what it would be:

Doubt.

It's the first word of TAXI's motto: "Doubt the conventional. Create the exceptional." And it's what drives every process the agency applies to building its clients' brands, and what powers its globally recognized creativity.

In the driver's seat at TAXI is Chairman and Chief Creative Officer Paul Lavoie, a shaven-headed 6-footer with a deep, baritone voice and an even deeper respect for smart, creative, independent thinking. Explains Lavoie:

"We have a reputation for bringing forward smart, unconventional thinking that gets results. Our mission is to create an environment that attracts bright people and challenges them to do great things that are socially and economically relevant. We think that in any world there are hunters and there are the hunted. Here, we attract the former. Smart, ambitious, agile minds with the spirit for winning in business."

In 1992, Paul Lavoie and Jane Hope created TAXI and its organizational philosophy as a response to the frustration they felt working at larger agencies where strict process and layers of personnel stripped away creativity. They've successfully done business according to their distinctive model in Canada ever since. In January of 2005, they turned the agency over to a very capable and seasoned management in Canada in order to devote their full attention and energy to creating TAXI's New York office, which will ultimately serve as their global hub.

The entire TAXI team in New York and elsewhere pride themselves on being a company of independent thinkers, working together. With many voices, viewpoints and ideas, they all strive toward the same goal: delivering sustained results for their clients' brands. As Lavoie puts it:

"TAXI brings together bright people who deliver bold ideas by integrating strategic and creative disciplines. There are no lines between account people and creative people. We only have creative minds. Creativity is about thinking and innovating, not about the skill of writing and art directing, it's ideas first and foremost. The way we define good work is when we solve the business problem and innovate somewhere along the chain. Creativity is a business tool; it's about seeing new opportunities and it's important for us to share that vision with our clients."

As Wylie Curtiss, Business Development Director in New York explains: "TAXI is more than a name; TAXI is an organizational philosophy. We believe a core team is composed of about as many people as you can fit into a cab—creative director, brand strategist, account director, media strategist and very importantly, the client. Five voices and visions functioning as one and heading toward the final destination."

Like the agency itself, the clients TAXI attracts are also hunters with aggressive goals, the ability to think big and a desire to make a difference in the marketplace.

For the agency, collaboration with its clients is critical, and also the key to creating a winning game plan that will achieve desired results.

TAXI starts its work by thoroughly investigating its clients' brand, product, consumers, competitors and industry. "We distill this information into one key insight which is the inspiration that drives the development of every piece of communication. Building brands is about telling stories. These stories should have the flexibili-

A

B

ty to evolve over time and to fit into all appropriate media venues," says Jane Hope, co-founder of TAXI and Design Creative Director.

That's exactly the route TAXI is taking for its client, Nike. The agency explains: TAXI was faced with the challenge of launching Nike Hockey in Canada. As a global brand with American roots, an attempt to appear Canadian would likely backfire. But as a relative newcomer to hockey, demonstrating the brand's under-

standing of the sport was the highest strategy priority in the long-term goal to be embraced as a true part of hockey's culture.

Hockey is in an ongoing state of evolution. A couple years ago, the big issue was The Trap, and the measured style of play it generated, where defense ruled and breakaways were almost non-existent. Fans and players alike bristled at this restraint, and the game and its athletes responded. Today, the game is about a short burst of glory, and what you can do

in a 45-second shift.

Nike is known for being tapped into the emotional frontiers of sport. The shift to all-out play in a short amount of time presented Nike with an ideal platform to introduce its new line of equipment. 45 seconds is all you have to make your mark; you'd better be prepared.

Starting with the rarely used and highly fitting format of 45-second television, TAXI created an example of the kind of off-ice training that helps players make the

A. Toronto World Wide Short Film Festival — A series of TV spots feature an egomaniacal director providing tips on how to get to the point quickly in a short film.

B. Flow 93.5 Afro — Wild postings used musical paraphernalia with a double meaning to communicate the musical genres featured on this urban radio station.

C-D. Nike — Urban geography was hijacked as ambient media to underscore that training can happen anywhere.

E. Nike — Murals were placed on consecutive buildings to suggest the force of distance runner Bernard Lagat bursting through.

C

D

E

most of their 45 seconds. The campaign extended to "super-human" outdoor, using the medium in unprecedented ways to show how determined athletes could find a training opportunity anywhere. For those who spend their lives thinking about hockey, a message that lets them know any spot they're in is a training ground for their "45" is incredibly motivating.

The campaign debuted when hope returned to hockey again. The airdate coincided with the end of the year-long strike, an alignment that signaled Nike's closeness to the sport.

TAXI also stresses that its business is built on a media-neutral approach that allows strategic and creative agility and a consistent brand experience across multiple consumer touchpoints. "TAXI has always used an integrated approach to building powerful brands," says Wayne Best, Executive Creative Director in New York. "Every piece of great creative starts with a blank page and without precon-ceived solutions. We push ourselves to go beyond the expected and create "category breakthrough" ideas that propel a brand and drive business."

When MINI asked TAXI to create a few posters for the entrance hall of an autoshow, TAXI saw a much bigger brand opportunity. As the MINI brand is all about mischievous fun, TAXI transformed the entrance hall into an obstacle course, turning pillars into pylons and placing skid marks on the floor.

A

B

C

To illustrate the gravity of the literacy problem in Canada, TAXI turned a traditional outdoor board into a conversation by inviting subway commuters to press a button rather than read anything. When the button was pressed, a branded message from the ABC Literacy Foundation explained that the poster had no words because 5 million adult Canadians wouldn't be able to read them.

TAXI's television launch for Rickard's beer portrayed a typical drinker ordering a pint only to witness the heavenly ritual that followed—the Rickard's choir singing Carmina Burana in all its glory. TAXI then took the choir on a tour, making inpromptu stops at bars across the country so that drinkers could get a taste of that glorious drinking experience too.

So where is TAXI headed? The agency's mantra will always be "doubt," which Lavoie likens to, of all things, cholesterol:

"Doubt is a bad word, it's negative. But I give you another one: "cholesterol." We all know there's good cholesterol and bad, and like cholesterol, there is good doubt and bad doubt. The good doubt is at the beginning of a problem-solving challenge. You should have a lot of it, you should never assume."

Yet there is one thing you can assume when you look to TAXI brand building strategies: They will never look for the usual route, they will always look for the smartest.

D

A. MINI — A dominatrix is your guide through this interactive experience featuring the superior control features of the MINI.

B. MINI — Access to the Toronto Auto Show was decorated to recall a obstacle course and the "go-cart" handling of the of MINI.

C. MINI — Urinals in men's washrooms at MINI retailers became mini slalom courses using 3D pylons. The adjacent poster copy challenged patrons to test their handling skills; both in the washroom and in a MINI test drive.

D. ABC Literacy Foundation — When commuters pressed the button they heard a recorded message: "You'll notice this poster has no printed words. That's because 5 million adult Canadians would have a hard time reading them. But help is available. If you know someone who needs help with reading, writing or math, just look under Learn in the Yellow Pages. This message brought to you by ABC Literacy Foundation."

E. Covenant House — Wild postings during the holiday season provoke a double take by juxtaposing the bright desires of most children with the harsh depravity of kids living on the street.

F-G. Rickard's Beer — Drawing a pint of Rickard's becomes literally music to your ears in this TV spot which was echoed in real bars with the impromptu appearances of a traveling choir.

NOT ALL KIDS WANT THE SAME THING FOR CHRISTMAS.

COVENANT HOUSE 1-800-HELP-308

E

F

G

CASE STUDY: Amp'd Mobile

A

B

It was not until after the holiday peak selling season that a new product in an over-saturated market was going to be available. Not a cheering thought. But those were the facts for Amp'd Mobile, the first fully integrated mobile virtual network operator offering a full range of conventional mobile telephone services along with a broad range of unique, compelling and original content targeted for youth, young professionals and early adopters.

Says TAXI, "While it was a great product to build communications around, we had these two huge challenges—bad timing and too many other wireless providers—to overcome.

"So our initial branding campaigns needed to convince potential customers—people looking to change their provider or upgrade their service—to wait for Amp'd Mobile to launch. Our second challenge was to stand out in an overcrowded category."

The strategic backbone for the branding campaign was the promise that Amp'd Mobile could do things that other mobile phones couldn't, and would never even try for fear of alienating their traditional and conservative investors. From its syndicated, original and user-generated content to its breakthrough technology, Amp'd Mobile offered users an experience they just couldn't get anywhere else. It represented the marriage of youth culture's two addictions: mobile phones and entertainment.

As a pre-launch campaign, TAXI offered a warning to potential consumers: "Try not to die—Amp'd Mobile is coming." The message was contained in a variety of irreverent executions: rich media ads, magazine and wild posting print, TV spots, and guerilla marketing stunts, all designed to generate expectation and buzz, as well as to drive traffic to a specially designed microsite. "Our key objective," points out the agency, "was to create immediate awareness that something new was coming in the area of mobile entertainment, which was worth waiting for, even in light of the looming holiday gift-giving season."

When it came time to launch, the campaign concentrated on selling the Amp'd Mobile product and brand points of difference: content and attitude. It was built around the theme, "Have the power to entertain yourself," and demonstrated the phone's unrivalled ability to let its young target audience exert total control over their mobile entertainment and communication choices. The spots communicated that Amp'd Mobile wasn't just a new cell phone, but an entirely new medium. The brand attitude was defined by the exclusive content carried by the product, paying off the promise that it would let consumers do things they couldn't with other mobile entertainment providers and see things they wouldn't with rival brands.

The strategic and creative tactics paid off. During the course of the pre-launch campaign, traffic to the Amp'd Mobile microsite averaged 1.8MM hits per week and requests for the service surpassed 30,000. Over a short two-and-a-half month period, the campaigns generated 16% consumer brand awareness, surpassing several already-existing brands. Perhaps most impressively, the company was able to generate significant incremental funding from investors due to the buzz generated from the marketing efforts.

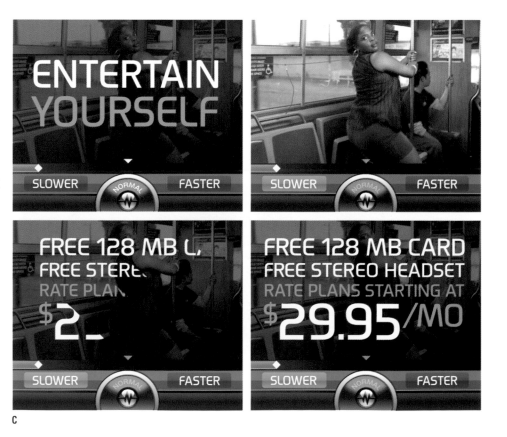

C

A-B. **Amp'd Mobile** — This pre-launch guerilla installation makes it appear as thought there's a gaping hole in the middle of the walkway. A sign urges people to avoid tumbling down the hole, lest they miss the Amp'd Mobile launch.

C. **Amp'd Mobile** — Following the launch, this interactive banner ad invited participation with controls that sped up or slowed down the command to "shake your junk!" Initially featured on content affiliates sites and sent as an email attachment to those who had signed up for the service online, the game took on a life of its own through viral distribution.

D. **Amp'd Mobile** — Double page spreads in youth culture and men's magazines, like ESPN Magazine, FHM and Thrasher, warn against exuberant fearlessness becoming fatal stupidity.

E-F. **Amp'd Mobile** — A series of web banners offer fictitious services with deadly consequences, anyone ruthless enough to click through lands on a warning page and an opportunity to link to ampd.com.

G. **Amp'd Mobile** — This TV spot portrays a hooker attempting to resuscitate a failing Senator with a combination of CPR and inducements to not miss the launch of a new phone featuring games, videos and really cool graphics.

CASE STUDY: Viagra

Viagra. Where does an agency begin?

Since 2001, TAXI has had the unusual challenge of developing a series of campaigns for Viagra, one of the best-known brands in the world. TAXI's challenge has never been to create understanding or awareness of the product (which is virtually universal) but rather to brand Viagra in Canada in a way that makes consumers feel more comfortable with it.

When Viagra launched in the U.S., it was perceived as a product for old guys and sex maniacs. This was a barrier for mainstream men, the actual target group. One in three men over 35 has Erectile Difficulties (ED), and the majority of them don't relate to either Bob Dole or Hugh Hefner.

In Canada, the challenge was even more unusual because of Canadian regulations that forbid advertisers from stating the connection between the product and the condition it treats.

A key insight the agency found when looking at men with ED was that although ED is a physical condition, its primary impact is emotional devastation. They found that sufferers could be persuaded by communication that portrays the emotions they

A

have lost and aspire to regain. Using that insight, the agency has helped the brand evolve over the five years that it's directed Viagra's image primarily using television, and some billboard and web activity:

Year 1: TAXI's launch effort was a bold approach, directly confronting the stigma of ED. "Good Morning" took one of the most everyday situations imaginable—a man on his way to work—and added a level of meaning to it that only Viagra could claim. The ad was an exuberant, over-the-top depiction of the brand's impact.

Year 2: "Good Morning" showed what Viagra had done for one man; in year two, TAXI expanded on this to demonstrate Viagra's relevance to men of all types. The universally recognized anthem, "We Are the Champions," reinforced feelings of success and ability, emotions the target group responded to very strongly.

Year 3: At this point, competitors to Viagra were appearing on the horizon. Knowing that nothing succeeds like

success, TAXI used Viagra's worldwide leadership to make a persuasive case to the target audience. "My Way" was the anthem sung in the shower by men all around the world whose lives had been changed for the better by Viagra, reinforcing its success at a critical time.

Year 4: Prior to competition, TAXI focused on the emotional benefits of Viagra, but the advent of competitive brands put an increased emphasis on performance benefits. To ensure Viagra competed on these attributes, the "Bleep" campaign featured men who couldn't quite keep their happiness to themselves and wanted to share their experience with the world. The particulars were 'bleeped' out, but the response of the audience made the conversation—and Viagra's performance—pretty clear.

Year 5: Always looking to lead the market, Viagra's most recent campaign looks at things from a woman's point of view, reinterpreting "Good Morning" in a way that combines both physical and emotional satisfaction.

The creative evolution of the brand has had a tremendously successful impact in the marketplace. Even in the face of intense competition, Viagra remains the number-one choice for consumers and doctors, retaining two-thirds of the Canadian market. Viagra in Canada also enjoys the second highest market share in the world.

....

A. Viagra — When advertising regulations disallow an explicit description of benefits, a implicit one serves very well on this billboard.

B. Viagra — Set to the 1939 classic "Good Morning!" this TV spot follows a impishly pleased fellow's journey to the office replete with stage show styled antics.

C. Viagra —The anthemic victory song "We are the champions" accompanies this over-the-top TV spot celebrating the benefits of Viagra.

D. Viagra — Unable to contain himself, this TV spot depicts a fellow recounting his exploits of the night before – bleeped out by the familiar blue pill.

B

C

D

Venables Bell & Partners

The World Belongs to the Brave

Founded in 2001

201 Post Street
San Francisco, CA 94108
415-288-3300
fax: 415-421-3683
www.venablesbell.com

KEY NEW BUSINESS CONTACT:
Bob Molineaux, President, 415-288-3302

SENIOR MANAGEMENT:
Paul Venables – Founder, Co-Creative Director
Greg Bell – Founder, Co-Creative Director
Bob Molineaux – Founder, President
Lucy Farey-Jones – Partner, Director of Brand Strategy

CLIENTS: Audi of America, HBO Video, Barclays, The Coca-Cola Company, Pacific Gas & Electric Company, iShares, Lucasfilm, Montana Meth Project, 24 Hour Fitness

Venables Bell & Partners

There's a four-letter word that Venables Bell & Partners has for every client and brand that's facing the daunting hurdles of today's marketing world:

Idea.

Yes! says VB&P, the idea is the answer. It can solve every single challenge listed in the CMO field guide. But, cautions the agency, it has to be great.

It can be said that the agency itself began with an idea. Paul Venables sets the scene:

"I was in LA on a shoot and I called my ex-client, Beth Kachellek, formerly of SBC, now UltimateTV, to tell her we had won 'Best of Show' at the ICON Awards. She said she was down in LA, too, and that we should meet for drinks. Well, over said drinks, we had the following conversation:

Me: Are you serious, you'd fire your big agency and give me and Greg Bell, the account?

Her: Are you serious, you'd quit your dream jobs at Goodby and open an agency for me?

Me: Are you serious?

Her: Are you serious?

"Well, I thought, come Monday morning, all would be forgotten. It wasn't. Beth called and set the wheels in motion for Greg and me to work on UltimateTV, which, by the way, was a sizeable national television account backed by a company called Microsoft. And that was the birth of Venables Bell & Partners."

A

B

C

Once VB&P got the account and were signed on, they got a call from their client, Beth, every week or so, adding to the scope of work. Could they also do product demos? How about interactive? In-store? Guerilla? What about corporate identity? And could they pull it all off, plus traditional advertising, in three months? Insane as it was, the agency sees it as the best thing that could've happened. Recalls Venables, "It forced us into a model where our best thinkers, creative

and strategic, worked on every piece of the brand puzzle. It became a model we never abandoned." Over the course of the past five years, the power of that model also has attracted Audi, HBO Video, Pacific Gas and Electric, Barclays, Robert Mondavi, Siebel Systems, Mervyn's, Lucasfilm, and The Coca-Cola Company's Fresca.

Venables and Bell had, though, abandoned arguably the two best jobs in advertising: both had been creative

directors at Goodby, Silverstein and Partners. They'd also managed to convince Bob Molineaux that he really didn't want a cushy job as head of the New York office of AKQA. So there they all were, with their own agency. Even more surprising was that they ended up with the blessing and support of two of the industry's greatest practitioners, namely Jeffery Goodby and Rich Silverstein.

"We had their emotional, intellectual

A. HBO Video — Rome

B. The Coca-Cola Company — Fresca

C. Barclays — Brand

D. Barclays Global Investors — iShares

E-F. PG&E San Francisco Green Campaign — This campaign, which featured everything from a couch made of grass (seen here with mayor Gavin Newsom relaxing on it) to an ad about getting energy from of all places—cow manure—served to build awareness around PG&E's efforts to make San Francisco the greenest city in the nation.

D

E

F

and financial support," says Venables. "That meant a great deal to us."

It turned out they were going to need it. As their new agency opened, budgets were being slashed, doors were being shuttered and dot.com-ers were bailing right and left. So how did VB&P manage to get through the storm? With ideas, answers the agency. And a branding philosophy to support each and every one. Here's the agency's take:

"It's got to be hard being a CMO. There's a new problem lurking around every PowerPoint deck. A fresh marketing challenge with every technological innovation.

"Nowadays, though, in addition to all your tried and true marketing problems, you have the increasing segmentation of audiences, a proliferation of media vehicles, including new ones you have to get an education about quickly, plus there are ad-skipping technologies and services to contend with. To complicate things further, we have the rise of new disciplines and specialties that need to be managed and integrated (CRM alone could fill your calendar). And let's not forget budget restraints. You have to pay more as you splinter the media plan to reach less people than you used to, and those restraints aren't going away—they're getting tighter."

Against this challenging backdrop, the agency insists, ideas need to work hard; to be nothing less than great. The good news is that they're (finally) entering, as they put it, The Age of the Idea.

As VB&P sees it, big ideas are the one sure currency in today's business climate. "In the old days, clients could choose to bludgeon people with massive mass media buys until people succumbed to a message. Not possible today. Today, people have the power. Brands must be magnets. They must entice and attract. Instead of using the stick to prod people toward their brands, advertisers need to dangle carrots. Given all the new media vehicles and fragmented targets, it's more like dangling countless carrots—zillions of them—every which way the target turns. And they need to be delicious carrots. So the target consumer is constantly discovering these little tasty bits in various places at various times; is literally looking for your brand. That's the game today."

So how does VB&P validate their creative/branding expertise? Lucy Farey-Jones, Partner, Director of Brand Strategy, "We've won 5 EFFIEs in three years of eligibility, so we're no strangers to

A

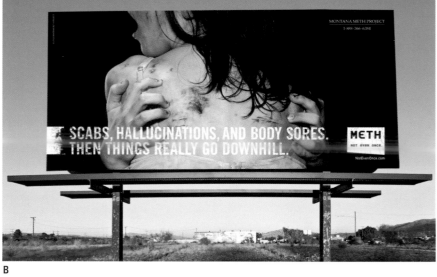

B

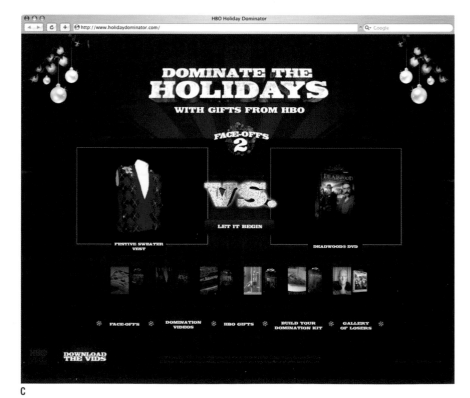

C

measurement. In fact, we insist on it. We may use a variety of different qualitative research techniques to get to our insights, but we bring out the quantitative guns when it comes to testing whether or not our insights worked. Only by measuring do we see if we truly hit our goals, and only by measuring year-one efforts, do we get the information we need to better these goals in year two, and on into the future."

But the agency recognizes that not all clients have bottomless pockets when it comes to research. For those clients, they've constructed what they refer to as 'some pretty nifty' research solutions. For instance, when Napster needed to demonstrate pre- and post- results, but didn't have the cash to command a huge quantitative study, VB&P designed a short but robust online study that helped demonstrate ROI to the Napster board. Once again, an idea that worked for the client.

"It's ROI that proves EFFIES, but our real pride and joy is in winning what we've coined the 'L'EFFIE' for a client: A Cannes Lion and an AMA EFFIE for the same campaign. In our world, creativity and results are not mutually exclusive, but happy bedfellows."

An idea whose time has come.

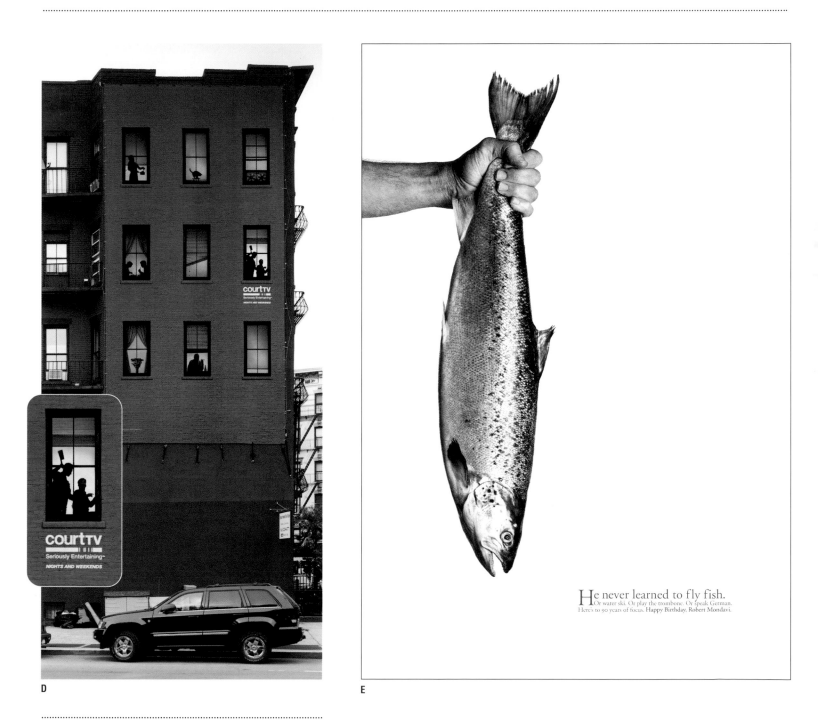

D

E

He never learned to fly fish.
Or water ski. Or play the trombone. Or speak German.
Here's to 90 years of focus. Happy Birthday, Robert Mondavi.

A. HBO Video — The Sopranos

B. The Montana Meth Project

C. HBO Video — Holiday Dominator Microsite

D. Court TV — Brand

E. Robert Mondavi Winery

In an age when strong branding is critical to the success of any product, the television series is no exception. For Venables, Bell & Partners, that challenge began in the land of OZ.

The prison drama OZ was an HBO show that was critically acclaimed, but less ubiquitous than bigger hits in HBO's formidable lineup. And a show whose first season HBO was ready to release on DVD/VHS.

VB&P explains the challenge:

"In the cluttered and highly competitive DVD retail sales market, a product must come strong out of the gate. Titles that fail to sell within the first week are quickly pulled from the shelves to make way for more profitable ones. No second chances. This presented a daunting marketing challenge for OZ, as the DVD success stories to date had been well-known series and blockbuster movies."

The agency quickly realized that, in order to reach HBO's 12-month sales goal, it needed to reach a wider audience than the strong, but small, loyalist OZ universe. VB&P also knew that HBO's respected reputation for original content would make the OZ collection appealing to an additional, secondary audience: content enthusiasts who are avid movie buffs with home collections of DVDs.

VB&P delved into its target and discovered two key insights. The first was that viewers of OZ felt completely immersed in the program when they'd watch it, almost as if they'd just completed a prison sentence themselves. The second insight: by framing the program as a cinematic experience (instead of 8 individual TV episodes), they could capitalize on the intensity of the show. The agency then used the media to full advantage to get the OZ message out.

With less than a 1% category share-of-voice to make an impact in these already crowded DMAs, the agency had their work cut out for them. OZ had to feel like a physical presence in the city. A heavy broadcast TV rotation was targeted at DVD buyers. Buzz and excitement were created in three OZ markets: Chicago, New York (including the boroughs) and Philadelphia. Once again, creative solutions were put to work.

"We used a dominant share of bus wraps, subway train car cards and platform posters, and fleets of message-wrapped SUVs to surround crowds at key entertainment events and popular destinations. The SUV drivers handed out OZ merchandise at movie premieres, at electronic retail outlets (Tower Records, Coconuts), local events and outside professional sports arenas."

Through a clear definition of two distinct audiences and a single, compelling, emotive creative strategy that appealed to both, this launch campaign for the release of HBO's OZ series demonstrated effectiveness beyond expectations. It managed to generate more short-term DVD/VHS sales in its first week than some of HBO's other more popular shows (both Sex and The City and The Sopranos), and hence protect retail listings long-term.

Venables Bell & Partners continued the hit-'em-from-all-directions formula with campaigns for the following OZ seasons. The release of OZ Season 3 included, along with a print campaign, a full-size prison guard tower, built above a bustling corner in Times Square. OZ Season 5 included a magazine sticker insert with prison character titles such as "Snitch," "Mule" and "Slave." A lottery-style scratcher card with undesirable prison outcomes was also passed out at points-of-purchase to encourage sales.

....

A. Magazine — "Cubicle"

B. TV — "Jaywalking"

C. Insert — "Sticker"

D. Go Card — "Scratcher"

E. Outdoor — "Guard Tower"

A

B

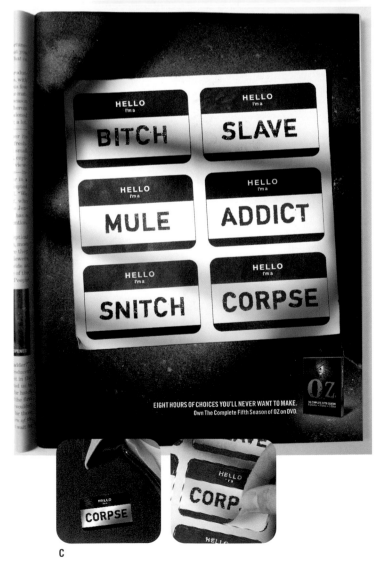

C

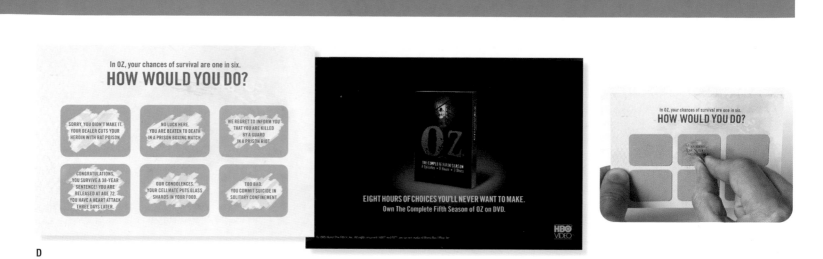

D

E

CASE STUDY: Napster

Napster was all set to relaunch as a legal service. The upside? 98% brand awareness. The downside? People equated Napster with stealing, not paying. In addition, Napster's brand strength lay in its grassroots appeal. Unlike CDs, which are a physical symbol of belonging to a particular band or genre, digital music is all about experimentation. It's all about trial, about being a chameleon, about not committing. Digital music is all about discovery. Thus, the real question was, could the service be commercialized without destroying the brand?

Client and agency both knew they had to deliver the message in a non-commercial insider tone or the brand would be written off as a total sell-out. Creatively, the unifying branding elements were simple: the ubiquitous kitty head and a healthy dose of irreverence. So it was decided to turn things on their heads by doing it backwards: the fully-integrated, multi-channel campaign started with a simple flick of a switch.

On June 25, 2003, Venables Bell & Partners did no marketing at all; they just quietly switched the home page of Napster.com to Napsterbits.com. Napsterbits.com was a microsite that housed the animation-based vignettes and told the story of the come-back. These vignettes were released sequentially every two weeks. At Napsterbits.com the fans could register, download screensavers and artwork, or forward the animations to a friend.

Next stop in the re-branding reverse launch: an email campaign. In a one-on-one communication with their core, the agency only gradually turned up the heat. They emailed the 197,183 Napsterites who had expressed an interest in finding out more about the new Napster to tell them the relaunch news. After the email came online banners, closely followed by print in books like Blender and XLR8, followed by wild postings. When this underground campaign had seeded, VB&P layered on mainstream music print and, finally—in the last part of the launch—tactical billboards were added in the media markets to capture the entertainment industry's attention, and 15- and 30- second versions of the original animations were run on select cable TV channels in the week leading up to the October 29th launch date.

The results were amazing. During the first three months Napsterbits had 2,190,829 visitors; 143,000 emails were collected, and 44,171 of these people forwarded the link to a friend. "I wasn't really even sure it was an ad. Cool." "You don't need any sort of pitch to cue you in to what they are selling. I like that cat, cool." was some of the feedback from Downloader focus groups. There was coverage of the animations on sites like USA Today, Hollywood Reporter, MTV, CNBC, Comcast.com, Filter.com, and beyondgeek.com. Also in its launch quarter, Napster.com had more unique visitors than Apple iTunes—on 9% of the spend. Napster sold its 5 millionth track just 4 months after its rebirth. Venables Bell & Partners' integrated approach meant that in its launch quarter, Napster attracted more visitors than any other music site.

A

B

C

D

A. **Magazine** — "Crazy Guy/Prophet"

B. **Webisode** — "Jailbreak"

C. **Magazine** — "Graveyard"

D. **Microsite** — www.napsterbits.com

Index of Case Studies

Image Index by Client